Heldentod

Dedication

For the memory of Janusz Korczak who courageously sought life in the face of death for the children of the Warsaw Ghetto until the very end.

West German postal issue 1978.

Heldentod

THE NAZI CULTURE OF DEATH

PAUL GARSON

FONTHILL

Fonthill Media Language Policy

Fonthill Media publishes in the international English language market. One language edition is published worldwide. As there are minor differences in spelling and presentation, especially with regard to American English and British English, a policy is necessary to define which form of English to use. The Fonthill Policy is to use the form of English native to the author. Paul Garson was born and educated in the United States of America and now lives in Los Angeles, California, therefore American English has been adopted in this publication.

www.fonthillmedia.com
office@fonthillmedia.com

First published in the United Kingdom
and the United States of America 2021

British Library Cataloguing in Publication Data:
A catalogue record for this book is available from the British Library

ISBN 978-1-78155-757-0

Typeset in Minion Pro
Printed and bound in England

"When you look into an abyss, the abyss also looks into you."

Friedrich Nietzsche

Dancing with Death

The woodblock print was one of several found in *Goldatengeist—Eine Deutung aus Bekentnissen der Front* (*Soldier Spirit—An Interpretation of Confessions from the Front*) published in Berlin in 1942 by Nieberlugen Verlag of Berlin. The book addresses via prose and verse various aspects of war including comradeship and the glory of death in battle. It also contains a number of woodblock style illustrations by Paul Weber.

The illustration appears to be drawn in imitation of the famous series of woodblocks created in 1498 by Albrecht Dürer, his artwork visually interpreting the revelations of Saint Jean who prophesied the end of the world, a theme resonating with the Great Plagues of the Middle Ages that decimated much of Europe. The "Dance of Death" genre began in 1424 in France and spread across the continent, the artwork appearing in many cathedrals, cloisters and burial vaults as well as in illustrated manuscripts. The images featured death as a skeleton claiming victims from all social classes, from peasants to kings. The renderings also carried commentary in verse, as it were the voice of Death speaking to his victim often in a threatening, accusatory or sarcastic tone.

Another earlier term associated with such imagery is *Danse Macabre*. During the Middle Ages, such drawings were sometimes seen as a warning for all "to lead a responsible and Christian life" More to the point, the theme recalls the shortness of life. Each succeeding generation produced its own versions of the Dances of Death, the one seen here following that tradition albeit with a Nazi twist of meaning, the "dance" to be regarded with anticipation and joy rather fear or dread ... the embracing of death as the gateway to *Heldentod* … the Hero's Death.

Contents

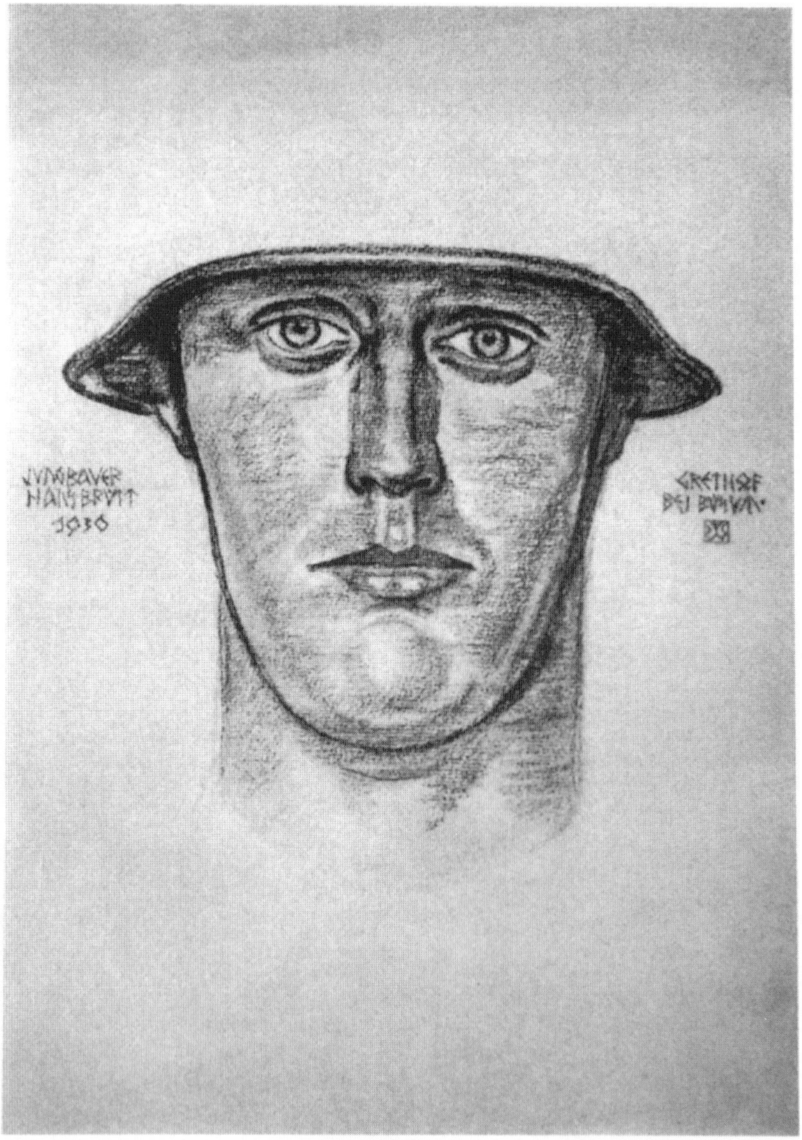

Deutsche Soldat—1936
Drawing by popular Third Reich era artist Wolfgang Willig whose art appeared on thousands of German postcards created as he traveled among the troops rendering illustrations of the high ranking as well as the average *landser* foot soldier. Then as a POW he earned money drawing U.S. servicemen. The image is striking on various levels. Some say its highlights the *Stahlhelm*, the iconic German iron helmet; others suggest it may relate to Hitler's emphasis on mindless emotion over thought to motivate his people.

Glossary of Military Ranks and Equivalents

German Army	SS	United States Army	British Army
Generalfeldmarschall	Reichsfuehrer-SS	General of the Army	Field Marshal
Generaloberst	SS- Oberstgrupenfuehrer	no exact equivalent	no exact equivalent
Generalleutnant	SS-Gruppenfuehrer	Lieutenant general	Lieutenant general
Generalmajor	SS-Brigadefuehrer	Major general	Major
General Oberst	SS-Oberfuehrer	Brigadier general	Brigadier
Oberst	SS-Standartenfuehrer	Colonel	Colonel
Oberstleutnant	SS-Obersturmbannfuehrer	Lieutenant colonel	Colonel
Major	SS-Sturmbannfuehrer	Major	Major
Hauptmann (Rittmeister)	SS-Hauptsturmfuehrer	Captain	Captain
Oberleutnant	SS-Obersturmfuehrer	1st lieutenant	1st lieutenant
Leutnant	SS-Untersturmfuehrer	2nd lieutenant	2nd lieutenant
Stabsfeldwebel	SS-Sturmscharfuehrer	Sergeant major	Warrant Officer
Hauptfeldwebel	SS-Stabsscharfuehrer	Sergeant major	no exact equivalent
Oberfeldwebel	SS-Hauptscharfuehrer	Master	Sergeant Major
Feldwebel	SS-Hauptscharfuehrer	Technical sergeant	no exact equivalent
Unterfeldwebel	SS-Scharfuehrer	Staff Sergeant	Colour Sergeant
Unteroffizier	SS-Unterscharfuehrer	Sergeant	Sergeant
Gefreiter	SS-Rottenfuehrer	Corporal	Corporal
Grenadier	SS-Sturmmann	no exact equivalent	Lance-corporal
Oberschütz	SS-Sturmmann	Private 1st class	Private 1st class
Schütze/Landser	SS-Mann	Private	Private

Introduction

Heldentod—The Nazi Culture of Death focuses on Nazi Germany's perspective on death, destruction, killing and dying, as reflected through both state-sponsored propaganda imagery and as captured by the amateur camera. In so doing it confronts the matter of subject *versus* observer and their intimate connection. The images also serve as both a conscious and unconscious documentation of man's inhumanity to man and the seeming ease with which tyrants can dehumanize and weaponize an individual or an entire population.

The German word *Heldentod* translates to "Hero's Death" and was a staple term of praise printed on hundreds of thousands of *sterbebild* or "deathcards" sent out in memory of fallen Third Reich soldiers.

Ich gab mein Leben in Gottes Hand Und starb als Held furs Vaterland

"I gave my life into God's hands and died a hero for the Fatherland"

. . . . .

As has been proffered by other observers, the history of civilization is the history of warfare. While militarism, with its adjuncts of expansionism, colonization and violent aggression, found expression in many cultures and nations, past and present, the underpinnings of the Nazi mindset toward conquest and industrialized murder could be traced back some 2,000 years. As one Roman military leader once remarked, "You don't know warfare until you fight the Germanic Tribes."

One hundred years before the rise of Nazi Germany, the famous German poet Heinrich Heine (1797–1856), wrote in his 1835 book *History of Religion and Philosophy in Germany*: "… that ancient German's eagerness for battle which combats not for the sake of destroying, not even for the sake of victory, but merely for the sake of the combat itself."

The general population's subservience to and support of endemic militarism is also linked to the advent of the 19th Prussian military code developed during the unification of Germany with its emphasis on duty and the sacredness of a superior's orders, in effect blind obedience. This was echoed by the often heard refrain voiced by those being brought to trial for war crimes, from the highest to the lowest in rank … "I was only following orders."

Words to Die By—"Live Bravely and Die Courageously"

The translated title of *Vom Mutigen Leben und Tapferen Sterben* by Waffen-SS soldier Kurt Eggers echoes the concept of *Heldentod*. Eggers, characterized as a warrior-poet by the Third Reich, was "deified" when a Waffen-SS unit was named for him after he died fighting on the Russian front. The book's chapters included: *The Awakening of the Life Will, One's Own Life, Overcoming, Reservation, Community, Valuation and Dialogue*, the last raising several questions including "How does the strong go to his death?"

An excerpt from the Pro-Nazi "hero's guidelines" translates:

> Whoever wants to strengthen the German, must force him to distress and deprivation. That is the secret of German nature: the German soul has never yet been endangered in wars, but often in cowardly times of peace. In prosperous times the German is unsuspecting and happy like a child. In such times it is easy for his enemies to tame him with theories and strange doctrines. Then they can dare to exploit him and force him to debasing slave tasks. German gullibility, upright trustfulness are the weakest spots in the fortress of German nature. **One has taught the German that hatred is despicable. And the German has believed this teaching. Only late did he come to realize that genuine hatred is just as noble as genuine love.** (Author's emphasis)

. . . . .

> All Freedom, all Greatness, all Culture is only maintained and spread aloft by wars … Today in Germany we write poems in steel and symphonies in ferro-concrete … War is the mightiest encounter of nations!

Nazi Party approved writer Ernest Jinger from his book of essays titled *The Inner Experience of Battle.*

. . . . .

During the era of the Third Reich, war heroes gained the status of celebrities and served as morale boosters, inspiration for young soldiers-to-be and instruments of Nazi propaganda. After the war and continuing into the current period, many of the highly decorated combatants, especially fighter pilot aces of the Luftwaffe, were accorded similar status and often made appearances on television programs and feted at special Second World War veterans and historical events, including those in the U.S. Their autographed photos continue to find a popular audience.

Damaged Battlefield Photograph
As civilization/warfare evolved so did its weapons of destruction, where once "warriors" wielded swords and axes, they now held machine guns and grenades, yet the concept of the "hero's death" continued through the millennia without interruption.

Face to Face Photos
The photographs and documents seen here, most one of a kind originals, are from the author's personal collection. They in turn were selected after the examination of over 500,000 images and chosen for both their intrinsic historical context and visual impact. In addition to several that were created during First World War and the Interim-War Period, the majority relate to the Second World War, specifically the era of Nazi Germany. Of those each records a fleeting instant of time within the twelve years of the Third Reich including six years of war that swept through Europe, an era that shook civilization to its foundations.

Optical Spectrums and Ideologies Collide
A 1920s German large format plate film camera compares to the compact Russian made copy of the revolutionary 1925 introduced German Leica 35 mm camera. The FED "clone" was first produced in 1934 at the F. E. Dzerzhinsky Labor Commune in Kharkov, Ukraine, the facility established as a "rehabilitation for youth" center by Stalin and named in memory of the infamous founder of the Soviet Secret Police. It was Russia's first 35 mm camera, and only the second camera made in the country.

. . . . .

The photos seen in this compilation, sourced from over 20 countries, were in most part taken by "ordinary" soldiers wearing the uniform of Nazi Germany and often gazing through the apparently ubiquitous personal cameras they had taken to war to document their experience. The image quality as presented depends on the original quality of the camera and film, the photographer's skill and the effects of decades upon ephemeral slips of paper.

Each image functions as a time capsule unearthed and previously buried away in a dusty drawer or glued into a moldering scrapbook, destined to remain unseen and unexplored. But now decades later they are brought to view in the hope that they may shed some light on those darkest of times and moreover lead others to their own further investigations. Any errors in identification remain the responsibility of the author. No accusations of war crimes are intended or implied against any of the individuals appearing here except in the documented cases as so noted in the text.

Camera Mania

At least six different cameras are detectable in this photo showing exuberant Luftwaffe personnel greeting the arrival of the Supreme Leader.

Hitler and Goebbels promoted the use of the "modern" compact 35 mm camera over the "old" large plate film and foldable cameras and in fact placed an effective ban on the older cameras by the state propaganda organs. Nazi Germany would also see the introduction of the first color 35 mm slide film.

German Officer Aims his Foth "Derby" Camera—August 17, 1941

On the photo's date, the U.S. launched its first daylight bombing raid on Nazi-occupied France, 18 B-17 "Flying Fortresses" taking part without a loss. Two months earlier, on June 22, Germany launched its invasion of the Soviet Union.

Point and Shoots—Foth and Friends
Four of the many cameras available to Third Reich era civilians and soldiers. (*Top left to right*): Agfa Karat 35 mm cassette film, *circa* 1938; Foth Derby, 127 roll film, Berlin, 1931-1940. (*Bottom left to right*): Icarette folding camera, 117 roll film, Dresden *circa* 1934; Voigtländer Brilliant, 120 roll film, 1930s, Berlin.

Amateur Photographer at Work
A soldier of the *Luftwaffe* flak force, wearing his ceremonial dress dagger, squints through the viewfinder of his folding camera.

SS Man Documenting History
An SS *Sturmbahnführer* (battalion commander) aims his movie camera at an unknown target. His tunic indicates his membership in a motorized division and his lapel ribbon denotes the awarding of the Iron Cross. The breast medal is the German Cross (introduced September 28, 1941), an intermediary award following the Iron Cross and prior to qualifying for the vaunted Knight's Cross. He wears a wedding ring on one hand, an SS "death's-head" ring on his other as well as an expensive wristwatch.

All Metal Construction
A variety of high quality amateur cine cameras were available to the German public including early 9.5 mm, 8 mm and 16 mm designs from Agfa, Pathex, Siemens and other manufacturers. (*Top left to right*): French 9.5 mm Pathé, German Pathex Motocamera H. (*Bottom left to right*): German made Agfa and Siemens. Their pre-motorized "clockwork" design required winding of the "key" seen on the side of the cameras to enable filming.

War Photographer—Everywhere!
The cover image appearing on the December 17, 1940 issue of the *German Illustrated* newspaper published in Berlin focuses on the war correspondent film maker.The caption in part reads: *Where German troops are in the fight or in preparation for the fight can also be found the War Photographer They convey to their homeland and posterity a powerful portrait of the heroic mission of the German soldier … and we should not forget that the war photographer has also sacrificed his life for his Führer and people.* By the end of 1940 Germany claimed new victories including the occupation of France. The soldier wields the industry standard Arriflex professional 35 mm movie camera, also the choice of notorious Third Reich filmmaker Leni Riefenstahl.

Nr. 51

Deutsche Illustrierte

PK. — überall!

Aerial Film Maker at Work
Sitting in the open cockpit of a biplane, a corporal in the Luftwaffe prepares his camera for either ground reconnaissance or plane to plane filming for training purposes. Special "gun cameras" were also developed to record aerial combat.

Professionals at Work—Words for the Photos
Somewhere in France, war correspondents (*Kriegsberichter*) at work with their typewriters ponder over their next feature articles for both military and civilian consumption.

Soldier and Grandmother Photographed with Photographs
No other war had been so intensely documented by film, in great part German film, both by official agencies and by the individual soldier himself via his personal camera, literally millions of images produced, many of them seen for the first time in the following pages.

Photo within Photo
A studio photographer has created a special photo-postcard for a soldier depicted as contemplating his wife and two young sons as he pens a letter. The original photo of woman and children is seen propped against the flower vase. The army private wears black ribbons on his shoulder epaulets indicating he is selected for NCO training and promotion. The "x" marks on the children's faces could have various meanings.

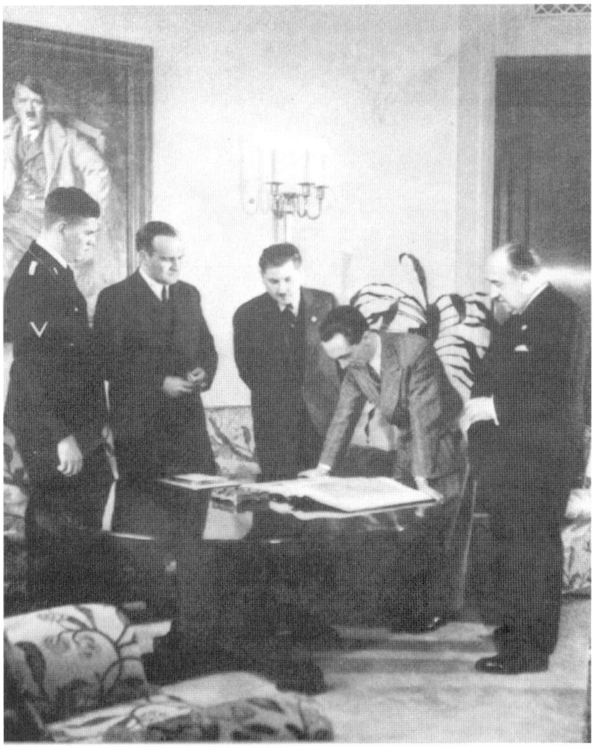

The Third Reich's Social Media Master
Examining a large book and seen here as the focus of a 1937 German newspaper feature "A Day at the Propaganda Ministry", Joseph Goebbels as its minister would marshal all the most advanced visual, auditory and printed media resources to promote the programs and ideology of National Socialism as imprinted by Adolf Hitler. As the air war ravaged German cities, it was Goebbels, not Hitler, who appeared in public to rally the population. Goebbels kept a detailed diary recording the maelstrom of Nazi inner circle competition and personality conflicts as well as the course of the war.

The Third Reich's Master of War Production—Testing All-Terrain *Kettenrad*

Highly accomplished architect Albert Speer would cater to Hitler's grandiose plans for the New Germania's building projects, creating the physical imagery of the Thousand Year Third Reich. Moreover as minister of armaments and war production Speer developed methods by which German manufacturing of war materials not only continued but increased despite incessant Allied bombing and by doing so lengthened the war by a year or more. Without both Goebbels's and Speer's efforts Nazi Germany could not have wreaked such incomprehensible destruction and mass murder. Goebbels and his wife would kill their six young children with poison then take cyanide themselves. Of all the high level Nazis on trial at Nuremberg, only Speer shrewdly admitted to responsibility. Although he denied knowledge of genocide, he also claimed to have procured Zyklon B poison in a failed attempt to kill Hitler at war's end by sending the gas into the Berlin *Führerbunker*. The gas was the same as used in the extermination camps. In the final Tribunal outcome, the man behind the German war machine was not condemned to death and survived his 20-year prison sentence, receiving friendly letters from Allied aviation experts and military leaders, eventually writing a best-selling book and living to the age of 76, dying during a visit to London in 1981.

Pre-War Portrait of Newly Married Couple
In 1936. summing up the role of imagery in Nazi Germany, art critic Fritz Zadow in the 41st volume of the publication, *Kulturbewußtsein und nationale Wirklichkeit* (Cultural Awareness and National Reality) wrote, "If anything, the new age of Germany will create the image of the German Man. There has never been a richer time for the presentation and interpretation of the German character. The Great War showed us how little mere strength, diligence, and conscience mean nowadays. **Everything depends on the persuasive power of the images provided so that a whole Folk can identify itself with them.** (Author's emphasis).

Transition of One Family, One *Volk*
Sometime in 1936, three years since Hitler took power and three years prior to the start of the Second World War, the Holfzappel family has gathered in their backyard for a family portrait, a table with a flower arrangement serving as a centerpiece. The father, a First War veteran wears his medals as well as a Swastika armband and Nazi Party pin. One son wears the uniform of the *Arbeitsdienst* para-military labor organization, another that of a Luftwaffe corporal. The youngest boy appears in civilian clothes although likely a member of the *Hitler Jugend*, the Hitler Youth organization.

A Country in Uniform

Under the umbrella of the *Wehrmacht*, Germany's military was composed of the Army (*Heer*), the Navy (*Kriegsmarine*) and Air Force (*Luftwaffe*), the latter also responsible for *Flak* anti-aircraft ground defense. Seen here are members of all three branches along with family and friends wearing a variety of expressions for the camera. Of a population of 80,000,000, some 18,000,000 would don uniforms of one kind of another during the 12 years of the Third Reich.

Along with Stalin's draconian "reconstruction" of the Soviet Union, the Nazi "social engineering" of an entire country and its population marked a pivotal point in human civilization. The military aggression conjoined by its racial "war within a war" waged by the Third Reich established a level of technologically-enhanced barbarity via its industrialization of genocide that placed the concept of human civilization itself in doubt.

Part I

The First World War—
Seeds of a Future War Sown

The Unending War

The carnage and brutality of the Second World War was deeply rooted in the previous European conflagration known as *The Great War* and *The War to End All Wars*. Many consider the second conflagration a continuation of the previous conflict fomented by the restrictions of the Versailles Treaty that severely penalized Germany, compounded by the global financial depression and rampant political unrest, the fertile breeding ground for the Nazi movement. In addition, the horrendous slaughter of the First World War affected the Allies' hesitation upon entering a new conflict. As a result, in the hopes of preventing more bloodshed, the British early on sought appeasement and the French ultimately capitulated after six weeks of fighting that began in the summer of 1940 a year after the mechanized *Blitzkrieg* had overwhelmed Poland in a matter of days.

While the veterans of the First World War on all sides were all too well aware of its abject horror and had some realistic understanding of what lay in store for them in the new war, the post-1918 generation of German soldiers now 18–21 in 1939 were literally "raw recruits" and like most young men they responded with one degree of enthusiasm or another to the drum-beat of their country's call to arms, a response summoned countless times throughout the centuries either to protect the homeland or to seek conquest and glory, apparently an endemic human trait.

But in the case of the Third Reich's military force, its youth had been relentlessly indoctrinated since 1933, some six years during which the Nazi programmers had worked their skills upon mind and body. A new brutality swept aside the norms of the past and while most young Germans did not go to war as pitiless automatons capable of crimes against humanity, the conflict's brutalizing effects, virulently infused with the Nazi supra-cultural arrogance and racial hatred soon metamorphosed into a cauldron of savagery beyond human civilization's ability to to comprehend. Even now some 75 years later, the questions remain … How could it have happened? How could an advanced culture step, so eagerly, into the abyss? How could other nations harken to its banner of nihilism and hatred? Was it some species catharsis of self-destruction, now excised, and the future safe some such madness? Or will there be new photos of new apocalypses?

1913—Strassburg Reserve 11th Company 105th Regiment
A year before the outbreak of the First World War, more than eighty members of a Reserve unit have gathered for a massive studio portrait complete with beer kegs and a forest of lances. The often contested Alsatian city of Strassburg (German) aka Strasbourg (French) lying on the Franco-German frontier was the capital of the province of Alsace in Eastern France. The "cross-roads city" was once considered the "capital of Europe" because of its shared cultures and would change nationality four times between 1870–1945.

Officers at the Center
The officers, including one with a chest full of Franco-Prussian war medals, are grouped in the center above the large crest signage bearing the motto "God Bless Saxony" and "Homeland—The Rallying Cry!" Four members of the unit's band flank the artwork, each wearing the distinctive *Schwalbennester* or "swallow's nest" shoulder insignia of a bandsman.

Beer and Watchwords
The shield-shaped signage translates to "Who has watched Germany's borders has done so as a soldier." Visible also are trays of beer steins, beer an intrinsic element in the *gemütlichkeit* of German military comradeship.

Lances at the Ready
More signage proclaims "The Military Barracks Bid Farewell—The Reserve's watchword is Peace!" As the young soldiers strive to appear grim and foreboding, at least one seems to face the camera with a smile.

Soldiers of the Austro-Hungarian Empire—Two Austrians and One Hungarian (*right*)—Studio Photo Postcard

The merger of the Austrian and Hungarian monarchies had taken place in 1867. After long standing nationalist movements sought to throw off the yoke of the Austro-Hungarian Empire, escalating Balkan tensions resulted in the assasination on June 28, 1914 of the heir to the Empire, Archduke Franz Ferdinand (and his wife) by a Serbian nationalist. Austro-Hungary then justified its attack on Serbia (to end Serbian nationalist insurrection). Russia soon joined Serbia resulting in Germany declaring war on Russia. With Germany on its side, the leaders of the Austro-Hungarian Empire were enboldened to expand their war.

Its standing army in 1914 at the outset of the First World War included 40,000 Austrian and 30,000 Hungarian troops, but could also initially draw upon some 350,000 troops from the Imperial and Royal troops scattered around the empire. After joining them, Germany would eventually mobilize some 11,000,000 while the Ottoman Empire (Turkey) would send forth 2,850,000; Bulgaria another 1,200,000. The coalition was known as the Quadruple Alliance, while more generally as the Central Powers.

In opposition to the aggression, the Allies aka the Entente Powers took form via the United Kingdom and its colonies, then joined by France, Russia, and Serbia, and after some wavering, Italy in May 1915, and then in April 1917, the United States.

As the war ground on for four years in virtual stalemate, the initial 20,000,000 troops mobilized by the various warring nations would swell to some 70,000,000. Of that number, 15–22 million men in uniform would die, another 23 million wounded. As many as 20,000,000 civilians also perished.

In the end, following the defeat of the Central Powers in 1918, the Austro-Hungarian Empire was dissolved .

German Emperor and King of Prussia Kaiser Wilhelm II of Germany

Postcard dated September 26, 1914 mailed from Coblenz to the Saar Region.

Wilhelm was the grandchild of Queen Victoria of Great Britain, the royal ties between the two empires illustrative of the connectiveness of several European dynasties. He secretly signed an accord with the Austro-Hungarians guaranteeing military support thus precipitating the First World War. He abdicated at war's end with Germany's defeat, dying at age 82 in the Netherlands on June 4, 1941, long enough to see Nazi Germany launch a second world war. He initially held hopes for the re-establishment of the monarchy by Hitler.

***The Illustrated History of the World War*—published 1916**

Striding side-by-side, Germans in tell-tale spike helmets (*pickelhaube*) and their Austro-Hungarian allies charge forth on the special issue's cover.

War was characterized as a glorious undertaking with combat rendered in heroic imagery. As shown in the illustration, even old, bearded men have taken up gun and bayonet for the sake of the Fatherland.

Once the truth behind the propaganda images became known, the carnage of the First World War with some 16,000,000 soldiers and civilians dead, civilization was shocked to its core. In the wake of bloodshed on such a vast scale, long secure worldviews of history, humankind, religion, economics and morality were left in a shambles. Whole generations of British, French, Belgian, German and Russian young men disappeared in the muddy mayhem of protracted trench warfare where the term "No Man's Land" took on a whole new meaning for the future of armed conflict. The toxic seeds of a future war lay sown into the mire of blood and flesh ground deep into the battle-scarred European landscape.

The illustration bears the signature of Anton Hoffmann of Munich, born 1863 in Bayreuth. He became well known for his paintings and drawings, particularly his military themed work which today is still offered by galleries and art auctions.

Anton Hoffman coincidentally bears the same last name as Heinrich Hoffmann (1885-1957), Adolf Hitler's premiere photographer, responsible for thousands of images glorifying *der Führer* and as a result a major contributor to the Nazi propaganda machine.

Child of the Previous War—In the Image of the Father

Militarism was sewn into the fabric of German society as it was in most European countries, children playing soldier the natural order of things. The glamour and glory of a soldier's life made its mark early on, linking one world war with the next with only changes of uniform while the carnage grew exponentially.

1914 Commercial Postcard

During the first year of the First World War, ten German children having donned a variety of uniforms while brandishing swords, toy rifles and flags for the camera. The accompanying poem translates:

> Our Fathers' victory is certain,
> Because they strike like the Blücher!
> The enemy, however, got away this time,
> but we'll settle it later.

The reference to Blücher refers to a First World War naval warship, a transitional design between armoured cruiser and battleship, and named after the famous Prussian military hero of the Battle of Waterloo. On January 23, 1915, the ship was sunk by overpowering British naval fire at the battle of Dogger Bank but the steadfast resistance by her crew enabled its comrade ships to escape. After its own sinking, a German Zeppelin by error impeded British efforts to rescue the German seamen. Of the Blucher's crew of nearly 1,400, only six officers and 275 enlisted men survived. The designation *Blücher* would be resurrected by Nazi Germany's *Kriegsmarine* as the name for a flagship heavy cruiser, it too meeting a similar fate.

Top of next page:

Off to War Souvenir

Young recruits pose for a "trick" photograph at the studio of Julius Graetz in the city of Magdeburg, The backdrop, in addition to the hurtling artillery shell, features in the lower panel an illustration of their military barracks located near the village of Dornitz in north-eastern Saxony–Anhalt Germany. If any of the soldiers survived the First World War, they may well have found themselves in the next war, only some 20 years later.

Studio Family Portrait (*Below left*)
The soldier's belt buckle is inscribed with the Imperial German Crown and the words *Gott Mit Uns* (God is with Us) the same phrase later found on Nazi era military belt buckles.

First World War Austrian Soldier—*Studio Elite* Photo—City of Linz (*Below right*)
Hitler who as a child lived in Linz, Austria, until 1907, considered it his "home town," the city also Adolf Eichmann's residence as a youth. Hitler had plans to transform Linz into the Third Reich's cultural center. A dozen miles outside the city was the infamous Mauthausen-Gusen concentration camp. In 1996 the city chose to confront its Nazi past, resulting in a public exhibition in 2001. At this point in time, the city also recognized the work of Simon Wiesenthal who had opened his Holocaust documentation center in Linz in 1945.

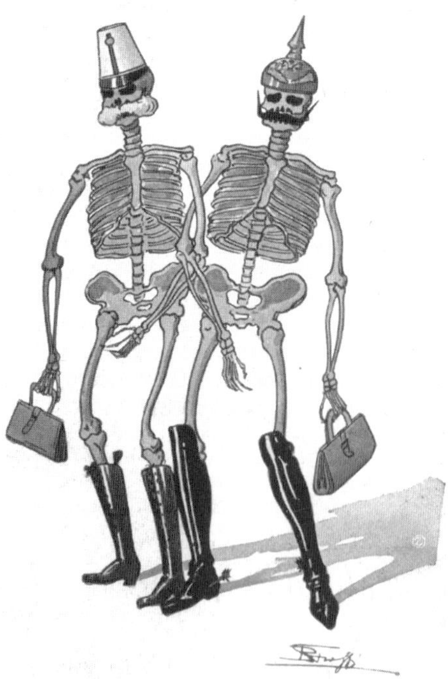

Verso la pace .... eterna.

Clockwise from top left:

German Cavalryman

Bedecked with flowers for his studio photograph, an unnamed young soldier's spur straps indicate his membership in the horse troop. He also wears his bayonet at his side as well as his flashlight on his chest while the number 77 on his helmet indicates his regiment. Such "floral" images were taken as a soldier was about to depart for the battlefield perhaps as a sign of good wishes or even a veiled hint of funeral decorations. Thousands of soldiers from all combatant nations were never identified, many remaining forever MIA (Missing in Action).

Photo Postcard

Wearing the iconic spiked *Pickelhaube* helmet a pair of young German soldiers stand at the ready.

"Toward Peace ... Eternal"

A colorized illustration characterizing the Austro-Hungarian and German military alliance and its fate appears on a commercial Italian postcard of First World War vintage. Italy would join the Allies in combating Germany and its allies during this initial world war.

"Away with the Barbarians! Subscribe to the Victory Loan"
A First World War Italian postcard depicts hand-to-hand combat between German and Italian soldiers, the captioning calling for the purchase of war bonds to support the war effort. The illustration shows the Italian overwhelming the German and relying only on his bare hands rather than the rifle and bayonet slung over his shoulder, apparently emphasizing the prowess of the Italian soldier. The postcard, printed in Milan, carries postmarks of March and April 1918, and addressed to the village of Ranzo in north-east Italy, some 50 miles southwest of Genoa.

German Soldiers Gear-up for Battle
Their spiked helmets, though distinctive, were fashioned in most part from leather which proved less than effective against flying shrapnel, machine guns and snipers. A new steel helmet, the *Stahlhelm* aka "the coal bucket" was soon designed and introduced as a replacement.

Handgrenatenwerfer
A First World War German commercial postcard features the image of a fir tree sprig camouflaged soldier armed with several "stick grenades," including a half dozen at his feet and ready for priming. He also wears the new steel helmet.

Trench Warfare
Troops of the Austro-Hungarian Empire battle hand to hand with soldiers of the Russian Imperial Army (white caps), the latter eventually withdrawing from the war, Russia falling into a state of chaos, the Bolshevik revolution taking place in 1917. The stalemate of the First World War warfare dragged on for years, the nonstop carnage turning the vast networks of trenches into mass graves for the combatants. Whole generations were consumed, the First World War leaving European societies festering with open wounds that never healed.

Seppl's War Report from Russia (*right*)
Originally printed in bright colors, this strange card carries a caption apparently translating to "I'm fine, an earwash needed, miserable Bazi." The earwash reference seems related to the injury involving his face. Seppl is a popular Bavarian nickname, while Bazi, also Bavarian, is the derogatory term for "clever or mischievous boy."

"The First American Prisoners"—Photo Postcard Dated December 23, 1917 (*below*)
It was a gloomy Christmas for six U.S. army soldiers (four without helmets, two with "pie tin" helmet) visible in the photo. Troops of the American Expeditionary Forces (AEF) had landed in Europe in June but not fully deployed until October with the arrival of the well-trained First Division then thrust into the French trenches at Nancy. In addition to the throng of German soldiers now wearing the new steel helmets, captured weapons including French machine guns have been placed on display for the photo. The commercially printed postcard was available to both soldiers and civilians.

The First World War found some 7,000,000 POWs captured from the various nations involved in the conflict, Germany itself holding some 2,400,000. Unable to handle the flow of prisoners, they were initially housed in make-shift camps often with poor food and hygiene conditions, very often all nationalities and ranks mixed together although the officers had better arrangements. By 1915 many camps had some sporting and cultural activities, even prayer rooms for Christians, Jews and Moslems. At one point British officers were allowed to go for group walks if they signed a document promising not to attempt escape. For the less cooperative, there were special "reprisal camps" where conditions were frequently fatal due to lack of food and arduous labor. Estimates of deaths in the POW camps range from a high of 70,000 for the Russians who received no food packages from home, to France with some 17,000 deaths and Romania with 12,500.

American Postcard—"Photo of First German Prisoner"—Dated 1917 (*above left*)
A seemingly relaxed, fully kitted young German soldier poses for an American soldier's camera or it may be a photo carried by the soldier himself and confiscated by his captors.

"The Final Blow"—German War Bond Drive Poster—April 6, 1918 (*above right*)

Top of next page:

Execution of a Deserter on the Ramparts of Straßburg—No Greater Crime
An apparently staged image of a condemned man about to face a firing squad is seen on a commercial German postcard that focuses on the shameful crime of desertion, punishable by death. The use of the word 'ramparts' refers to the historic city's famous defensive fortifications.

The poem loosely translates:

> An hour well into the night you have called for me
> You presented me right before the captain's house
> Oh, God, they fished me from the river!

Straßburg aka Strassburg aka Strasbourg, home to German speaking peoples was claimed by Germany both during the First World War and the Second World War, though eventually repatriated to France after both wars.

During the Nazi-era the Germans created the Natzweller-Struthof concentration camp some 30 miles southeast of Strasbourg. By 1943 victims of the infamous "Night and Fog" decree were sent there including many members of the French Resistance. The skeletons of Jewish prisoners gassed at the camp were forwarded to the large collection studied at the Strasbourg University. Roma prisoners were also gassed to test poison gas. Eventually some 50-subcamps were established in the area. By war's end, at least 20,000 had died in them.

The postcard writer, a Richard, has dated the card as June 3, 1914. It bears a Posen postmark and addressed to Anna Haruh in Rakwitz. The town would become a flashpoint many years later in the days of the Second World War. Up until 1939 it had been a Polish frontier station near the German border. In the first few days of the invasion of Poland, beginning on September 1, 1939, large numbers of ethnic Germans then living in Rakwitz (Rawicz) were rounded up by Polish civilians, many badly beaten or killed by them and also by Polish soldiers taking their revenge for Nazi Germany's attack. The survivors were rescued by German troops after the ethnic Polish Germans were driven toward the front lines.

Sniper's Target

Commemorating *Der Weltkrieg (the First World War)*, this "collector" card (No. 54) was one of a series found in Nazi era packages of German "Mokri Superb" cigarettes. The illustration depicts German troops tempting their Russian enemies. Titled "In the Trenches," the caption further reads "… at the end of September our East Operation came to a standstill. The difficulties of replenishing supplies along the Riga–Czernowitz Front brought great privations. However the German soldiers' sense of humor, including all kinds of banter aimed at 'Ivan' made it impossible for the enemy to break down our troops."

"My Hand Guards Your Steps"
Chosen by a soldier of the 25th Infantry Regiment, 1st Company, this postcard was
stamped in Austria and sent to an address in Morava, then part of Czechoslovakia.
Despite guardian angels, over 2,000,000 German soldiers died during the First World War.

The Sun Sank in the West
"And will she be guided from another to the altar, shall she remember the one who once was faithful to her?"

A colorized postcard pulls at the heartstrings for a dying soldier and his wife not-to- be at home. It was postal stamped via *Feldpost* (military mail) on July 28, 1915 addressed to an Anna Shalber—Famer's Daughter—in Oberhaching, Bavaria from a Alois Huber. The date is one year to the day that the Archduke was assassinated in Sarajevo thus igniting the war.

***Stolzenfels am Rhein*—"Proud Rock on the Rhine"**

Stolzenfels is a strategic area on the Rhine River near the city of Koblenz and the location of a famous late thirteenth-century castle Schloss Stolzenfels.

The staged studio photo montage of angels and wounded soldier has been incorporated into a First World War era postcard that also featured a poem that read:

> In the field of battle in the dead of night
> Dying is a German Hero.
> For the emperor's honor and the country's military
> Leaving the world to the fellow who is kneeling with him,
>
> He lifts his dying eyes and says, 'If you return home
> Then search for my love,
> Give her back this ring and say that my faith was true,
> true unto death—
> However I do not return home,
> from the Proud Rock on the Rhine.

. . . . .

On a daily basis during the First World War, some 9.9 million postal mailings were sent to the front and some 6.8 million returned home. About half of the postings were in fact postcards, many like this example, composed of melodramatic photo-montages, then a popular format.

Zur frommen Erinnerung im Gebete
an den ehrengeachteten Herrn
Moritz Bichlmeier,
Schreinermeister in Mauern,
Pionier d. 5. Reserve-Pionier-Kompagnie,
gefallen am 17. Nov. 1915 auf dem Felde
der Ehre im 27. Lebensjahre und dessen
im Tode vorausgegangenen Schwagers,
des tugendsamen Jüngling
Bartholomäus Dausch,
Schreinermeisterssohn in Mauern,
Soldat beim 2. Inf.-Regt.,
gestorben am 2. Oktober 1915 als Held
fürs Vaterland im 22. Lebensjahre.

Schlaft wohl im Feindesland bis wir
uns wiederseh'n.

Druck v. J. Pichlmayr (G.m.b.H.) Moosburg

Cabinet Makers from Mauern—Related in Death—KIA 1915 (*left*)

Two young men, brothers-in-law from the Upper Bavarian village of Mauern both shared a trade and "fell on the field of honor." Bartholomaus Dausch of the 2nd Infantry Regiment died at age 22 on October 2, while Moritz Bicschlmeier, age 27, died on November 17 while serving as a combat engineer. Together in death, they shared one memorial card printed by their families. Based on the dates listed, Dausch likely died during the Second Battle of Champagne (September 25—October 6), a French offensive against German positions. French losses were 145,000 men, while the Germans lost 72,500.

***Den Heldentod furs Vaterland*—A Hero's Death for the Fatherland—May 28, 1917** (*below*)

Johann Reiterberger was the son of a large landowner from the Bavarian town of Oberpirach some 45 miles east of Munich. He died at age 22 from wounds while being treated in a field hospital in Hungary "after 15 months of loyal military service." A member of the 3rd Rifle Regiment, 15th Company, he is shown via a formal studio photo in full uniform including a club hanging at his left side, a weapon well-used in the brutal, close-quarters trench warfare encountered on the Western Front.

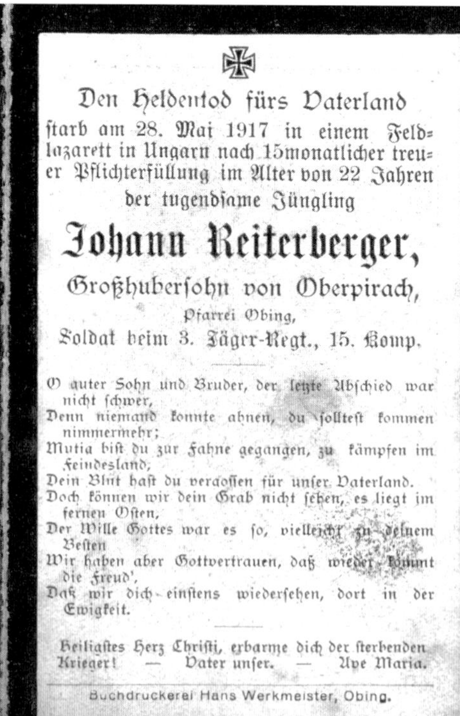

Den Heldentod fürs Vaterland
starb am 28. Mai 1917 in einem Feld-
lazarett in Ungarn nach 15monatlicher treu-
er Pflichterfüllung im Alter von 22 Jahren
der tugendsame Jüngling
Johann Reiterberger,
Großhubersohn von Oberpirach,
Pfarrei Obing,
Soldat beim 3. Jäger-Regt., 15. Komp.

O guter Sohn und Bruder, der letzte Abschied war nicht schwer,
Denn niemand konnte ahnen, du solltest kommen nimmermehr;
Mutig bist du zur Fahne gegangen, zu kämpfen im Feindesland;
Dein Blut hast du vergossen für unser Vaterland.
Doch können wir dein Grab nicht sehen, es liegt im fernen Osten,
Der Wille Gottes war es so, vielleicht zu deinem Besten
Wir haben aber Gottvertrauen, daß wieder kommt die Freud',
Daß wir dich einstens wiedersehen, dort in der Ewigkeit.

Heiligstes Herz Christi, erbarme dich der sterbenden Krieger! — Vater unser. — Ave Maria.

Buchdruckerei Hans Werkmeister, Obing.

"I had a Comrade"
The commercially printed First World War German postcard, one of the series titled *Unsere Feldgrauen* (Our Soldiers) referring to the field grey uniforms of the German infantry, commemorates the fallen and reads: *I had a comrade, a better one you could not find. The drums called to arms. He went to my side, in the same pace and step.*

Memorial Card Artwork—1918—
Heavenly Approval
"You Will Wear a Glorious Crown in the Land of the Lord" reads the inscription on this funeral announcement issued in the memory of a fallen soldier. The invocation confirms that his hero's death in war will find be crowned with heavenly reward.

Illustrierte Geschichte des Weltkrieges 1914/16.

Phot. Berl. Illustrat.-Ges. m. b. H.

Österreichisch-ungarische Kriegsbeute: Italienische Fliegerwaffen.

"Spoils of War"
A German special edition magazine chronicling the then current war features an image of captured Italian weapons including a machine gun and "flying bombs." The war would spur the creation of more effective weapons of mass destruction including aircraft and rocketry that would be further developed for the next conflict.

Special Aerial Effects
The designer of a commercial postcard printed in France has added the images of a dirigible and an airplane, both introduced initially for reconnaisance then soon as platforms for the aerial bombing of ground targets. At first the pilots would simply drop grenades by hand; purpose-made bombs soon developed.

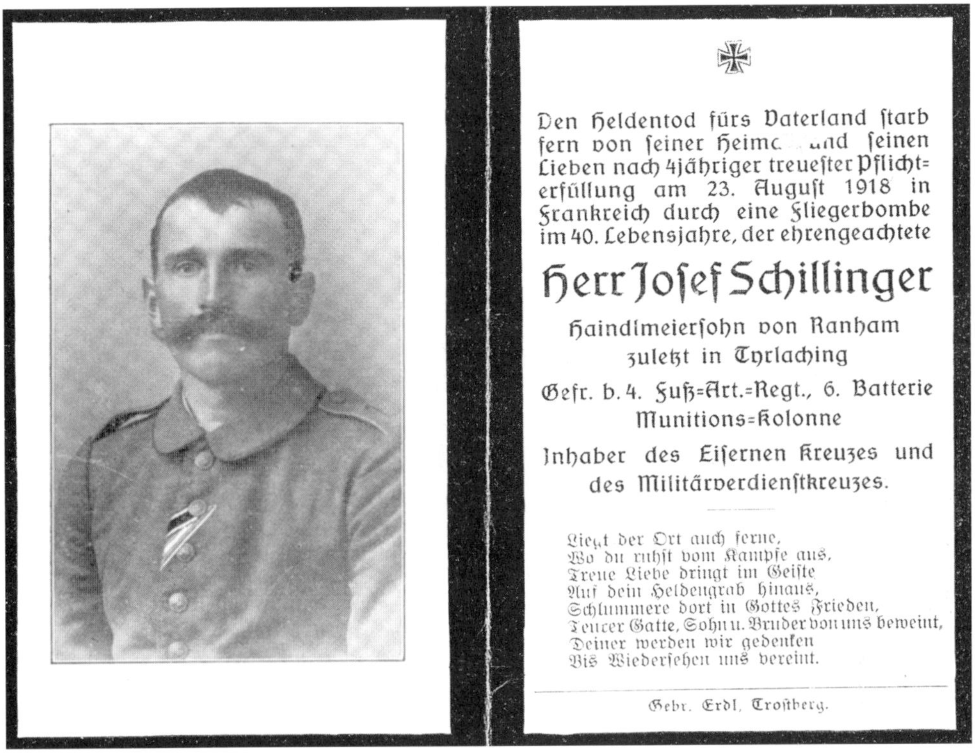

Den Heldentod fürs Vaterland starb fern von seiner Heimat und seinen Lieben nach 4jähriger treuester Pflicht=erfüllung am 23. August 1918 in Frankreich durch eine Fliegerbombe im 40. Lebensjahre, der ehrengeachtete

Herr Josef Schillinger

Haindlmeiersohn von Ranham
zuletzt in Tyrlaching

Gefr. b. 4. Fuß=Art.=Regt., 6. Batterie
Munitions=Kolonne

Inhaber des Eisernen Kreuzes und
des Militärverdienstkreuzes.

Liegt der Ort auch ferne,
Wo du ruhst vom Kampfe aus,
Treue Liebe dringt im Geiste
Auf dein Heldengrab hinaus,
Schlummere dort in Gottes Frieden,
Teurer Gatte, Sohn u. Bruder von uns beweint,
Deiner werden wir gedenken
Bis Wiedersehen uns vereint.

Gebr. Erdl, Trostberg.

Death by "Aerial Bomb"- August 23, 1918

The use of fledgling aircraft as a weapon of war claimed one of its newest victims when the 40-year old Josef Schillinger, a member of an artillery munitions battery, after four years of service and winner of the Iron Cross, died a *Heldentod*—a hero's death for his Fatherland in France, three months before the war ended.

Heavy Machinegun Team in Trench Position—1916 German Postcard

Zur frommen Erinnerung
im hl. Gebete
an den ehrengeachteten Jüngling
Franz Klaunzler,
Schütze bei einer M.-G.-K. des 12. bayer.
Res.-Inft.-Regts.

Geboren am 17. Dezember 1898 in Amberg.
Gestorben am 4. Oktober 1918 den Heldentod fürs Vaterland in Frankreich.

Stolz als junger tapfrer Krieger
Zogst du von uns hinaus in's Feindesland.
Doch Gott, der Lenker aller Mächte,
Er hatte anderes im Sinn!
Nicht im großen Schlachtgetümmel —
Durch eine Explosion gabst du dein Leben hin.
Schwer ist der Schlag, der uns getroffen,
Zerrissen ist das zarte Band. —
Doch süßer Trost ist uns geblieben:
Du starbst als Held für's Vaterland!

Barmherziger Jesus, gib ihm die ewige Ruhe! (7 Jahre 280 Tage Ablaß.)
Jesus, sei ihm gnädig!
Mein Jesus, Barmherzigkeit!

Vereinigte Druckereien Buchloe.

Death of a Machine Gunner

Franz Klaunzler, seen here in his formal uniform, died *den Heldentod* in France a month before his 20th birthday on October 4, 1918. Germany would formally surrender on November 11.

English Gas Bomb—German Photo Postcard—November 2, 1916

While first employed on the battlefield by Germany, the U.S., Britain and Russia also developed their own gas weapons.

The first battlefield experiment by British forces against German troops took place at the Battle of Loos on September 15, 1915, but led to a disaster due to wind changes and malfunctioning containers, many hit by German artillery. While Russia produced quantities of poison gas, it was not deployed. The British in contrast actually used it more often than German forces during 1917–1918 due to increased production, including the entry of the U.S. which also produced and stockpiled some 1400 tons of poison gas.

Mutual Assured Destruction
The caption of the 1917 German magazine illustration translates: *Defense against English Gas Attack with Hand Grenades* though it is difficult to discern who is dispensing the gas and both sides are lobbing grenades.

Nach einer englischen Darstellung
Abwehr eines englischen Gasangriffes im Handgranatenkampf.

American Commercial Postcard—1918
Photo-Cards of The Great War's carnage appeared along with series of steroview cards visually chronicling the battles. This card was printed and marketed by A. C. O'Neil of Akron, Ohio.

Zur frommen Erinnerung im Gebete an den tugendsamen

Jüngling Max Knott

Bauer von Kuppel,

Landsturmmann im 14. bayer. Reserve-Infanterie-Regiment, 1. Kompagnie, Inhaber des Eisernen Kreuzes 2. Kl., welcher am 11. Juni 1918 in Frankreich im 39. Lebensjahre infolge Gasvergiftung sein Leben für sein Vaterland hingab.

R. I. P.

Nicht wir allein, die um dich weinen,
Nein wer dich kannte, liebte dich,
Der Herr auch kennt und liebt die seinen,
Drum nahm er frühe dich zu sich.

Mein Jesus Barmherzigkeit!
(100 Tage Ablaß.)

Süßes Herz Jesu, sei meine Liebe!
(300 Tage Ablaß).

Süßes Herz Mariä, sei meine Rettung!
(300 Tage Ablaß).

Druck von J. Wein, Cham i. W.

Grave 242—Death by *Gasvergistung*—June 1918—France (*Previous page, above*)

A farmer from Kuppel, Hessen, Max Knott, 39, served in the 14th battalion of the Reserve Infantry Regiment, 1st Company and had been awarded the Iron Cross 2nd class for bravery. He was killed in action by poison gas on June 11, 1918 in France. According to the German Graves Registry, his body was buried in the Military Cemetery in St. Quentin in France, Block 11, Grave 242. The June 11, 1918 death in combat indicates Max Knott fell during the major German offensive that began at midnight on June 7. The assault had been known in advance as French intelligence had broken the German code. As a result the German attack was met by a massive French artillery barrage. In response, German artillery fired thousands of rounds of poison gas—mustard, phosgene and diphenyl-chlorarsine—into the French trenches, incapacitating some 4,000 French soldiers and killing 32. A shifting wind may have brought death to Max Knott as well, but also recorded was a large American gas attack on German targets in the Bois de la Sonnard area. It was also the timeframe of the historic Battle of Belleau Wood (June 1–26, 1918), during which U.S. Marines made their famous stand against repeated German attacks, one of the most brutal engagements of the entire war.

"Fog Sprayers" (*Previous page, below*)

A collector card packaged inside German cigarettes bears the image of soldiers with a caption on the reverse referring to the production of a smoke screen. The text translates, "Artificial fog is produced toward troops and equipment to reduce the effects of enemy fire." The portable unit bears some resemblance both to a poison gas canister as well as a flame weapon.

During 1915 trials with gas-infused artillery shells and running short of the shells, the Germans began experimenting with the direct release of chlorine gas from industrial cylinders. The poison gas testing was code-named "Disinfection," a term that would herald ominous future meanings. The first field test on January 25, 1915 at the battlegrounds at Ypres in France proved inconclusive due to the vagaries of wind direction. However the October 19, 1915 first-time use of phosgene gas saw 14,000 gas cylinders expended by the Germans against a 7.5 mile French entrenchment resulted in 750 dead, more than 2,000 injured.

The Face of Gas Warfare—First World War French Monument

190,000 tons of chemical weapons were produced during the First World War. Mustard gas, first used by German forces in July 1917 at the Third Battle of Ypres, is most often associated with the poison gas warfare of the First World War. It was considered a "harassing" weapon rather than having a lethal intent as it most often caused lingering injury including blindness. It was also a toxic pollutant that remained active in the soil often for weeks or longer.

Improvements Made
However, credit for the development of the even more potent phosgene poison gas goes to French chemists seeking to improve on chlorine for which some countermeasures had been developed. It was virtually colorless and thus less easy to detect. Phosgene proved far more lethal producing some 85 percent of the 100,000 First World War chemical weapons related deaths. Of that number a reported 56,000 were among the Russian troops gassed on the Eastern Front.

Children's Toy Soldier—Germany
Adolf Hitler, then a member of the 6th Bavarian Reserve Division, was both gassed and later wounded, a bullet in the leg, the latter during the Battle of the Somme that ground on until November 18, 1916 with little accomplished, the Allies gaining about eight miles of territory. However, the losses on both sides were astounding … a final total of some 420,000 British casualties, 200,000 French casualties, and 500,000 German casualties … more than 1,000,000 casualties in three and a half months. This level of attrition and its psychological impact would have far reaching effects during the early phase of the First World War.

Plaything—Portable Weapons of Mass Destruction—1920s–1930s
The designer has accurately rendered the actual flamethrower weapon, both the doughnut-shaped fuel reservoir and the nozzle end. Produced in Germany by the Gloria company, most of the red "flame" paint has worn away. (author's collection)

***Flammenwerfer*—Portable Unit—From the Battlefield to Berlin**
The image of the military response to the General Strike demonstrations appears on commercial postcard printed in 1919.

While the history of the delivery of flame as a weapon of war stretches back to the Ancient Greeks and the semi-mythical "Greek fire", flamethrowers as an effective and portable battlefield weapon first appeared during the First World War. On February 26, 1915 the German flame weapons were unleashed upon French troops near Verdun. The French fled in panic. A few months later on July 30, 1915, during one of the battles of Flanders, German troops used flame attacks against British troops defending Hooge. While initially terrified, the British regrouped and held their ground, but the two day engagement cost them 31 officers and 751 enlisted men. The *flammenwerfer* equipped "shock troops" became an integral part of the *Reichswehr* battlefield tactical strategy, later incorporated into Nazi Germany's pantheon of weapons.

First World War French Soldiers Examine German "Liquid Fire Gun" captured during the Battle of the Somme
The larger "cannon type" flame thrower or *Grossflammenwerfer* was adapted as a wheeled fieldpiece, one of several variations in size that came into use. The original text that accompanied this 1916 photograph that had been transformed into a viewable stereoscopic card read as follows:

> This gun instead of firing shot and shell shoots forth liquid fire, one of the barbaric methods of fighting used in modern warfare. The idea of throwing liquid fire upon an enemy's trench was planned and perfected by the Germans several years before the war, and its history may be traced in the German patent office. This is proof that they intended making this war as hideous and horrible as in their power.

Top of next page:

***"Frits" Fini" Near Belloy (Oise)*—Souvenir Photo Postcard**
A First World War era German soldier is photographed where he died, perhaps on his way to bringing ammunition to his comrades. "Fritz" is one of the derogatory names given the German soldiers while "Fini" is French for "the end." The "Belloy (Oise)" captioning refers to the Oise department located in Northern France and the commune of Belloy, which in sound and spelling appears similar to the famous battleground of Belleau Wood some 95 km southeast.

"Remains of a Boche"

Boche is a pejorative French term for German. An American veteran has returned home with a First World War souvenir photo from Europe. The German soldier appeared to have been resting on a water or petrol can when he died, perhaps placed there by a comrade.

On May 28, 1917 the U.S. enacted the Selective Service Act, America joining the war on April 6, 1917. The war ended with an Armistice on November 11, 1918 but not before bringing death and destruction on an unprecedented scale.

Even today, the "body count" for both World Wars is still in a state of re-assessment with the total number of estimated First World War casualties varying greatly. According to the Robert Schuman European Center (Scy-Chazelles, France) military and civilian casualties reached as high as 40,000,000 including 20,000,000 deaths, and 21,000,000 wounded. Of that number 9,700,000 million were military personnel who died in combat or by disease, accidents or while POWs. The estimates of 10,000,000 civilian deaths, many resulting from famine and disease, also incorporated the Ottoman Empire's genocidal campaign against the Armenians. The most conservative estimates from other sources for total deaths incurred by all war-time belligerents stands at 8,500,000 military dead as well as six to thirteen million civilian deaths.

Exhuming a Battlefield Corpse
German soldiers use a wire mesh frame to extricate the human remains. The machine gun, poison gas, aircraft, tanks and flamethrowers increased the mayhem wreaked by "modern warfare" as experienced during the First World War.

"The Shattered Remains of Russian Heroes"
The Underwood & Underwood Company founded in 1881 eventually produced ten million such stereoviews that documented world events, travel, fauna and flora, art, religion, and education. A popular form of entertainment, extensive collections could be purchased for home use and were also made available in public libraries. The coverage of the First World War was one focus of their productions; this image recording the aftermath of a battle between poorly equipped and equally poorly led Russian forces when meeting their German enemy. The Russian Tsar Nicholas II had officially abdicated the Imperial throne in March 1917, after large scale protests demanded the end of the monarchy and withdrawal from the disastrous war. A provisional government took control but only briefly until the Bolsheviks under Vladimir Lenin and Leon Trotsky's leadership overthrew it in the following June while the war still raged on the Eastern Front. On December 15, 1917, an armistice was signed between Russia and the Central Powers and fighting stopped. Lenin succeeded in formally withdrawing Russia from the war itself with the signing of the Brest–Litovsk treaty in March 1918, basically having capitulated to German demands in exchange for ending German attacks. However, Russia immediately found itself engaged in a bloody civil war between the "Reds" aka Bolsheviks and the "Whites," comprised of the Monarchists, counter-revolutionaries and anti-Communists. The struggle for control of the country continued until October 1922 with final victory going to the Red forces followed by the Bolsheviks eventually becoming the Communist Party of the Soviet Union.

1914—The Battle of Flanders—La Basse—German Trench Dead

A photograph records the true nature of trench warfare.

South-west of Lille and some ten miles from the Belgian border lies the area of France known as La Basse. In the autumn of 1914 it was the scene of one of the bloodiest battles of the First World War, in great part a continuation of the previous engagement at Ypres. Here the German army, thwarted in its initial drive on Paris, regrouped and shielded by a massive artillery bombardment, launched a new offensive westward. The targets were the French ports in an effort to cut off British delivery of men and supplies. A million German troops were thrown into the effort, the ensuing several battles collectively called the Battle of Flanders effectively converted the area into a massive cemetery … becoming the famous Flanders Fields.

Direct Hit

An artillery shell has turned a trench into a mass grave for several German soldiers, their bones strewn amongst their broken rifles, helmets and boots. The photo was sold as a commercial postcard.

Among the protracted battles of Flanders was the struggle in the trenches of La Basse lasting two months of continuous attack, counter-attack and stalemate. As reported at the time:

> The dead lay thick, bodies without heads, without arms or legs, human flesh plastered by the explosion of shells against and actually into the walls. The dead lay for days, decomposing under the feet of the living. Throughout these battles the Germans advanced in solid formation, often six or seven deep, and their losses were almost beyond belief. They carpeted the ground. Not a shell hole but had its quota.

For Home Viewing—"Ghastly Mementos of Battle at Verdun—A Pile of Human Bones"—1916

A First World War era Keystone View Company stereoscopic image captures the carnage at Verdun, the last eastern stronghold preventing the fall of Paris to German forces. It was also the site of the longest battle of the war (300 days) and fought from February–December 1916 with French forces eventually repelling a massive German offensive. Total casualties have been estimated at some 800,000, almost equally divided between opposing sides. Of the dead, 230,000 were identified, the remaining 70,000 lying in unmarked mass graves.

The caption on the obverse of the stereoscopic card reads:

> It would be impossible to imagine such a ghastly scene as this anywhere else than on the World War battlefield. In no other conflict of history were there such vast numbers of dead whose final identification proved impossible. Sometimes they were blown to pieces by high explosives and sometimes they were blasted out of their original graves and their bones scattered by recurring bombardments.
>
> The broken bits of skeletons heaped up before us were sifted from the soil of Verdun fields almost as if the latter had been raked with fine tooth combs. The slaughter which occurred from February 21 to December 21, 1916, on this small territory seems almost incredible. Looking from the parapet of Fort Douaumont southward across the shallow valley, possibly 2½ miles wide and 4 miles long, lying between the Douaumont Ridge and St. Ant where stood Forts Vaux, Souville and Belleville, the observer may reflect that on this ground which he can see in one sweeping glance, approximately 300,000 men were killed in the space of ten months, while hundreds of thousands were wounded. Thus did the generation of the World War pay in blood for the hatreds and rivalries of governments.

Boneyard

The Douaumont Ossuary memorial was erected near Verdun, the famous First World War battleground in northeast France, the city located on the Meuse River west of Metz. Within the structure, and visible through its windows, lie the jumbled bones of 130,000 unidentified dead, both French and German, as it were the largest mass grave of unknown soldiers in the world. From the 130-foot tower one can view the entire 20 square kilometre battlefield. The structure was dedicated on August 7, 1932. While the Verdun landscape today still bears the scars of battle, the city was christened "World Capital of Peace, Freedom, and Human Rights" in 1987.

Lingering Death in the "Forbidden Zone"

As reported in July 2016, it will take some 300–700 more years to remove the unexploded munitions festering in the 460 square mile area in north and eastern France known as the Zone Rouge or The Red Zone. Over the years hundreds have been killed by unexploded shells and mines. Moreover, like some nuclear wasteland, the area will be uninhabitable for at least 10,000 years due to the non-biodegradable and toxic elements leeched throughout the soil from the chemical remains of the exploded shells including lead, zinc and mercury found in the untold tons of shrapnel left from the battles. The area also tests for 300 times the tolerable levels of arsenic. Some areas of the Red Zone have lost 99 percent of its plant and animal life.

Death Oozing from the Sea

Recent reports have emerged of the growing danger from a variety of First and Second World War munitions dumped into the ocean that are now leaking toxins. In addition to tons of poison gases, thousands of artillery shells and other explosives were simply thrown into the sea, their metal casings now eroded by the water and time. For example, in the Baltic an estimated 80,000 mines occupy one mass dumping site. In some areas, due to the risk of explosion and toxicity, fishing is still banned a century later. It may take decades to remove the threat.

The Face of War—1918
His face mutilated by a war injury, a French soldier wears one of the exceptional prosthetic masks sculpted by American artist Anna Coleman Watts Ladd.

Born in the U.S., raised in France, followed by 13 years in Rome, Ladd then became one of Boston's major sculptors of city artworks. Her bronze works, especially the treatment of faces, were praised for their 'spirit of youth and hope." Shown in major galleries, she was commissioned by celebrities of the time including the famed dancer Anna Pavlova. She was also a writer, having published two books on her travel adventures. During the First World War at age 39 she relocated to the Latin Quarter of Paris where in 1917 she established *The American Red Cross Studio for Portrait-Masks* as part of the French Bureau for Reeducation of the Mutilated. Her studio came to the aid of badly disfigured soldiers by crafting individual masks specific to their conditions, accurately matching their original appearances.

With cosmetic and reconstructive surgery in its early stages of development, her talents surpassed the surgeon's efforts, her lightweight, finely detailed masks fashioned from copper, metallic foil and paint, were literally works of art. Her compassionate efforts brought a measure to relief to some 100 French soldiers as well as other war wounded nationalities and for which she was celebrated with the awarding of the *Légion d'Honneur Crois de Chevalier* and the Serbian Order of Saint Sava. A British observer wrote, "Deformed by the weapons and fires of war, these patients found relief in the artistry of a woman who had previously sculpted only the faces of lifeless statues."

Anna Coleman Ladd passed away a few months before the outbreak of the Second World War, on June 3, 1939 in Santa Barbara, California.

"We Will Never Forget"—*Kriegerdenkmal Munchen*—The First World War Munich War Memorial
The now ironic words etched into the stylized funeral bier commemorate German military losses in the First World War. While estimates vary because of the number of unidentified and missing, France lost over 1,400,000; Britain and its Commonwealth nations 1,115, 000; Russia 1,800,000 and Germany over 2,000,000 as well as millions more wounded.

Rustic Memorial
A motorcyclist, a camera case carried over his shoulder, visits an unidentified First World War battlefield. The archway carved with images of medieval weaponry carries an inscription that reads: "Remember your ancestors who fell here in the struggle for Freedom and Homeland."

Postcard—Model of the National Memorial and Hindenburg Internment
Built in 1927 in Hohenstein, East Prussia, (now Olsztynek, Poland), the *Reichsehrenmal Tannenberg* was a massive German memorial to the fallen soldiers of the 1914 First World War Battle of Tannenberg and the historic defeat of Russian forces by German troops under the command of General Paul von Hindenburg, then age 66.

National Hero—Generalfeldmarschall von Hindenburg
Referred to as "Father of the Fatherland," Hindenburg became an iconic and much beloved leading figure of post-war Germany even overshadowing the Kaiser. Although he retired in 1919, he was called back to public service in 1925 at 78 and elected the second President of Germany. Although in poor health, he was then asked to campaign for the 1932 election as the only candidate capable of defeating Hitler who was seeking the presidency. Hindenburg won in a runoff although the German public as well as members of the military and industry demanded Hitler be given the chancellorship. It appears that Hindenburg's own strong anti-communist stance may have shifted him toward supporting Hitler. Hindenburg gave way and signed the Enabling Act of 1933, which gave start to Hitler's takeover of the government and the country.

Tannenberg Memorial—Monumental Sarcophagus
What appears to a scale model for some epic film is an actual structure, its immense size illustrated by the barely visible figures of soldiers moving toward one of the white stone crosses on the upper tier.

Hindenburg died on August 2, 1934, his coffin and that of his wife then interred at the *Reichsehrenmal Tannenberg*. With the President's office vacant as a result of Hindenburg's death, Hitler took over its possession and authority, thus sealing the Nazi takeover.

OLD GRAVES AND TRANSITION TO A NEW WAR

A Visit to the Tomb of Germany's Heroes (*Next page, above*)
A group of Third Reich Army troops pose for a photo in front of their massive First World War forebears.

Germans adored Hindenburg to the point of a cult of personality, his aura even permeating the Third Reich. As a result Hitler staged a funeral on a grand scale leading up to the internment of his coffin and that of his wife at the memorial. Some ten years later as the Red Army penetrated the area, the coffins were moved to another location prior to the destruction of the *Reichsehrenmal*. Initial damage was caused by some 30 tons of explosives planted in late January 1945 by retreating German demolition teams, their targets including several of its eight 20-meter tall towers. Additional destruction was caused by the Soviets who re-purposed the materials to build post-war Soviet memorials. Along with further looting over the years of usable materials, the Polish government in 1949 ordered the dismantling of the remaining rubble, the process continuing into the 1980s. As a result of years of attrition, the truly monumental Tannenberg structure, perhaps rivaling the work of the Pharaohs, finally disappeared without a trace.

Re-Visiting the First World War Dead (*Next page, below*)
Luftwaffe soldiers have visited a French veterans' cemetery shared by both sides in the aftermath of the First World War.

Located in Ambleny in northern France and also known as the *Bois Roger* after the nearby woods, the Ambleny French National cemetery established during 1920–24 contains four "communities" referring to different combatant nationalities. In the German *Soldatenfriedhof* section there are 9,229 burials; of that number only 3,672 have individual graves. However, the majority of the dead are identified with only 13 remaining unknown (*Unbekant*). Most died in the last year of the war during the final great German offensives of 1918. There are also 67 civilian and one Russian grave from the First World War era. Two British soldiers had lain there but later moved to another French cemetery. Following the First World War an additional 555 graves were added.

AMBLENY
1914 - 1918

First World War Canadian National Vimy Memorial—France

German soldiers visit a monument to their past and present enemies. Unveiled on July 26, 1936, the massive structure was dedicated to the memory of the unknown dead of the Canadian Expeditionary Force who fought in France during the First World War. An eleven-year construction project, it is situated on the 250-acre battlefield park near Calais that includes trenches, tunnels, bomb craters as well as unexploded munitions closed off for public safety. The monument was rededicated after restoration in 2007 on the 90th anniversary of the Battle of Vimy Ridge which became a symbol of Canada's national unity and coming of age as a nation. The Canadians suffered some 10,000 casualties during the battle including 3,598 KIA.

Points of First World War Interest—French Graves

German soldiers visit the imposing pyramidal *Ferme de Navarin* memorial and Ossuary (boneyard). Upon entering one descends into the crypt that contains the remains of 10,000 soldiers killed during the September 1915 second battle of Champagne. The surrounding area was left pockmarked with bomb craters.

France— New German Graves for a New War
The neatly laid out garden cemetery shows two orderly rows of ten graves, each with the Third Reich soldier's name and his helmet. As the war progressed, especially on the Eastern Front the cemeteries would grow exponentially in size and without as much adornment. Such was the intensity of mutual hatred; the Russians often destroyed German cemeteries when their tanks came upon them. Neither side spared the wounded or medical personnel when overtaking field hospitals.

Gebetsandenken
an den Gefreiten
Peter Karl
Bäckermeisterssohn von Oberalteich,
Feldzugsteilnehmer 1914-18 und 1939-42,
welcher am 3. August 1942 bei den schweren Kämpfen im Osten im Alter von 43 Jahren sein Leben für unser Vaterland opferte.
Er ruht auf dem Heldenfriedhof Borißow.

Mein Jesus Barmherzigkeit!
Jesus, Maria und Josef, mein Trost u. meine Stärke!
Jesus, Maria und Josef, steht mir bei im letzten Streit!
Jesus, Maria und Josef, möge meine Seele mit Euch im Frieden scheiden!

Herr, gib ihm die ewige Ruhe!
Das ewige Licht leuchte ihm.
Laß ihn ruhen in Frieden!

Peter Karl—A Bridge between Wars
Peter Karl was a health spa attendant's son from Oberalteich in Bavaria. He had previously served in the First World War 1914–18 and then again from 1939–42 when he, at 43, was killed on August 5, 1942 in Russia. In the preceding June, German forces were successful in their push through the Ukraine, the 6th Army preparing for its assault on the Caucasus and the fateful siege of Stalingrad. Peter Karl, who had survived one world war, was "buried in a Hero's Cemetery in Borikov."

. . . . .

The Third Reich dictated even the design and graphics permissible on the memorial cards including what information including military details was printable. Naturally no anti-war sentiments appeared, such written or even vocal acts punishable by imprisonment or even death.

A Father Found—A Grave Bridges the First and the Second World War

The grave of Bernard Luttner, a driver in the Germany army, who died during the last days of the First World War on August 7, 1918, has had a note attached to it that translates: "The mother of two of your sons sent them looking for you! Hans and Heinrich in the War 1940–41."

The two young soldiers, fighting in the Second World War, have apparently discovered and photographed the grave. They were either small children during the First World War or were born to their mother via a second husband.

The date of Bernard Luttner's death marked a pivotal moment in history. On August 8th, the Allies launched a series of offensives against the Central Powers on the Western Front that lasted until November 11, 1918. It became known as "The Hundred Days Offensive" that saw the German retreat beyond the Hindenburg Line and the resulting armistice, ending the war and the German Empire. Germany's losses were estimated at 30,000 on the single day of August 8th, Allied dead numbering some 6,500 killed, wounded and missing.

Kinder—From the Cradle to the Grave

Inter-War Discontent—Past and Future Soldiers (*above*)
Children carrying rifles have joined a demonstration by members of the *Freikorps*, the First World War German veterans disillusioned and discontent with post-war conditions. They would form the nucleus of the SA "Brownshirts" that would help the Nazi movement take control of Germany.

Breeding for the New Order—Nazi Germany's Progeny (*right*)
In seeking to replenish both the horrific losses incurred during the First World War and the casualties mounting on the new war's battlefields, the Third Reich encouraged high birth rates via various incentives including financial inducements and honorific medals including the German's Mother's Cross in bronze, silver, and gold, the latter for those who produced eight or more children.

†

Christliches Andenken

an die geachtete Frau

Theresia Knoll

Mitbesitzerin des Mayr-in-Wald-Gutes in Teufelsgraben Nr. 111, Pfarre Kronstorf

Trägerin des Goldenen Ehrenkreuzes der deutschen Mutter

welche am 10. Jänner 1941 um 12 Uhr mittags nach kurzem, schwerem Leiden und Empfang der heiligen Sterbesakramente im 64. Lebensjahre selig im Herrn entschlafen ist.

Als Gattin, als Mutter, als Freundin,
Ruht hier, von vielen beweint,
Eine Mutter, die Tugend stets übte
Und Treue und Redlichkeit liebte.
Schlumm're sanft, o gute Mutter,
Das Grab entriß Dich uns zu früh,
Du warst uns Helfer, treuer Rater,
Ach, wir vergessen Deiner nie.

Leichenbestatt. Stigler, Steyr, Enge.

..ruckerei Steyr.

Gold Medal Mother

Theresia Knoll, co-owner of a guest house, died "at noon after a short, painful suffering" on January 10, 1941 at the age of 64.

During the period of December 1939 through May 1940, four months into the war including the invasion of Poland and France, some 121,853 Gold Mother's Cross medals were awarded indicating the birth of some 1,000,000 children. However, none would be old enough to wear the Nazi uniform as the promised 1000 Year Reich lasted but twelve.

"In Recollection of Our Wedding—from Ingeborg and Walter"

This photo produced as a postcard was dated March 20, 1943. The Stalingrad disaster had taken place the previous month with Germany now on the defensive on the Eastern Front. These children, eventually too young to go to war, were however caught in the midst of the intense aerial bombing of Nazi Germany, their fate as are their names, unknown.

On the next page:

May Day Parade (*above*)

Several children have prepared for the annual celebration and carry traditional Bavarian flower poles while two boys serve as the wagon's "horsepower". Three of the boys wear traditional *lederhosen* leather shorts. One of the swastika banners carries the name of a local newspaper while the other relates to the SA. The image, processed by a Hans Hofer at his photography shop possibly in Munich, appears to have been taken in the early 1930s, the boys eventually of age to join the military.

On the Knee of the SS (*below*)

In a photo dated June 22, 1940 three children join three SS men and their machine gun in the French city of Orgeville, German forces having occupied France in the previous May after a six week campaign.

Panzers by the Hundreds—War Toys for the Young

The photo taken in 1943 finds members of the 504th Infantry Grenadiers enjoying themselves in a toy factory. While two stand among a display of wooden wheelbarrows, their comrades seem drawn to the field of miniature tanks, very likely they the foot soldiers who advanced with and give support to the panzers in their full battlefield size. A large model of what appears to be a four-engine Focke-Wulf 200 Condor bomber hangs suspended over the legions of tanks. The airplane began life as a long distance commercial airliner that could fly nonstop from Berlin to New York. Later weaponized as war planes, they wreaked havoc on Allied shipping but their thin armor, non-battle-hardened design and construction saw them return to transport duties in 1944.

Third Reich Toy Soldiers— "Brown Shirts"—Early 1930s (*above left*)

These rare figures depict members of the SA (*Sturmabteilung* or "Storm Detachment"). Toy soldiers had become popular at the beginning of the century and advanced from simple tin and cast metal figures such as these to more detailed three-dimensional figures, tens of thousands produced.

Mayhem in Miniature (*Previous page, below right*)

A First World War *Reichswehr* era soldier throws the distinctive "stick grenade" or "potato masher" hand grenade while wearing a gas mask as highly toxic and often fatal chlorine, phosphene and mustard gases were used in battle by both the Germans and the Allies. Several more grenades are strapped to the soldier's waist, a Mauser rifle slung over his shoulder.

Pre-war and Third Reich German children alike played with these popular toys which came modeled after army, navy and air force personnel brandishing a variety of weapons and equipment as well as tools, musical instruments, etc.

Elastolin was a trademark of O&M Hausser (*O&M Haußer*) founded in 1912. During the Third Reich it would go on to produce images of the Nazi leadership as well as personnel from all branches of the *Wehrmacht*. This particular example bears the signs of age and perhaps trauma as it was found at a post-Second World War German home in Nuremberg.

HITLER JUGEND—HITLER YOUTH

Tabula Rosa for the Iron Forge of the Hitler Youth

The term Hitler Youth *(Hitler-Jugend)* came into official use in July 1926 when German youth groups were placed under the control of the SA and divided into several geographic areas or *Obergebeite*, specifically *Nord, Sud, West, Ost, Mitte* and *Sudost,*. The female section was labeled the League of German Girls (BdM or *Bund Deutscher Mädel*). By 1936, three years after the Nazi takeover, the *Hitler-Jugend* would count 5.4 million members aged 10–18. Almost all pre-Third Reich youth groups, both for boys and girls, were assimilated into the Nazi collective organizations.

Some groups balked, particularly the religously affiliated, but all eventually fell under the thrall of the State whose control and conditioning of Germany's children was a top priority, its goal the suplanting of the traditional family as the controlling force.

Hitler Youth for boys was divided into sections based on age: the so-called "Little Fellows" known as *Pimpf* recruited 6–10 year-olds; the *Deutsche Jungvolk* (German Young People) required the age of 10–13 for admittance with a focus on outdoor sports and para-military training. At 14 they transferred to the regular Hitler Youth, remaining there through the age of 18 during which they received more martial training before transitioning to their mandatory civilian labor service via RAD *(Reichsarbeitsdienst)* and finally on to military service in the Wehrmacht (army, navy, air force or SS). Girls aged 14–18 joined the *Jungmädel* (Young Maidens) with training emphasizing healthy habits, duties of the housewife and child-raising. Emphasis was also placed on Nazi racial dictums inflamed by its anti-Jewish virulence. Between 14–21, girls took part in further State sponsored motherhood training via the BdM (*Bund Deutsche Mädel*), the League of German Maidens.

HJ Comrades-in-arms

> I want a brutal, domineering, fearless, cruel youth. Youth must be all that. It must bear pain. There must be nothing weak and gentle about it. The free, splendid beast of prey must once again flash from its eyes. That is how I will eradicate thousands of years of human domestication. That is how I will create the New Order.
>
> Adolf Hitler

. . . . .

The pilots that flew the Stukas over Poland and carried the paratroopers over Crete and fought in the Battle of Britain had a few years earlier been among the 135,000 boys trained yearly as glider pilots prior to the war. Listed as members of the National Socialist Flying Corps, it circumvented the Treaty of Versailles designed to prevent German re-militarization. Another 300,000 boys trained in motorized units while others were enrolled in the Hitler Youth Navy.

Top of next page:

Summer Camp

Adult supervisors and offiicials gather at the entrance to a Hitler Yourth Camp.

> He who marches in the Hitler Youth is not one among millions,
> but a soldier of an idea.
>
> Baldur von Schirach
> Reich Youth Minister

Olympian Heights

An HJ squad, having brought their banner to their rooftop vantage, pause for a group photo. As highly indoctrinated "true believers" many would join elite units and fight with a fanaticism and vicousness that often surpassed older troops. Many German military as well as Hitler Youth songs contained virulently anti-Semitic lyrics, a popular HJ example contained the following: "Yes, when the Jewish blood splashes from the knives, things will go twice as well."

"The Captured Tommy"—Photo Dated June 6, 1943
Along with the Mayor (in suit and Nazi party pin), the town's moustachioed leading citizen and a elderly member of the *Volkssturm* carrying an antique shotgun, a throng of Hitler Youth have gathered for the photo op with the English prisoner, perhaps wearing his escape disguise, shown handcuffed and held at bay. Two days previously the massive German–Soviet tank battle at Kursk had taken place, Germany unsuccessful and no longer on the offensive in the East.

Zur Erinnerung
an
Josef Tischberger
Reichsbahn-Junghelfer
in St. Georgen an der Gusen
welcher am 20. Oktober 1943, um ½9 Uhr früh, im 15. Lebensjahre, verunglückte.

In der Blüte meines Lebens
Ueberraschte mich der Tod,
Meine Eltern und Geschwister, trauert
nicht vergebens,
Denn das Schicksal kam von Gott.
Wir sind ja noch verbunden
Durch ein Band, das nie zerbricht,
Liebe hält uns fest umwunden
Und die Liebe stirbt ja nicht.

Besteller: Seidel, St. Georgen a. Gusen

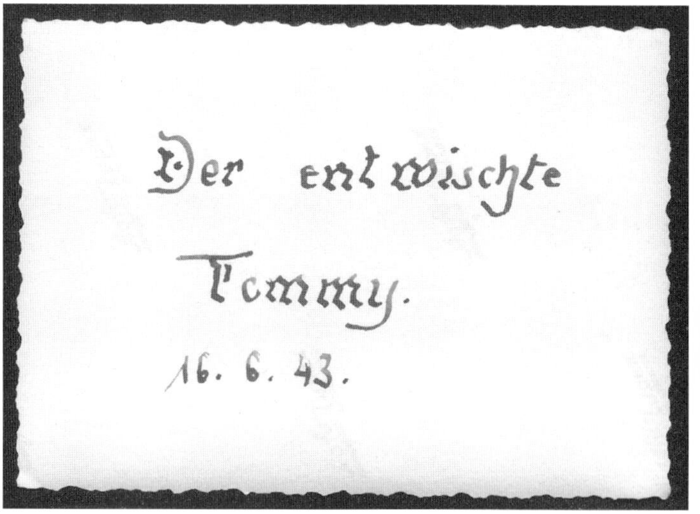

Accidental HJ Death—Age 15 (*previous page, below*)

The card states the time of the 15-year old's death on October 20, 1943 as "about 9:30 in the early morning" and due to an "unfortunate accident" while serving as a "train helper."

Seen in his Hitler Youth uniform, Josef Tischberger lived with his family in *Sankt Georgen an der Gusen* (Saint George's Town on the Gusen River), a small picturesque market village in Upper Austria situated near the city of Linz. It became the administration center for exploiting the slave labor of the Mauthausen-Gusen concentration camp system, including the infamous granite quarries, the camp set in operation in the summer of 1939.

It also was the location chosen for Gusen 2 described as the most brutal sub-camp. The slave laborers dug by hand some 50,000 square meters of tunnels and caverns beneath St. Georgen. The subterranean factories included a massive modern assembly plant for the radically new Messerschmitt Me 262 jet fighter and remained in production until the end of the war in May 1945, assembling some 1250 planes per month. An earlier introduction of the planes as promoted by Speer may have altered the outcome of the war but Hitler stymied the effort, more intent on bomber production.

Unser über alles geliebter hoffnungsvoller Sohn

Robert Diebold

Gebirgsjäger / Abiturient der Adolf-Hitler-Schule

geb. am 11. August 1926 · gest. am 25. Juli 1944

Joſef Rieß

†

In Chriſtus Jeſus
erwartet ſeine Auferſtehung unſer
einzig geliebtes Kind

Joſef Rieß

Fabrikantenſohn

der im 17. Lebensjahr nach langem ſchwerem Leiden im Oktober 1945 aus dem ruſſiſchen Kriegsgefangenenlazarett zu Brandenburg zu ſeinem himmliſchen Vater berufen wurde.

Wir bitten dich, o Herr, komme deinem Diener Joſef zu Hilfe, den du in deinem koſtbaren Blute erlöſt haſt.

O Herr, gib ihm die ewige Ruh und das ewige Licht leuchte ihm; o Herr, laß ihn ruhn in Frieden. Amen.

Mein Jeſus, Barmherzigkeit!
(300 Tage Ablaß.)

Süßes Herz Mariä, ſei meine Rettung!
(300 Tage Ablaß.)

Druckerei Waidhofen a.d. Ybbs Leopold Stummer

Death Card for a Top Hitler Jugend Student—Age 17—1944 (*above left*)

The family of Robert Diebold from Trostberg have commissioned an extra-large *sterbebild* commemorating his short life.

The card opens to show three pages of text describing his accomplishments as a school leader (Staff Sgt. in the Hitler Youth) and top graduate of the prestigious Munich Adolf Hitler School as well as his aspirations to become a "political leader." He died four months after enlisting in the Wehrmacht apparently joining the mountain troops (*Gebirgsjäger*). The card states "his biggest wish was to serve on on the front, but it was not to be." The vague reference may indicate he died from some other cause, perhaps an accident or from Allied bombing, as it states he underwent surgery in the military hospital at Hallein, Austria. Although no further details as to his death are supplied, a few days earlier the German Army Group Center was annhilated by Soviet forces in Belorussia. The card states "He was the idol of his comrades; with his clear-cut attitude, he was a born leader. He was always opposed to wrong-doings. He never forgot his hometown, and adored his mother above all others." Diebold died 17 days before his 18th birthday and five days after the failed assassination attempt on Hitler at his bunker in East Prussia.

War's End Plus Five Months—Age 17 (*above right*)

After a "long and difficult illness" Josef Kiess died sometime in October 1945 in a Russian POW hospital at Brandenburg. Information from the Soviets regarding German prisoners was not forthcoming or accurate. He is shown in civilian clothing rather than that of Hitler Youth.

Last Minute Soldiers of the Third Reich—21 October 1944—Aachen
The U.S. Signal Corp Radio press release photo carried the following caption: *Three small German boys were picked up on a road near Aachen for firing on advancing American soldiers. From left are Willy Eischenburg, 14, a Hitler Youth; his brother, Bernard, 10; Hubert Heinrichs, 10, and another Eischenburg brother Victor, 8.* (No final disposition of the boys' fate was stated.)

R. C. K. Ensor, author of the 1945 Oxford University Press publication *A Miniature History of the War—Down to the Liberation of Paris*, concerning the war in its final months, stated that "Hitler believed that the warlike qualities of a nation could be stimulated by teaching (in the broadest sense) to a decisive extent. Hence from the moment of his advent to power he set about controlling every avenue to the German mind—books, press, radio, films, theatres, schools, universities, and churches. By such methods he blinded, brutalized, and fanaticized his people, producing through the *Hitler Jugend* organization a whole generation of young barbarians, whose psychology may for long blacken the shadows of his country's future."

On the next page:

***Das Deutsche Mädel*—December 1941** (*above*)
The cover of the official magazine for the Federation of German Girls (BdM) of the Hitler Youth shows a young girl bringing flowers to a a bedridden soldier. The text of the insert reads: "With song and play, young women and young girls carry the glad tidings of Christmas eve to our wounded in military hospitals." The young soldier's left arm and chest seems to be held in some form of traction, the outline of a cast visible beneath the sheets. A chart behind the bed shows a long list of entries.

Helping Hands (*below*)
Two BdM girls in uniform have joined volunteers bringing refreshments and flowers to a troop train.

A popular BdM song went as follows:

> *We've given up the Christian line,*
> *For Christ was just a Jewish swine,*
> *As for his Mother-what a shame-*
> *Cohn was the lady's real name.*

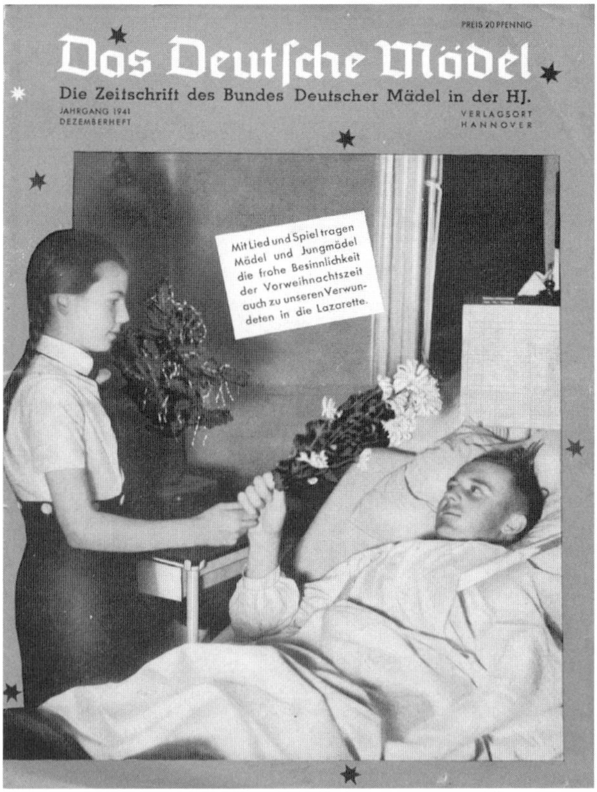
PREIS 20 PFENNIG
Das Deutsche Mädel
Die Zeitschrift des Bundes Deutscher Mädel in der HJ.
JAHRGANG 1941
DEZEMBERHEFT
VERLAGSORT
HANNOVER
Mit Lied und Spiel tragen Mädel und Jungmädel die frohe Besinnlichkeit der Vorweihnachtszeit auch zu unseren Verwundeten in die Lazarette.

***Blitzmädchen*—"Lightning Girls"—Female Auxiliaries** (*above left*)
Young women who served in the Luftwaffe communications detachments (*Nachrichtenhelferinnen*) were known as *Blitzmädchen* referring to the lightning bolt uniform emblem designating their role. Less complimentary nicknames created by their male colleagues included *Blitzmaus* (lightning mouse) and *Blitznutte* (lightning prostitute).

Out of Uniform (*above right*)
A woman has donned a man's formal (*waffenrock*) uniform.

Italian journalist Filippo Bojano who spent years living in Nazi Germany commented on Hitler's effect on women after attending an early camnpaign speech:

> I could see the seething masses of women who were becoming ever more and more mesmerized by him as they listened to every word he uttered, and who kept up a prolonged orgy of cheering when he had finisihed. Strange to say, Hitler's first supporters came from the masses of the female electorate. His first and most enthusiastic audeinces were women, and I am firmly convinced that the German women will be the last to admit that Hitler's political career has been disastrous to Germany.

Hitler however was strongly opposed to women in the military or even in industry for that matter, regarding them as the "incubators" for German future soldiers. Special medals were awarded mothers who were honored as equals to their men fighting on the Front in consideration of their contribution to the State. The awards were given out on the annual Mothering Sunday celebrated on the second day in May. As Germany needed to accelerate the production of military personnel, Nazi programs sought to remove the stigma of children born of wedlock and in fact encouraged it with financial stipends and state care facilities. SS men were particularly encouraged to take part in the so-called "*Lebensborn*" repopulation efforts where females were gathered at such facilities specifically established to encourage so-called *Ubermensch* breeding.

Top of next page:

Women at the Well
Dressed in overalls, an all-female team labors on a construction project somewhere in Germany. As the war ground on, more women were funneled into the military industrial workforce.

Berliner

Illustrierte Zeitung

†

Zum
Andenken
im Gebete
an

Alberta Speckner
von Rieding

Fliegerhelferin in einer fliegertechnischen Schule in München.

Am 7. Januar 1945 mußte sie im Alter von 18 Jahren bei einem Terrorangriff ihr Leben lassen.

ACH es ist ja kaum zu fassen,
Daß du nimmer kehrst zurück.
So jung mußt du dein Leben lassen,
Vorbei ist unser aller Glück.
Ein jeder, der dich hat gekannt
Und auch dein gutes Herz,
Der drückt uns jetzt nur stumm die Hand
In diesem tiefen Schmerz.

Kameraden der Flak (*above left*)

Appearing on the cover of the March 4, 1943 issue of the *Berlin Illustrated News*, several women are shown contributing to the war effort at a Luftware anti-aircraft fire control center. The caption states, "In command and evaluation positions, women and girls take the place previously used by soldiers. With the light throwing device, they determine the exact flight path of the advancing enemy aircraft."

January 7, 1945—Female Auxiliary—Flight Technical Training School (*above right*)

Alberta Speckner, age 18, "lost her life" during an Allied raid when bombs fell on her flight technical school in Munich where she served as a *fliegerhelferin*. Three days previously, U.S. troops withstood the German assault on Bastogne during the Third Reich's last ditch effort to thwart the Allied advance into western Germany. 20 days later, on January 27, Soviet troops would discover the Auschwitz–Birkenau slave labor and extermination center in Poland and evidence of over one million murdered men, women and children.

Gott Mit Uns—An Ambivalent Faith and a Twisted Cross

The Crucifix and the Swastika
Germany was a deeply religious country, divided between Catholics and Protestants. A group of young people have apparently made a pilgrimage outing, the event captured by camera.

* * * *

"Peace is a dream and not even a pretty one at that, while war is a link in God's own order of the world."
Count Helmuth von Moltke—Chief of the German General Staff 1857–87

On the next page:

Family Corner Shrine (*above left*)
Religious icons watch over the photograph of a lost son.

Public Approval of the New Messiah (*above right*)
Issued in the 1930s this German trading card carries the title "Under Adolf Hitler's Leadership" and shows the image of a cheering civilian crowd giving the Hitler salute. The caption relates to the Third Reich's re-acquisition of the 1,000 square mile Saar region including its valuable coal mines, previously under the administration of the French as a result of the First World War and the Treaty of Versailles. The change occurred in 1935 after a plebiscite of the area's residents, some 528,000 voting to return to Germany. It was considered another major success for Hitler while others viewed it as but a stepping stone to another German war.

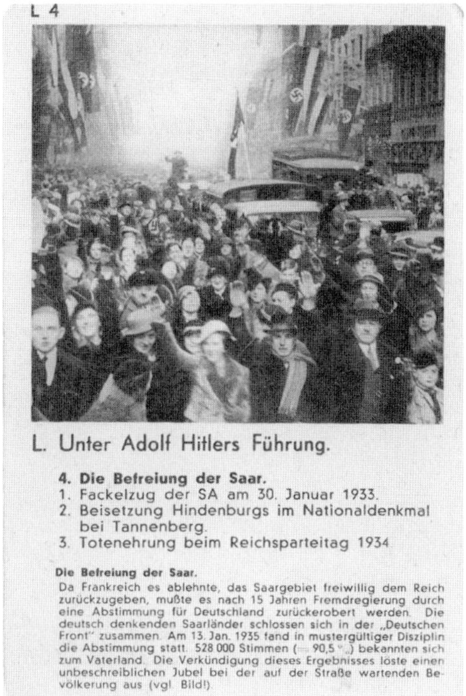

L 4

L. Unter Adolf Hitlers Führung.

4. Die Befreiung der Saar.
1. Fackelzug der SA am 30. Januar 1933.
2. Beisetzung Hindenburgs im Nationaldenkmal bei Tannenberg.
3. Totenehrung beim Reichsparteitag 1934

Die Befreiung der Saar.
Da Frankreich es ablehnte, das Saargebiet freiwillig dem Reich zurückzugeben, mußte es nach 15 Jahren Fremdregierung durch eine Abstimmung für Deutschland zurückerobert werden. Die deutsch denkenden Saarländer schlossen sich in der „Deutschen Front" zusammen. Am 13. Jan. 1935 fand in mustergültiger Disziplin die Abstimmung statt. 528 000 Stimmen (= 90,5 %) bekannten sich zum Vaterland. Die Verkündigung dieses Ergebnisses löste einen unbeschreiblichen Jubel bei der auf der Straße wartenden Bevölkerung aus (vgl. Bild!).

Church in Flanders—Art by the Führer-to-be

Drawn in 1917 during the First World War by Hitler, the image was later printed as a 1930s commercial postcard. Captioning on the reverse touted a book containing other artwork, its publication orchestrated by Hitler's photographer, Heinrich Hoffman. Hitler was a lapsed Catholic who however did espouse a connection to Providence which he thought protected him, having survived some purported 44 attempts on his life.

The sketch, though technically competent, has a sterile quality and is devoid of human characters. When he did incorporate human figures into his artwork, he had trouble creating faces. One of Hitler's favorite movies was the 1937 Disney film *Snow White and the Seven Dwarfs* and he reportedly often drew images of the dwarfs.

Meeting Room—German Restaurant—1939—Shrine to the Nazi Party
Along with portraits of Göring and Hitler, a pair Swastika banners frame a painting apparently of German horses fighting off Russian wolves, the walls are hung with images of farming life as well as a map of Germany's African colonies, most lost as a result of the First World War .

"Can you create a new religion which will
Support the bloody murder of a son?
Do you agree to sow this notion
Throughout all Europe?"

Spoken by the King to the Grand Inquisitor
in the play *Don Carlos* by Friedrich Schiller 1787

Top of next page:

German soldiers pose with a bullet ridden religious monument
The German poet Heinrich Heine commented in 1835: "Christianity … subdued to a certain extent the brutal warrior-ardor of the Germans, but it could not entirely quench it; and when the cross, that restraining talisman, falls to pieces, then will break forth the frantic Berserker rage whereof Northern poets have sung so much … The old stone gods will then arise from the forgotten ruins and wipe from the eyes the dust of centuries, and Thor with his giant hammer will arise again, and he will shatter the Gothic cathedrals … When you hear a crash such as never before heard in the world's history, then know that at last the German thunderbolt has fallen.

Zur frommen Erinnerung
im Gebete
an Hochw. Herrn

Pater Josue OM. Cap.

von Haibühl

geb. am 12. Juni 1914
feierl. Profeß 21. 4. 1939 in Dillingen a. D.
Priesterweihe 18. 2. 1940 in Dillingen a. D.
erstes hl. Meßopfer am 25. 2. 1940

Besser ist es im Kriege zu sterben als das Vaterland dem Untergange preiszugeben.
(1. Makk. 3, 59)

Gebets-Andenken
an meinen lb. Sohn u. unseren guten Bruder

Anton Mühlbauer

San.-Uffz. bei einem Gebirgsjäger-Regt.
welcher am 25. Januar 1944 im Osten
bei den schweren Kämpfen den Heldentod starb

Ordained in February 1940 as Father Josef from the Bavarian town of Haibuhl, he then resumed his civilian name of Anton Muhlbauer as a clean-shaven medic with the rank of Sgt. in the mountain troops (*Gebirgsjäger*) and earned the Iron Cross. He died "from severe wounds" at age 29 on the Russian front during the winter of 1944. He retained wearing his glasses in both photos.

In the time frame of death, January 25, 1944, Germany's last, and failed, offensive had been launched in the Ardennes, known as "The Battle of the Bulge," while the Soviets had reached the Polish border and discovered Auschwitz, the war in its final convulsions.

Der greise Kardinal gab seine Seele seinem Heiland zurück zur gleichen Stunde, da am Fronleichnamstag, 12. Juni 1952, der Officiator der Fronleichnamsprozession in der Nähe seines Hauses kurz zum Segen innehielt. Fronleichnam war eines der liebsten Feste des Kardinals. „Immer wieder freue ich mich auf das Fronleichnams-Offizium".

Wir gedenken unseres Kardinals in tiefer und dankbarer Treue.

✝

GEBET

O Gott, Du hast Deinen Diener Michael, Kardinalpriester der Heiligen Römischen Kirche, mit der Würde und Kraft des Bischofsamtes ausgezeichnet. Gib auf unsere Bitten, daß er bald in die Gemeinschaft Deiner Heiligen aufgenommen werde. Durch Christus, unsern Herrn! Amen.

J. Pfeiffer's Kunstverlag, München 2

Modified Defiance—German Cardinal Faulhaber—June 5, 1952

The controversial legacy of Michael Cardinal Faulhaber, the Archbishop of Munich for 25 years including the Nazi era, was highlighted by a speech given August 21, 1934 during which he declared, "Persecution will never eradicate the ancient Jewish people, which has been suffering and which always suffers because of its deep devotion to religion. Let us Catholics take an example from the Jews and honor them because they gave the world the best gift, which is the Bible. Catholics, educate your brothers that racial hatred is the wildest poison in our life." He also stated that "no Catholic had ever agreed to the persecution of the Jews in Germany" and that "God always punishes the persecutors of the Jews." The Nazi controlled press did not publish his statements.

In fact, Faulhaber had as early as 1923 spoke out against anti-Semitism and sought to amend Catholic prayers that contained anti-Jewish rhetoric. However, ten years later, during the 1933 Nazi boycott against Jewish businesses, Faulhaber stated that the Catholic Church would not intervene to protect Jews because, "This is not possible at this time because the struggle against the Jews would at the same time become a struggle against Catholics and because the Jews can help themselves as the sudden end of the boycott shows."

While in general a staunch anti-Nazi in the political sense, finding Hitler's ideology anathema to Christianity, he was not pro-democratic but rather favored a monarchist government, and thus opposed the Weimar Republic preceding Hitler's rise. Faulhaber had served in the First World War as a frontline clergyman and was awarded the Iron Cross. He publicly recognized the Nazi government as legitimate and required Catholic clergy to remain loyal to its authority as he believed this stance, by its association with the Church, would help ameliorate the harsher aspects of fascism.

He also spoke out against the Nazi euthanasia program aimed at eliminating the mentally and genetically afflicted and against the persecution of individual Catholic priests. Nazi thugs raided his offices and shouted threats against him as he was considered a "reactionary" and "friend of the Jews" by the Nazi ideologues. Unlike the Protestant religious leader Martin Niemöller who spent seven years in Nazi concentration camps for his outcries against Nazism, Faulhaber was never imprisoned although interrogated by the Gestapo after the failed assassination attempt against Hitler, but reportedly affirmed his loyalty to the Führer.

Faulhaber joined the Church in supporting the struggle against Soviet Bolshevism/Communism, but opposed the 1933 Papal Concordant believing it would give Hitler a propaganda victory, but then agreed feeling the fate of the Catholic Church in Germany was at stake.

Faulhaber also added an appeal for amnesty for victims in concentration camps. In his Advent 1933 sermon, in response to Nazi racist policies, he stated, "Let us not forget that we were saved not by German blood but by the blood of Christ!" But in general he also refrained from directly raising the matter of the "Jewish Question" in regards to the Nazi extermination programs, rather focusing his attention on protecting the Church.

Postwar, he called for German Jews to be welcomed back to the country, offering to pay for their transportation costs to Germany from the Theresienstadt concentration camp. He remained as archbishop and in 1951 ordained Joseph Ratzinger, the future Pope Benedict XVI. Faulhaber passed away on June 10, 1952 at age 83.

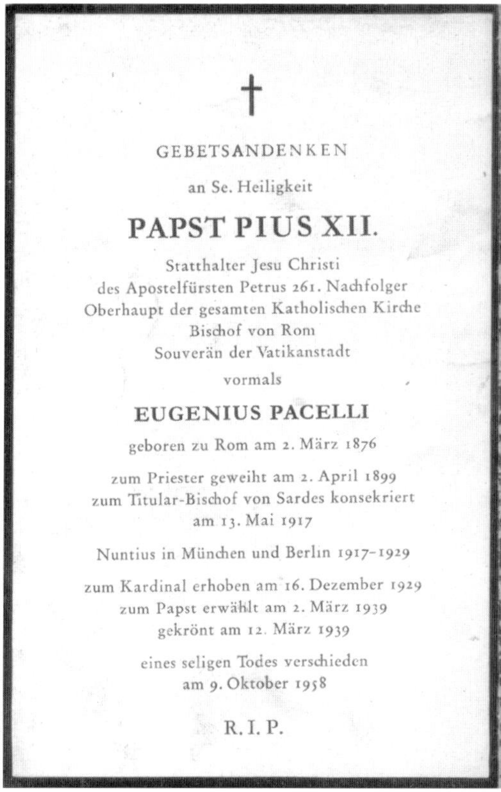

†

GEBETSANDENKEN

an Se. Heiligkeit

PAPST PIUS XII.

Statthalter Jesu Christi
des Apostelfürsten Petrus 261. Nachfolger
Oberhaupt der gesamten Katholischen Kirche
Bischof von Rom
Souverän der Vatikanstadt

vormals

EUGENIUS PACELLI

geboren zu Rom am 2. März 1876

zum Priester geweiht am 2. April 1899
zum Titular-Bischof von Sardes konsekriert
am 13. Mai 1917

Nuntius in München und Berlin 1917-1929

zum Kardinal erhoben am 16. Dezember 1929
zum Papst erwählt am 2. März 1939
gekrönt am 12. März 1939

eines seligen Todes verschieden
am 9. Oktober 1958

R. I. P.

Memorial Card for a Pope—Emissary to Germany—RIP October 9, 1958
Pope Pius XII, the Vicar of Rome, head of the Catholic Church, passed into history at age 82. The Italian born prelate had been known by his birth name Eugenio Pacelli when serving as the Papal Nuncio in Berlin and Munich from 1917–29. Ten years later, on March 12, 1939, when the white smoke rose from the Vatican, the ballots cast by the bishops confirmed Pacelli's ascension to Pope.

The *Reichskonkordat* signed between the Church and the Weimar Republic was a pivotal treaty established at the rise of Nazi Germany. While it protected the Roman Catholic Church in Germany, it was construed as providing moral validity to the Nazi cause and as such was linked to the lack of intervention against the Holocaust by the Pope and the Church. It was signed on July 20, 1933 by Nazi Vice Chancellor Franz von Papen and by then Papal Secretary of State Pacelli. Even after the war and the fall of Nazi Germany, and despite the Allies terming the agreement "inappropriate," Pope Pius XII retained the Concordat which remains in force today. He was the last Pope to add "Pius" to his name upon his election as head of the Holy See.

Sermon of Sacrilege
The police unit has taken over what appears to be a Russian Orthodox Church, one member donning the priest's vestments while pontificating for the amusement of his comrades.

Top of next page:
The Church Mocked
In a "skit" mocking religion as well as British and African colonial subjects, soldiers parade for the amusement of their fellow soldiers. While Nazi Germany promoted their own "ideological" religion, especially the SS, many Germans remained steadfast Catholics and Protestants, at least in affiliation.

Hitler's secretary and power wielder Martin Bormann summed up the Nazi Party's stance on religion on June 6, 1941 when he stated, "National Socialist and Christian concepts cannot be reconciled. The Christian churches build on the ignorance of people and are anxious so far as possible to preserve this ignorance in as large a part of the populace as possible; only in this way can the Christian churches retain their power. In contrast, National Socialism rests on scientific foundations." Later, on December 10, 1943, he added this caveat, "Make sure that none of our children gets depraved and diseased by the poison of Christianity, in whatever dosage."

Artwork Selected for Johann Ernst (*right*)
The family of Johann Ernst has chosen to add an illustration of the gravesite of their dead soldier, a grave they will never see as it lay somewhere in Russia. The generic drawing they have selected to which his name has been added shows a merging of the Christian cross with a non-Christian design, one preferred by Nazi ideology and shaped in the form of an ancient Runic letter, the symbol of life inverted to form the symbol of death. Many such markers were favored in place of the Christian cross, particularly by the Waffen-SS, and often hewn from white Birch trees found in abundance in parts of the Soviet Union.

Tourists of Rubble
An NCO seems to lecture his troops concerning a bomb pockmocked and bullet-riddled Catholic church somewhere in France.

* * * * *

SS policemen were "anti-Judeo-Christian" and would desecrate both foreign houses of Christian worship and Jewish synagogues often turning the latter into stables or brothels or setting them on fire in order to incinerate their congregations.

On the next page:

Kopfschusses (*above*)
Described as a "Catholic Theologian," Siegmund Kammermayer wore the army uniform of a corporal when "he fell because of a headshot" on October 8, 1941 near Wolotscheck (Vyshny Volochyok) in Romania while fighting on the Eastern front front. The day prior to his death German forces had invaded Romania seeking its all-important oil reserves that could fuel its motorized forces.

A Martyr's Glory in Russia—Betrayal in Holland (*below*)
A number of priests, monks and ministers served as military chaplains and medics, many dying in battle. Priest/Medic Alois Weichselbaum entered the priesthood in 1931 and served the community of Diersbach beginning in 1937. He was also a professor of mathematics and physics at the Petrinum College in Linz. In February 1941 he began his military service with much time spent on the Eastern Front. He was awarded the Eastern Service medal and the War Service Cross with Swords 2nd Class. Serving as a medical sergeant and while coming to the rescue of his wounded comrades, he was killed in action on September 3, 1944.

The funeral card includes a quotation from Thomas Aquinas, "When a soldier falls in the fulfillment of his duty, he falls in the Army of God. He will enjoy the Glory of the Martyrs."

* * * * *

On the day Weichselbaum died in Russia, Anne Frank was betrayed and rounded up among 1019 other Dutch Jews and sent the Westerbork transit camp prior to shipment to Auschwitz where she was not immediately gassed because she was 15. She was spared, momentarily, while 14-year olds and younger were subject to death upon arrival.

Wer im Herzen seiner Lieben lebt,
der ist nicht tot, der ist nur fern.

In nie erlöschender Liebe und
zum frommen Gedenken
an unseren unvergeßlichen,
lieben Sohn und Bruder

cand. theol.

Siegmund Kammermayer

**Gefreiter
in einem Inf.-Rgt.**

gefallen infolge eines Kopfschusses am 8. Oktober 1941 in einem Gefecht bei Wolotschek im Osten im Alter von 22 Jahren.

„Ich aber in Gerechtigkeit darf schauenDeinAntlitz, mich sättigen am Anblick Deiner Erscheinung.
Ps. 16, 15.

Zur lieben Erinnerung

an den Hochw. Herrn

Alois Weichselbaum

Kooperator in Andorf

geboren am 11. Mai 1907 in Pierbach (Mühlviertel), am 29. Juni 1930 im Dom zu Linz zum Priester geweiht, 1931 bis 1937 Kooperator in Diersbach und zugleich Lehramtskandidat auf der Hochschule in Graz, 1937 bis 1938 Professor der Mathematik und Physik im Kollegium Petrinum in Linz, 1938 bis 1940 wieder Kooperator in Diersbach, 1940 bis 1941 Kooperator in Andorf, seit Februar 1941 im Wehrdienst, davon größtenteils an der Ostfront, Inhaber der Ostmedaille und des Kriegsverdienstkreuzes mit den Schwertern 2. Klasse, gefallen als Sanitäts-Unteroffz. am 3. September 1944 nordwestl. Ostrow (Rußland) während der Bergung von verwundeten Kameraden.

+

Eine größere Liebe hat niemand, als wer sein Leben hingibt für seine Freunde.
(Joh. 15, 13)

Wer als Soldat fällt in der Erfüllung seiner Pflicht, fällt in die Arme Gottes. Er wird die Glorie des Martyriums genießen.
(Hl. Thomas von Aquin)

War Games and Deadly Diversions

Gallows Humor
Soldiers and civilians stage a mock lynching. Note as one soldier assists, another carries an accordion strapped to his chest.

* * * * *

Humor of a sort existed during the Third Reich, both the Nazi Party approved variety and that which could prove fatal. For example, in 1943 a woman told the following joke:

> Hitler and Göring are standing atop the Berlin radio tower, several hundred feet up. The war in progress, Germany being heavily bombed, Hitler asks Göring what he, Hitler, could do to cheer the Berlin inhabitants. Göring replies, "Why don't you jump?"

The joke-teller was overheard and reported to the Gestapo. She was arrested, found guilty of treasonous provocations, and executed by guillotine.

Construction Project (*above left*)
Placing a rope around a comrade's neck, soldiers enjoy a playful break while building a fully functional execution scaffold.

Effigy—Army Barracks (*above right*)

***Vorsicht*—"Warning"**
A death's head warning marks either an electrical junction box or the Luftwaffe building itself. The smaller drawing of a chicken dropping eggs is joined by a plaque with the words "Boom-Boom" and may indicate the structure warehouses aerial munitions.

Dark Humor in a Gray Uniform

One of a series of humorous commercial postcards commenting on military life, the soldiers are chorusing "*Von der Wiege bis zur Bahre, sind die schoensten Lebensjahre*" that translates to "From the cradle to the grave are the most beautiful years of life."

Point Blank

Lying prone before several corporals, a private of the 16th infantry smiles at the cameraman from behind his standard issue Mauser rifle; the group posing at a target range.

Man-sized Missile
A Luftwaffe corporal embraces an aerial bomb.

Focal Point
Naval marines point their bayonet-equipped carbines at a comrade, the focal point of their "war game."

Hitting the Nail

An army *unteroffizier* (NCO) poses with his young hammer-equipped charges taking a break from their fence building. The subject of the hammer blows wears his denim fatigue jacket and thick gloves for protection from the barbed wire. The ubiquitous war-time material in its first successful form was patented by an American farmer Joseph Glidden in 1874 after looking for an inexpensive fencing solution during the westward expansion. Glidden became a millionaire. His invention changed the future of the U.S. and eventually the world at war.

***Panzermann* at Play**

Wearing their distinctive short black jackets and berets, young members of a tank crew practice brave deeds in this pre-war photo.

Axmen Replay
Soldiers echo the dark humor of war, a comrade clowning on the chopping block.
In reality, one of the common instruments of execution employed by Nazi Germany was the guillotine, often with the victim forced to face upwards in view of the blade as it descended.

Circus Act
A soldier feigns fear in an apparently staged "knife throwing" demonstration, his comrade preparing to fling a bayonet. Its scabbard has been embedded next to the target's head as a simulated knife adding to the image's intended impact.

Obstacle Course
Recruits negotiate a series of field exercises reflecting battlefield conditions including moving along narrow roof beams. The soldiers are wearing white denim fatigues to protect their uniforms as they join hands to both keep their balance and form group support bonding.

Leap of Faith
After Hitler Youth and labor service, induction into the Wehrmacht brought on new challenges of physical fitness. The intensity of training frequently resulted in injury, even death but was considered the price paid to hone superior warriors.

Synchronicity
Focus on group unity and team work was relentlessly drilled into the young German recruits. Units were often formed from members of the same village to further strengthen group coherence.

NCO Training School Candidates
As in most armies, the sergeant was the backbone of the German army. As non-commissioned officers the *Unteroffizier* took orders from their superior commissioned officers, but in the heat of battle many NCOs took over commands as the officers fell.

Symmetry of Three-Headed Fighters
As two soldiers flail away, their comrades enjoy the impromptu boxing match. Aggressiveness and physical competition were an integral part of training.

Combat in Earnest?
What may be an actual personal altercation has been photographed as two soldiers wrestle in the mud while their rifle-carrying comrades take notice but seem to ignore their antics.

Deadly Play
While one young *soldat* pretends to use his boot to disengage his bayonet from the stomach of the "enemy," another prepares to club him from behind, a scenario for real battles to come.

Luger Proxies
Re-enacting a classic duel, two soldiers face off with wooden guns as a third prepares to give the command to fire. Both men appear to holster standard issue sidearms, mostly like the Luger P08. Prior to its banning by Nazi authorities, young soldiers often fought with sabers seeking the status achieved by incurring a facial scar across the cheek, a traditional sign of Prussian prowess.

Pre-War Practice
Sometime in 1938, prior to the onset of war, a group of German naval cadets pray over the sandy tomb of one of their comrades, apparently a drummer. The location is Stolpmunde, a coastal town in the Pomeranian region.

Soldier and Friend

Germans were fond of animals, in particular dogs, many joining them in their battlefield bunkers as pets or serving in guard and attack roles. Hitler himself had a favorite German Shepherd (Alsatian) he called Blondi. Prior to his own death in the Berlin *Führerbunker* at 3:30 p.m. on Monday, April 30, 1945, he administered a vial of cyanide to his faithful companion ostensibly to spare her the fate of being captured by the Red Army. However, according to testimony by Gertraud "Traudl" Junge, Hitler's youngest personal private secretary, Hitler was also testing its effectiveness concerned that the cyanide that had been supplied via Himmler might have been altered to render him unconscious in order to then give him over to the enemy. Himmler had betrayed Hitler when he sought to make his own deal with the Allies, thus Hitler's suspicions. However, the poison proved full-strength, Blondi dying instantly after one of Hitler's doctors, SS-*Obersturmbannführer* (Lieutenant Colonel) Ludwig Stumpfegger, pressed the vial into the dog's mouth. Stumpfegger who had previously taken part in medical experiments on women at Ravensbrück, also reportedly helped Joseph Goebbels poison his six young children. Eva Braun would also use cyanide, while Hitler both used the poison and a gunshot to the head during their joint suicide, not long after the two were married as Soviet troops closed in.

Betrayal or Play?

A dog turns its head in a questioning manner, perhaps unsure of the soldier's intentions, be it in jest for the camera or otherwise, apparently aware of the function of the pistol, in this case a Walther P-38. The 9 mm semi-automatic pistol was issued in replacement of the more costly to produce P08 "Luger" that had been in production since 1900. The soldier wears a special winter issue lamb's wool leather coat, the type issued belatedly during the second winter in Russia.

Camouflage (*above left*)
An odd looking dog leaps in play with a Luftwaffe man, a flak battery concealed by camouflage webbing visible in the background.

Army NCO and Doberman (*above right*)

SS Mascot (*above*)
A small dog steadies itself on the barrel of a machine gun as SS cycle troops ride in triumph through Prague, the capital of Czechoslovakia.

A Soldiers' Best Friend KIA—Russian Front (*right*)
The handwritten inscription on the wooden cross reads "Here Lies Our Beloved Company Dog Wipp of Field Unit 63 Regiment 93—Killed in Action July 5, 1941."

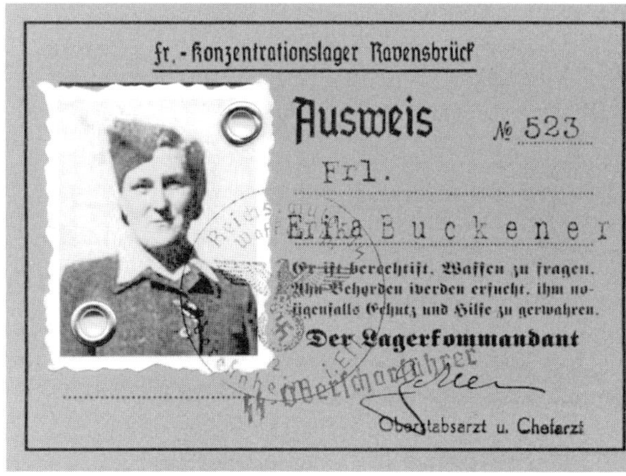

SS Guard Dogs—Ravensbrück Concentration Camp (*above left*)
The female guard identified as Erika Buckener poses with her uniformed companion. Nazi Germany trained some 200,000 war dogs as sentries, guards, messengers and scouts, the largest number serving with SS units in concentration and POW camps.

German Navy Admiral Wilhelm Canaris, director of the *Abwehr*, the High Command of the Armed forces counter-intelligence department, enjoyed pet dogs as well. He once said, "Rely on the goodness of animals. Look at my dachshunds. They're discreet. They'll never give me away."

Canaris, holding longstanding anti-Nazi sentiments and a leading member of the military inner resistance, was later implicated in the July 20, 1944 Plot to kill Hitler. He was imprisoned in the Gestapo cellars at Prinz Albrechtstrasse, kept in solitary confinement in chains and starved. On February 7, 1945, he was taken to Flossenbürg concentration camp where his brutal treatment continued. Even after long interrogations that went on for weeks, he denied all personal complicity in the conspiracy and never betrayed his fellow participants in the Resistance Movement. During the very last weeks of the war, Himmler, failing to extract the information he wanted, and receiving Hitler's permission, ordered Canaris killed. On April 9, 1945, Canaris was executed by members of the SS and his body left hanging to rot. Flossenbürg was liberated two weeks later by American forces.

In three post-war West German court trials, his known killers were acquitted each time. The 1956 West German High Court judges, by some gymnastics of thought, ruled that the Nazi Regime possessed the right to legally execute Canaris since he was a traitor.

Ravensbrück SS Identification Card (reproduction)—**Erika Buckener** (*above right*)
Ravensbrück was established by Himmler in May 1939, the camp located near scenic Fürstenberg some 50 miles north of Berlin. It was the only major Nazi KZ designed specifically to imprison women. Between 1942–43, it was also the center for the training of 3500 female SS guards in methods of torture and murder prior to their employment in other camps.

Prisoners were brought to Ravensbrück from Poland, Germany, Austria, France and other countries … anti-fascists, communists, criminals, Soviet POWs, homosexuals, gypsies, resistance fighters, Jews. Of the 132,000 women and children that entered the camp, an estimated 92,000 were worked to death, shot, hanged, beaten to death, gassed or killed by torturous medical experiments including those involving infants and children. Ravensbrück became a major slave labor network of some 70 satellite camps where prisoners made components for V-1 and V-2 rockets for the Siemens Electric Company. Others produced munitions and explosives, made prisoner uniforms and clothing for the Waffen-SS, or paved roads by manually pulled heavy rollers which also became of a form of execution. Russian troops liberated the camp on April, 30, 1945. Today the picturesque lake nearby still contains the ashes of the thousands cremated then dumped into its waters. Erika Buckener survived the war and lived to a comfortable old age.

Heroes of the Third Reich and Lethal Leadership

***Heldentod* Heritage—90th Birthday Celebration of an Old Warrior** *(above left)*
His chair crowned with the number 90, a veteran resolutely faces the camera, his coat pinned with awards dating back to the Franco-Prussian War of 1870–71.

The Iron Cross he wears was first introduced by King Friedrich Wilhelm III of Prussia on 17 March 1813 to rally his countrymen against the threat of French invasion led by Napoleon. Kaiser Wilhelm II reintroduced the *Eisernes Kreuz* during the First World War, Hitler doing so again after the invasion of Poland, the Iron Cross marked with "1939." The old soldier has survived long enough to see the beginning of the Second World War.

Hero of a Lost War—"Uncle Hugo" *(above right)*
The photo postcard was dated November 29, 1932 from the city of Köln (Cologne). The veteran of the First World War proudly wears several medals including the 1st and 2nd Class Iron Cross and Wound Badge. Pivotal events took place in Germany during this month. General Kurt von Schleicher toppled the Franz von Papen Weimar republic government but served only 57 days as Chancellor as a result of running afoul of Hitler, threatening an anti-Nazi political alliance. His plan fell apart and when he called upon war hero Hindenburg to assume the Chancellorship, Hindenburg refused. Germany's streets were filled with pitched battles between the socialist, communist and Nazi supporters, creating the turmoil that Hitler used for his election campaign for January 1933 during which he succeeded in realizing his goal of becoming Chancellor of a new Nazi-controlled Germany. Hitler also ordered the murder of Schleicher and his wife on the Night of the Long Knives, June 20, 1934.

The New German Hero—Hitler Youth Security Leader (*above left*)
As the new breeding stock of Nazi officers-to-be, the Hitler Youth had been instilled with absolute loyalty to the *Führer* and a virulent hatred of Germany's enemies. The more fanatical policed their fellow HJ and often matriculated into the ranks of the SS.

Hero's Rewarded (*above right*)
The Third Reich produced a wide spectrum of accolades, medals, badges, emblems, branch designations, decorations and rank insignia in vivid designs, colors and materials. A soldier's tunic served as his visual display from which an observer could distinguish his status and achievements. Awards indicated participation in combat, wounds, special battles and technical proficiencies.

The best known was the Iron Cross, a carry-over from the First World War, and awarded in 2nd and 1st Class categories. More than two million German soldiers earned the 2nd Class while some 300,000 1st Class Iron Crosses were awarded. One must keep in mind that over 18,000,000 Germans were in uniform of one kind or another.

The Knight's Cross (*Ritterkreuz*) was the senior award of the Order of the Iron Cross series of awards. Only some 7,500 were awarded. Due to the chaos of the war's closing months, some did not learn of their commendation until as late as the 1970s. A further iteration, the Knight's Cross with Oak Leaves was awarded to KC winners for additional accomplishments. Only 862 (some sources 883) were awarded. On June 3, 1941 the German High Command issued the following Guidelines for the awarding of the Knight's Cross.

> The Knight's Cross of the Iron Cross can be awarded for exceptional acts of gallantry which decisively affect combat actions.
>
> The conditions for this are: "Individual decision to act on own initiative, outstanding personal bravery and decisive success in the context of the overall conduct of the action."

In addition to surviving the war, the Knight's Cross winner's post-war celebrity status often grew over the years well into the 1980s and until their passing. While bravery in combat is evident, the patina of history has provided a false gloss of honor to their exploits, providing as it were a form of dispensation, at least to Western attitudes. *Continued on next page.*

Regarding those post-war "heroes," as time passed, the concept that "a hero is a hero in whatever uniform he wears" seemed to take hold, complemented by the prevailing Cold War attitude that much of the war saw the German military combating the forces of Communism, all of which appeared to modify and mollify attitudes toward elements of the Third Reich's war machine. Some individuals once wearing the Nazi uniform thus gained international status in the West.

However, a review of some of the Third Reich heroes' actions such as anti-partisan campaigns leads to a historical record that often involves the mass murder of civilians, not to mention a war of aggression that caused the death of some 10,000,000 Soviet military personnel including 3,000,000 POWs deliberately starved to death, a fact somewhat ignored in the West as well as the sacrifice of Soviet troops that accounted for 80 percent of the Nazi war machine casualties. Yet the autographed photos still sell well.

Front Page Hero—Knights Cross with Oak Leaves (*above left*)
The Third Reich propaganda machine capitalized on the Hero's Cult as seen here on the cover of an October 1942 issue of the *Cologne Illustrated News* which featured Lt-Colonel Walter Gorn then commanding Motorcycle Battalion 59 in Russia specifically in the area of Orel, some 220 miles south-west of Moscow, a scene of much heavy fighting. On August 27, 1942 he had been awarded the even more exalted form of the Knights Cross of the Iron Cross (*Ritterkreuz*) with the addition of Oak Leaves of which only 862 were awarded within all branches of the German military.

High Command (*above right*)
Posing with his secretary in front of a map of Europe, a Luftwaffe Major of the Anti-Aircraft division wears a full ribbon bar of decorations as well as the Iron Cross 1st Class, Ground Combat badge and Wound Badge in Black.

Signs of Glory (*above left*)
Army Lt Johann Heyer of the 109th infantry sits for a formal portrait, his uniform displaying the Iron Cross, 1st and 2nd Class, the Combat Assault badge, the Wound Badge and the Spanish Cross with Swords, the latter for his service during the Spanish Civil War. The Assault badge appears to be the silver version indicating at least three combat engagements.

Bravery Noted (*above right*)
Signs of combat experience are indicated by the NCO's two awards worn on the left side of his uniform, the General Combat badge (eagle with crossed swords), and the Wound Badge in Silver, indicating three to five wounds. The motif of the Wound Badge was a *Stahlhelm* or steel helmet with cross swords. A Silver Wound Badge could also be awarded for the loss of a hand, a foot or deafness. A Wound Badge in black was given for one or two wounds while a Gold Wound Badge went to those who sustained five or more wounds, permanent blindness, permanent disability or "loss of manhood." As the war raged in the Russian winter, a wound badge could also be awarded in cases of frostbite, the only illness or disease so recognized. A special Wound Badge was issued for the injured survivors of the abortive July 20, 1944 assassination attempt on Hitler.

On the next page:

Franz Weber—Knights Cross Recipient—War Survivor
Corporal Weber was born in the Novi Sad district of Yugoslavia in 1921. As a *Volksdeustche* he attended a *Volkschule*, then after earning his journeyman's papers as a baker moved to Germany in 1941. Called to service and posted to the 8th Kompanie of Jäger Regiment 28, he saw first combat in Demjansk, the scene of the celebrated successful defense of Soviet encircled German troops south of Leningrad in early 1942, and where he was promoted to *obergefreiter* (senior lance corporal) on April 1, 1943. His Knight's Cross was the result of action seen in Romania as Red forces continued their advance. Captured by the Russians, he escaped, was recaptured in May 1945 a few days after Germany surrendered. Released in the following September, he settled with his family in Munich and returned to baking.

(*Note:* The following commentary was supplied along with his autographed photo by the subject Franz Weber. It is the product of the individual's own memory and perspective. They are presented without editorial comment.)

The Action that Earned Me the Knight's Cross

I was part of the Eighth Company which received orders in fall 1944 to take Hill 1587 at Rodna Pass from the Russians. The grass covered pyramid-shaped hill featured an extensive trench system as well as machine gun nests, originally built by the Hungarian army. The Hungarian army was to hold the position to preserve it for use as an intercept position. The hill was strategically very important as it offered a good view off the roadway that was to be used by our reserves. Unfortunately the Russians had overtaken this position, and our company received orders to reclaim it."

Our much weakened company, reduced to about 40 men, prepared for this task. As we reached attack range over the coverless terrain, we took Russian machine gun and grenade fire. Due to this we were forced to halt. My group was led by a young officer cadet on the left wing of the company. Together with my Second Machine Gunner I immediately started to look for an adequate machine gun position. On a small hill I found a ruined fortification, most likely from the First World War, and in it I saw the most useful position.

The distance to the enemy's heavy machine gun was about 40 m as the crow flies. And also I had a great field of view, due to a low area between myself and the enemy, and as a result was almost horizontally across the enemy machine gun. Under the cover fire of my Second Machine Gunner who operated my machine gun, I was able to close in on the enemy heavy machine gun and attack it with grenades. After the first hand grenades the Russians showed resistance and threw the hand grenades back. More hand grenades from me finally drove the Russians into retreat. My Second Machine Gunner immediately seized their position. After this I returned to my company leader and reported that we had captured a part of the position. Our company, due to the coverless terrain and the enemy fire received could not continue the attack at this time. I took some hand grenades with me and explained that I would try to attack the heavy machine gun from the left side. After I was able to smoke out the second enemy's heavy machine gun our company was able to effortlessly take over half of the position. The other side was then quickly taken. At this fight I was wounded."

Autographed Photo of Luftwaffe Aces Walter Krupinski (left) and Erich Hartmann both wearing their Knights Cross.

Beating the Odds—Two Hero Survivors

Erich "Bubi" Hartmann was considered the "Ace of Aces" of the Second World War, at least by the Germans. His final tally: 352 downed enemy aircraft, mostly Soviet, for which he was ultimately awarded the Knights Cross with Oak Leaves, Swords and Diamonds, (one of only 27 Germans to receive the latter). Painted on the side of his Bf-109 within a red heart was the name *Usch* which referred to Usch Paetch, his fiancée.

Having survived the last air battles of the war, he surrendered to American forces in 1945 but was turned over to the Soviets and spent ten years in Siberia. Refusing to cooperate with the Russians, he was not released from captivity until 1955, but would go on to take an important role in the development of the post-war West German Air Force. He passed away in 1993 at age 71.

His companion in the photo Walter "Graf Punski" Krupinski flew combat missions over France and England but had no "kills" until he was sent to the Eastern Front in September 1941. He ended the war with 197 confirmed victories recorded during 1,100 missions including two while piloting the revolutionary Me-262 jetfighter near the end of the war. Wounded seven times, he survived to pursue a successful career in the post-war West Germany *Bundeswehr* rising to the rank of *Generalleutnant*. He passed away on October 7, 2000 shortly before his 80th birthday.

Top of next page:

Eastern Front Hero—Knights Cross Winner Adolf Schmahl

Seen here in an autographed photo dated July 7, 1942 and now a lieutenant, previously as a sergeant major in the 6th Regiment of the 30th Infantry Division, he had led a squad during fighting south of Ilmen Lake in northwestern Russia. In January–February 1942 the 16th German Army and the Morozov 11th Soviet Army clashed over control of the strategic city of Stelaia. As a result the German forces were encircled in the Demjansk pocket. During its defense, Schmal led a smaller force repulsing heavy Soviet attacks in the process capturing 40 prisoners and several machine guns. He fought in Poland, Holland, Belgium and France prior to the Eastern Front. Prior to the war he was a baker and also an Olympian team member in gymnastics. He received his Knights Cross personally from Hitler during a ceremony in Berlin.

Adolf Schmahl—October 1993 (*above left*)
Adolf Schmal (*left*) with fellow Knights Cross of the Iron Cross winner Troffer join other veterans for a gathering in England after he emigated to the UK in the early 1990s. He received many requests for his autographed photo up to to his death in 2004.

Major Ernst-August Wick—Knights Cross with Oak Leaves (*above right*)
Featured in the December 17, 1940 issue of the Berlin published pictorial newspaper *Deutsche Illustrierte*, the highly decorated *Oberstleutnant* Frick is extolled as the epitome of Luftwaffe standards. Three years later he would be killed in action, dying at 32.

"Between Life and Death"—The Fate of Luciano Serra
Produced in 1938, the Italian film *Luciano Serra Pilota* was co-released in Germany. It told the story of the First World War fighter pilot Luciano Serra and like many Axis era films extolled the virtues of bravery and self-sacrifice in battle.

The character of Luciano Serra (played by Italian matinee idol Amadeo Nazzari) struggles with problems adjusting to ordinary peacetime life. He leaves his family and makes his way to America where for 15 years he takes up barnstorming to both earn a living and keep flying.

It should be remembered that during the First World War Italy had joined the Allies to fight Germany, but apparently the switch in allegiances posed no problem for Nazi censors or the German audience. The film takes place against the backdrop of Mussolini's Italy where Serra's son Aldo, whom he has never met, is also seeking his pilot's wings. On his way home to Italy to meet his son, Serra crashes in the Atlantic and is presumed dead. He takes the advantage to assume a new identity and joins the new Fascist Italian air force then fighting in Ethiopia. The younger Serra, now an Italian combat pilot, is shot down by the Ethiopians just as his father, a passenger in a troop train, happens to be passing by. Aware of the dire situation with the Italian troops outnumbered, the elder Serra must find a way to get help. Then he learns his son has been shot down and presumably killed while trying to protect him. With various twists and turns, the story thunders on from there.

Rather than an overt propaganda piece as were many German films of the era, the Italian film focused on Italian nationalism and bravery rather than ideology. It also sought to highlight the excellence of the Italian fighting forces, a stance the German military would no doubt debate.

The film's director Goffredo Alessandrini was responsible for several patriotic, highly successful films during the Fascist era. "Between Life and Death" won acclaim in the form of the Mussolini Cup Award (Best Film) at the 1938 Venice International Film Festival (sharing the award with the iconic Leni Riefenstahl's two-part film "Olympia 1 and 2" concerning the 1936 Berlin Summer Olympics). The Italian film, one of the most successful of the decade and an innovation in neo-realism, also happened to have been produced by Benito Mussolini's son Vittorio Mussolini and neglected to focus on the genocidal treatment of the Ethiopian people by Italian forces including the use of poison gas attacks on civilian populations. (The film is still available and with English sub-titles although some critics have described it as an "absurdly contrived, bloated parody.")

Conformity, Uniformity and Leadership Lethality

Deaths-Head Legacy—German "Black Hussar"—Postcard dated November 23, 1916
The iconic, now historically indelible deaths-head (*Totenkopf*) insignia appeared in use many years prior to the Third Reich's adoption for its SS and Panzer uniforms. It first came into German military use during the era of Frederick the Great initially for a cavalry formation in 1774. It was in use during the First World War as well as the inter-war period by members of both the Freikorps and the *Reichswehr*, then by Hitler's SS unit, later by the concentration and camp guards as well as Waffen SS tank units. Perhaps not coincidentally, historical German films titled *Der Schwarze Husar*, "The Black Hussar" were released in 1915 as a silent film, then again in 1932 in a revamped sound production released in the last days of the Weimar Republic before the Nazi takeover and Goebbels domination of the film industry.

A Matter of Uniforms
Here the line between uniform and costume is blurred as volunteers collect for the annual Winter Relief drive for the needy.

It has been observed that the "advanced theatricality" of Nazi Germans contributed to their projected image of power and terror. A plethora of colors and blandishments were brought to a legion of Third Reich uniforms in effect most of Germany wearing one kind or another. While several of the Nazi high command like Göring were prone to wearing ostentatious uniforms, Hitler himself wore a plain army uniform with little decoration. He apparently was uninterested in his attire and was frugal on all counts, including having his worn socks darned and repaired while he ordered millions spent on his various monuments and architectural adventures.

Much has been written about Nazi Germany's uniform designs, many created by the fashion house of Hugo Boss, but it was the Prussian military leader Frederick the Great who some 200 years previously had taken a rabble of mercenaries and through rigid discipline and relentless drill melded them into the polished fighting force that earned the status of the best-trained in the world. But it was also the effect upon the men when given their handsome new uniforms that helped instill a new level of confidence and *esprit de corps* that would become part of the German cultural fabric.

On the next page:

Postcard Dated November 20, 1933—White Uniform (*left*)
The lyrics accompanying the theatrically uniformed soldier and his love interest reads:

> The Honourable Lieutenant fell in love today, and while he serving his duty loyally, his heart is not with it, but he does not show it.

During this month of November, 1933, Hitler's personal bodyguard, the *Leibstandarte SS Adolf Hitler*, was formalized. Its now 105 members and their commander "Sepp" Dietrich swore personal allegiance to Hitler, bypassing SS leader Himmler. On the 12th of the month a pivotal referendum concerning Nazi policy received approval by over 95 percent of the German public. One of several such referendums pomoted by the Nazi Party, it involved withdrawing from the League of Nations. The referendum coincided with elections to the governing body of the *Reichstag*. All "candidates"were supporters of the Nazi Party, and all 661 "voted" into office.

Leibstandarte-SS Adolf Hitler (*right*)

Death's-head SS

As evidenced by his Iron Cross 2nd Class and Assault Badge, the SS *Untersturmführer* member of the Bodyguard Regiment has seen combat. The grey uniform of the regular army was standard for the SS, the black uniforms usually reserved for ceremonial functions.

The double lightning bolt symbol associated with the SS insignia had a rather prosaic derivation. Known as the SS Sig Runes, the design was accidentally designed in 1931 by Walter Heck, then an SA company commander, later a member of the SS. He happened to notice the similarity between the two sig runes and the SS (*Schutzstaffel*) initials. He offered the design to the SS who paid him a mere 2.5 Reichmarks, the symbol destined to become one of the most feared and hated in European history.

The SS motto was "Loyalty is My Honour" which reflected unquestioning obedience. The Waffen-SS was considered an elite organization, its soldiers highly motivated and disciplined with a reputation for bravado in battle as well as abject ruthlessness toward both enemy soldiers and civilians.

The *Leibstandarte-SS Adolf Hitler* was initially employed to attack anti-Nazis and rival SA "Brownshirts" during street demonstrations and later as battlefield commandos acting as raiding parties including actions at Dunkirk in France and later against Soviet defenses in the Crimea.

Ideological Clones—*Leibstandarte-SS Adolf Hitler*—German Toy Soldiers (*above*)
The SS, initially Hitler's 8-man strong personal bodyguard, grew into a vast empire unto itself, its every move orchestrated by SS *Reichsführer* Heinrich Himmler. As Hitler's ideological soldiers, the SS functioned as the implementers of mass murder on an industrial scale, literally "instruments of terror." They envisioned themselves as the rightful masters of Europe, all others either their slaves or subject to annihilation. Responsible for internal security, intelligence gathering, operating the slave labor and death camps, the SS also formed fanatical combat divisions, the Waffen-SS, some 900,000 strong and among the last to defend Berlin even after Hitler had committed suicide.

Third Reich Collector Card—SS *Gruppenführer* with Adjutant—Uniforms introduced October 1933 (*left*)
Describing the black SS uniform's impact, SS *Reichsführer* Heinrich Himmler stated, "I know there are many people who fall ill when they see this black uniform; we understand that and don't expect that we will be loved by many people.".

A General and his Staff Officers gather before a requisitioned HQ—Russia—October 1942

Of the 2,500 German Generals serving in various branches of the Third Reich military, 768 died during the war years 1939–45. Of that number 253 were KIA (the majority on the Eastern Front), another 44 dying later as the result of wounds, while 81 committed suicide; several when overrun by enemy forces. 23 were executed by Hitler, most for real or suspected complicity in plots to assassinate him. 326 died from accidents, illness and other reasons while 41 were executed by the Allies.

General Werner Freiherr Von Fritsch as a Collectible Card #75

The image, originally printed in color, depicting the monocle wearing von Fritsch appeared in a series of collectible cards titled "Who Leads the Third Reich" included as "perks" in cigarette packets produced by the Bremen based Oriental Cigarette Company.

Walking into the Fog of War
Giving the regular army salute instead of the Hitler salute, General von Fritsch takes part in a pre-war training event.

Von Fritsch, embroiled in trumped up charges of homosexuality levied by Himmler and Göring when contriving to displace him, resigned in disgrace as Commander of the Germany Army in 1938, although vindicated in a court trial. But as war loomed, he was returned to the 12th Artillery regiment, his old unit, and assigned the role of honorary commander.

Three weeks into the invasion of Poland, on Sept. 22, 1939, while accompanying members of a forward observation group, his brightly colored general's uniform attracted the attention of a Polish sniper, a bullet striking him in the thigh. Other reports listed his wound as caused by deliberately walking into Polish machine gun fire. But when another officer, coming under fire, went to his aid, von Fritsch ordered him back to safety. As a result of his wound, he soon bled to death on the battlefield, statistically becoming the first German general killed in the Second World War. Many concluded that he had deliberately allowed himself to find an honorable death on the battlefield, thus erasing the dishonor previously attached to him.

Top of next page:

Death by Cyanide
Günther Adolf Ferdinand "Hans" von Kluge, seen with an unidentified Hungarian officer, attained the vaunted rank of General Field Marshal. Although purged in 1938 for his support for Gen. Werner von Fritsch during the latter's squabbles with Hitler, von Kluge was recalled in 1939 at age 57 and served on the Western Front before being sent to the Eastern Front in 1941 where he was given command of Army Group Center. He was known by his troops and fellow officers by the nickname "*der kluge Hans*" or "Clever Hans," the word Kluge in German translating to clever.

Considered an opportunist and currying favor with Hitler from whom he received large financial gifts, von Kluge vacillated in his support of the anti-Hitler plots and eventually aligned himself with Hitler. In the fall of 1943 he suffered serious injuries in a car crash but recovered sufficiently to take command of efforts to stop the Allied invasion at Normandy, but was removed because of subsequent military failures blamed upon him by Hitler. On August 19, 1944, after being recalled to Berlin due to his failures and possible involvement with the July Plot, and fearing a trial and execution, he walked into a French field and bit into a cyanide pill. Vacillating to the end, he did however leave a farewell letter praising Hitler and proclaiming his own loyalty unto death but did call for an end to the "hopeless struggle."

Figurehead Acquitted (*right*)
Hugo Sperrle was so frightening looking that Hitler would bring him along to meetings and events just for the intimidation factor. He would eventually rise to a General Field Marshal of the Luftwaffe. Previously he commanded the German Condor Legion when it fought for Franco's fascist forces in the Spanish Civil War. Aircraft under his control would take part in the infamous 1937 bombing of the Basque town of Guernica and its civilian population, the event immortalized by Pablo Picasso's painting in the same year. Sperrle also led Luftwaffe attacks on France and would end up stationed in Paris. Though charged with war crimes by the Allies he was acquitted. He died, age 68, in 1953 in Munich.

General Franz Ritter von Epp—Master of Bavaria *(above left)*
The appellation "Ritter" translates to "knight," the title bestowed upon von Epp in 1916 as a result of his military exploits during the 1900–1901 Boxer Rebellion in China, then also for serving as a company commander in the genocidal campaigns against the indigenous peoples in Colonial German Southwest Africa, and later as a Bavarian regiment commander in the First World War.

Collectible General *(above right)*
The image of von Epp appears on a cigarette card, #59, wearing a First World War design helmet, indicative of his "Old Guard" lineage.

Joining the post-First World War right-wing groups he took part in the frequent street clashes with communist factions, and then as a member of the SA eventually funded the Nazi acquisition of the *Völkischer Beobachter* newspaper as its party organ. He became a Nazi Party member of the German Parliament, headed the Nazi Military Political Office, led efforts to regain German African colonies, and was appointed the *Reichskommisar* for Bavaria. While he wielded dictatorial powers, he was at odds with other members of the Nazi hierarchy, even arrested in 1945 on suspicion of being a member of an anti-Nazi Bavarian group that sought to surrender to the Allies. At war's end he was arrested by the Allies, and while in a Munich American prison camp died on New Year's Eve 1947 at age 78.

Top left of next page:

Died in Captivity
As a General Field Marshal in the Third Reich, Ernst von Busch was a career military officer and fervent supporter of Hitler. He saw action in the Polish, French and Russian invasions but although his forces were decimated by the Russians, losing some 300,000 men, he was still promoted Field Marshal in February 1943. Apparently showing signs of depression he was relieved of military command by Hitler and posted to defend the North Sea Coast against the British to whom he surrendered on May 4, 1945. Detained as a POW at Camp Aldershot in England he died at the age of 60 while in captivity on July 17, 1945.

Anti-Nazi German Hero—Feldmarschall Erwin von Witzleben *(above right)*
Known to be a staunch anti-Nazi, Witzleben, a career Army officer, was forced to retire in 1938, but was recalled to service with the outbreak of war. From September 1939 to October 1940, Witzleben served as Commander of the German First Army, then of Army Group D until March 1941, and lastly Commander in Chief of the Army until February 1942 when he was again retired from active duty.

As a major member of the anti-Hitler conspiracy, he was slated to become Commander in Chief of the German armed forces after Hitler was deposed. Brought to trial as a conspirator in the July 20, 1944 assassination, he was judged guilty and executed the same day.

Von Witzleben, the first of the major conspirators to be tried, appeared in the infamous Nazi *Volksgerichtshof* or People's Court where he was forced to stand without his belt or false teeth. Although harangued by the chief judge, the virulently vitriolic Roland Freisler, he spoke out, saying, "You may hand us over to the executioner, but in three months' time our disgusted and harried people will bring you to book and drag you alive through the dirt in the streets!" (His prediction proved incorrect, as the people did not revolt, but the arch-Nazi Freisler was subsequently killed during an Allied bombing raid.)

An eye-witness to the executions of some of the conspirators at Plötzensee Prison on August 8, 1944 later described what he saw.

> Imagine a room with a low ceiling and whitewashed walls. Below the ceiling a rail was fixed. From it hung six big hooks, like those butchers use to hang their meat. In one corner stood a movie camera. Reflectors cast a dazzling, blinding light. At the wall there was a small table with a bottle of cognac and glasses for the witnesses of the execution. The hangman wore a permanent leer, and made jokes unceasingly. The camera worked uninterruptedly, for Hitler wanted to see and hear how his enemies died. He had the executioner come to him, and had personally arranged the details of the procedure. "I want them to be hanged, hung up like carcasses of meat." Those were his words.

As recounted in Samuel W. Mitcham, *Hitler's Field Marshals* (1990):

> Witzleben met his death with courage and with as much dignity as was possible under the circumstances. A thin wire noose was placed around his neck, and the other end was secured to a meat hook. The executioner and his assistant then picked up the sixty-four-year-old soldier and dropped him so that his entire weight fell on his neck. They then pulled off his trousers so that he hung naked and twisted in agony as he slowly strangled. It took him almost five minutes to die, but he never once cried out. The other seven condemned men (Robert Bernardis, Albrecht von Hagen, Paul von Hase, Erich Hoepner, Friedrich Karl Klausing, Helmuth Stieff and Peter Graf Yorck von Wartenburg) were executed in the same manner within an hour. They were followed over the next eight months by hundreds of others. (Von Stauffenberg and several others had escaped that fate having previously been shot.)

British War Propaganda Forgery
As part of their own war effort, the Allies produced several stamps aimed at causing discord among the Nazi leadership. These so-called 'propaganda forgeries' involved removing Hitler's portrait from a regular stamp and substituting that of another Nazi leader. Following the execution of General von Witzleben, the British war department created a stamp wherein von Witzleben's portrait replaced Hitler's which had previously appeared on a special November 1943 postal issue commemorating the 20th anniversary of the Munich uprising.

Hitler Bomb Plot Participant—Gen. Fritz Lindemann
A page from an unknown soldier's photo album carries a rare snapshot of General of the Artillery Fritz Lindemann making an 'on-location" report from somewhere in Bosnia. In addition to the war correspondents conducting the interview, two cameramen also appear in the photo who in turn are being photographed by a third camera.

Soldier Journalist (*above left*)
Lindemann, a career soldier, joined the military in 1912 at age 18, eventually decorated and promoted during the First World War. Although harboring anti-Nazi sentiments, he joined the Party in 1938 after his promotion to Colonel. He also began making reports as a journalist via radio for the Department of Military Policy.

Serving as a commander of both artillery and infantry regiments, he was promoted to the Army General Staff in October 1943. He took part in German operations in Poland, France and the Eastern Front and awarded the Knights Cross. As the result of his growing opposition to the war, he later joined the anti-Nazi resistance, and as spokesman for the planned post-Hitler government, he was scheduled to give the planned radio proclamation to the German people announcing Hitler's overthrow.

After the failure of the bomb attempt, Lindemann gathered his family and made an attempt to elude capture by hiding out in Dresden, then Berlin. On August 5, 1944 he was sentenced to death *in absentia* by the infamous People's Court (*Volksgerichtshof*). With a 500,000 *Reichsmark* bounty on his head, he was betrayed, then hunted down by the Gestapo during which he was shot and badly wounded on September 3, 1944. Although the medical staff reports remarked on his strong will, the bullet wounds to his stomach led to acute peritonitis, the General dying as a result on September 22, thus escaping the fate of his fellow conspirators. However the three civilians, Erich and Elisabeth Gloeden and the latter's mother who attempted to hide him, also arrested by the Gestapo, were beheaded.

Survivor—General Maximilian Freiherr von Weichs (*above right*)
A son of the German aristocracy who had served in the First World War with the 3rd Bavarian Army Corp's General staff, von Weichs initially commanded Nazi Germany's 1st Panzer Division, later taking part in the Polish invasion. Selected as Commander-in-Chief of the 2nd Army prior to the invasion of France, his success earned him the Knight's Cross. He took part in the invasion of the Balkans and the Soviet Union as commander of the 2nd Army, then in 1942 given command of the new Army Group B which included German, Hungarian, Romanian and Italian troops.

At Stalingrad he notified Hitler of weaknesses in the lines and when Russian troops encircled the German forces he counseled withdrawal which brought him into disfavor with *der Führer*. As a result von Weichs was relegated to a reserve position though promoted to General Field Marshal in February 1943. In March 1945 with Nazi Germany collapsing as the Allies closed in, Weichs was officially retired from service then arrested by American troops. Implicated in war crimes, he managed to escape trial purportedly due to ill health, dying nine years later near Bonn in September 1954.

On Weak Footing—General Werner von Blomberg
The Third Reich produced some 26 Field Marshals including Senior Field Marshal Hermann Göring, the only level higher than General Field Marshal and the only person ever to hold that rank. Of the 25 "regular" Field Marshals, a dozen were awarded that rank on July 19, 1940 as a result of Germany's victory over France. Field Marshal of the *Heer* (Army) was equivalent to a Grand Admiral in the *Kriegsmarine* (Navy).

Field Marshal Blomberg—Unlucky in Love
First World War hero and the Third Reich's first General Field Marshal of the Wehrmacht, Blomberg was appointed Minister of Defense in 1935, but eventually dismissed in 1938 purportedly for marrying a prostitute of which he later said, "I could not help myself. She was the great passion of my life." His loss of reputation and position has been credited to the machinations of Göring and Himmler as well as Hitler who wanted him out of the way, Hitler then appointing himself Commander of the Wehrmacht.

Before falling out of favor, Blomberg had promoted the Army's commitment to pledging itself to the *Der Führer* after the SA was purged. He died in March 1946 in American captivity at the age of 68. Summing up his fellow officers in 1945, he said, "Before 1938–39, the German generals were not opposed to Hitler. There was no reason to oppose Hitler, since he produced the results they desired."

Luck of the Draw—General Georg von Küchler (facing camera)

Georg von Küchler would spend his life in the German military swearing allegiance to the German Empire, the Weimar Republic and lastly Nazi Germany.

Initially a commander of artillery in the First World War, he would later side with Hitler in 1938 in the removal of von Blomberg and von Fritsch. He then served under Himmler in the occupation of the Lithuanian port of Memel, then in Poland and as army group commander on the Western Front as the Second World War began. While an ardent Nazi Party supporter, he took action against SS soldiers complicit in civilian atrocities, at least until 1940 when he came out in support of the racist programs of "ethnic struggle" including the Final Solution and the execution of Red Army political officers. While conducting several successful operations on the Western Front, he was eventually dismissed for his failure to take Leningrad. Post-war he was sentenced to 20 years in prison specifically for the treatment of "partisans" but was released by the West German courts after only eight years supposedly for poor health and old age. He lived another 15 years dying in 1968 at age 86.

General Friedrich Christiansen (center)—War Criminal

While born of a naval family, he learned to fly in 1913, then during the First World War while piloting a seaplane was credited with 13 confirmed victories over enemy aircraft. The only seaplane pilot recipient of the "Blue Max" he eventually rose to General's rank in Nazi Germany's Luftwaffe, then became Supreme Wehrmacht Commander of the Netherlands 1940–45 and one of the few awarded the Golden Party Badge. He was convicted of war crimes for his complicity in the burning of a Dutch village and the shooting of several of its civilians as well as the deportation of 661 men to labor camps where most perished. Sentenced to 12 years in 1948 he was released after only three years in 1951. His home town of Wyk auf Föhr celebrated his return by reinstating a street in his name, that act only revoked in 1980 after protest. Christiansen lived until 92, dying in March 1972.

The Fog of War—General Krebs in Consultation—Death in the *Führerbunker*
Army Infantry General Hans Krebs, center facing camera, confers with fellow officers on a foggy morning in a forest clearing, a stack of rifles in the foreground. Krebs would be one of the last to remain in Hitler's Berlin bunker, committing suicide as the Soviets captured the city, *der Führer* having previously killed himself. (There was another Hans Krebs, an SS General who became chief executive officer in the Reich Ministry of the Interior, known for harshly suppressing opponents to the Nazi Party in Czechoslovakia and later executed in that country for his crimes.)

Last Minute Fatality—Field Marshal Fedor von Bock
Bock commanded Army Group North during the Polish invasion, Army Group B during the French invasion, then Army Group Center during the invasion of the Soviet Union and lastly commander of Army Group South. He is seen wearing his Knight's Cross award. Though outspoken, even to Hitler, he raised no objections to the mistreatment of civilians nor took part in any anti-Hitler plots. Along with his second wife and stepdaughter, Bock was killed at the very end of the war, on May 4, 1945, while driving by car to Hamburg when strafed by a British aircraft.

Waffen-SS
As their comrades sing a marching song, a phalanx of NCOs lead the way somewhere on the Eastern Front. While two carry standard messenger pouches, their boot spurs identify them as horse-mounted troops.

Voices of the Heldentod Present Past—1995 Funeral Oration for Waffen-SS Panzer Major General Theodor Wisch

Theodor Wisch was an SS-*Brigadeführer*, a Major General of the Waffen SS who fought on both the Western and Eastern fronts eventually as commander of the First *SS* Panzer Division *Leibstandarte SS Adolf Hitler*. The son of a farmer, he rose in the ranks, joining the SS in 1930 serving in Poland and later the Balkans as well as the invasion of the Soviet Union including the monumental tank battle at Kursk. Recognized for his bravery and audacity, he was awarded larger commands.

Though severely wounded in both legs by grenade shrapnel during the August 1944 battle of the so-called Falaise Pocket, he was still able to rescue his troops from the Allied encirclement of British, American, Canadian and Polish forces that had trapped some 150, 000 German troops in Normandy near the town of Falaise, itself some 20 miles south of Caen. Wisch spent the remainder of the war confined under care in a military hospital prior to being taken prisoner. Although a member of the SS and Waffen-SS, he was considered an honorable soldier and never charged with war crimes. He was released from captivity in 1948. In 1990, he published a book, *Twelve Years 1st Company Leibstandarte SS Adolf Hitler*. His nickname was "Teddy."

On January 19, 1995, a funeral ceremony was held to commemorate the passing of Wisch who had died on the 11th, a month after his 88th birthday. The location was the cemetery hall in Ojendorf where the funeral oration was performed, as stated in the original text published for the ceremony, by "former SS-*Obersturmbannführer* Hubert Meyer of the *Leibstandarte* SS."

One copy of the funeral document passed out to attendees was signed by Hans Hotter, described as a German operatic bass baritone known for his singing of Hitler's favored Wagner operas. The memorial ceremony began with Wisch's own favorite song "*Wo die Nordseewellen treffen an den Strand*" or "Where the North Sea waves meet the beach."

A basic translation of the funeral oration given by Meyer reads:

> My dear Ladies and Gentleman, my dear Comrades,
>
> We have to say goodbye to our General and we will again say thank you. He was one of the first who entered the Leibstandarte in 1933 taking over the leadership of the First Company in the same year. Often he welcomed high foreign state politicians. He became famous, entered history and we've seen him in many photos. He led his company in Poland where he took his baptism of fire. After the campaign he received orders to create and lead a new battalion. When the Russian campaign began, he was Commander of the 2nd Battalion of the Leibstandarte.
>
> After many successful battles, the Leibstandarte pushed forward to Rostov and the Don River where they were able to establish a bridgehead. This famous action was accomplished by Heinz Spring, the former leader of this company.
>
> In the winter 41/42, Theodor Wisch was still in Russia with his battalion when ordered to France, but returned to Russia in February as Commander of the 2nd Panzer Grenadier Regiment of the Leibstandarte which took part in heavy defensive fighting in Charkov where they achieved decisive victories. Thereafter, the Leibstandarte took on a new corps staff position as the division "Hitler Youth" in which Theodor Wisch became leader of the 1st SS Panzer Division Leibstandarte. He led this unit during the Zitadelle (Operation Citadel) mission and achieved many successes until the division was ordered to break off engagement because of the loss of Italy. Then again in Russia, he was present during the encirclement battle of Tscherkassy and Tarnopol.
>
> More or less refreshed, his company arrived in Normandy at the end of June 1944 and again fought major battles. During the outbreak of the Falaise pocket, as the Division Commander, he was badly wounded, but succeeded in bringing out his men. Because of his serious injuries, he could not continue his military activities.
>
> After the war he had—as we all had—a hard time dealing with the indignities, but he also re-experienced a time of grand reconstructing. And he never forgot his old comrades, with whom he fought during the war. And when the Comrade's Union of First Tank Corps was founded, he was with us of course. Although he didn´t have an official function, when all the comrades met, he was always in the middle of our circle as a grand personality.
>
> As long as we live, we will keep our General in our mind—as a brave soldier who was awarded with both Iron Crosses and with the German Badge in Gold—and as a grand troop leader who received the Knight's Cross of the Iron Cross, the Knight's Cross with Oak Leaves and the Knight's Cross with Swords and Oak Leaves. We will keep him in mind as an exemplary comrade, faithful to us and faithful to our German fatherland.
>
> Dear family Wisch, you may be proud of you father, father-in-law and grandfather. Keep the memory of this fantastic man in your hearts. He and his achievements are established forever in the books of history. We, my comrades want to thank our General for everything he

did for us. We will now sing again our traditional song "Wenn alle untreu werden, so bleiben wir doch true … (Author's Note: singing ensued as the coffin was lowered into the ground. The song, a mainstay of the SS, became known as the Treuelied or Song of Faithfulness).

When all become disloyal, we remain loyal ... That always on Earth remains one battalion for you will be Companions of our youth, your vision of a better time, that for us you have consecrated with manly virtue and fearlessness of death.

Never weaken, always be True as German oaks, as the moon and the sunshine! Once again it will become clear to all our brothers' spirits ... They will return to the source in love and loyalty.

They have struggled well, the heroes of this time ... And now have found their victory, though Satan uses new tricks. But however these times may turn out in life You will never grow old for us, o dream of glory!

Your stars are our witnesses, calmly looking down ... When all the brothers fall silent and trust in false idols, we won't break our word, nor become like knaves ... We want only to speak in praise of the holy German Reich!"

The Generals Write the "History" of the War

For decades a perspective of the war, particularly on the Eastern front, was one filtered through the "memory" of not the Allies, but by the aggressors themselves. Though difficult to understand, the Americans called upon leading high ranking German military leaders to compile the history of the war years. In June 1946 some 328 German officers, mostly Generals, and all of them POWs, were engaged in writing for the American's Operational History Section program.

The work continued into March of 1948 at which time their efforts had produced some 34,000 pages of "documentation" that was henceforth relied upon by the Allies. The German officers were lead in the project by Gen. Franz Halder, former chief of the army general staff. Other contributors included Admiral Dönitz to whom Hitler prior to his suicide passed leadership of the Third Reich and Gen. Reinhard Gehlen, head of the German secret service and an "anti-Communist expert" and thus of major interest to the Americans in the post-war Cold War.

The writing of the history of the war by its main architects allowed them certain advantages, for example, the whitewashing of the regular Army's co-responsibility for the Holocaust. They depicted themselves as "honorary" soldiers who had fallen victim to Hitler and that the common German soldier (as compared to the SS) were guilt-free. In all their thousands of pages of "history" writing, the German military hierarchy makes no mention at all of war crimes or the Holocaust as in any way the responsibility of the Wehrmacht.

This charade maintained its façade, much encouraged by West German military and political leaders as well as the general population, until revelations in the 1980s and 1990s by German researchers shattered the myth of the "honorable" Wehrmacht. The problem of accepting responsibility, and guilt, lay in the fact that of Germany's 60 million population during the Second World War some 20,000,000 had been in uniform and thus every German family was directly or indirectly affected/implicated in the war of aggression and its core program of racial extermination. Denial was much more palatable for all concerned as a form of personal and national psychological survival.

On the Path to Heldentod—
The Wounded and Wound Healers

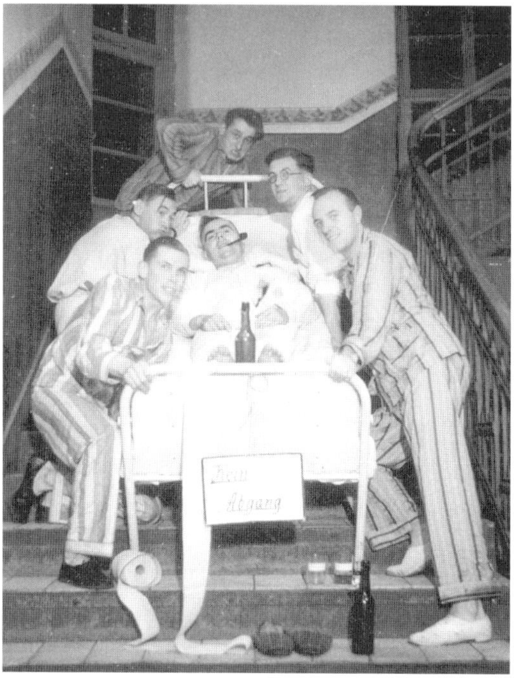

Kein Abgang

Soldier jokesters have brought one of their bedridden comrades out on the stairway. Along with with the beer and toilet paper decorations, the signage, in military parlance translates to "No Casualties" but can also mean "No Departure."

Propaganda Ministry Photo Postcard—Veteran's Benefits

Soldiers recovering in a military hosipital are shown dining with attractive companions sourced from a local woman's organization. The accompanying caption translates:

> Naturally, the wounded were cared for with even greater zeal. Our picture shows happy faces everywhere.

Wounded Wedding

Surrounded by relatives, an army officer and his new bride exchange a glance, perhaps at the bidding of the photographer. His uniform tunic carries both the 2nd and 1st Class Iron Cross and the Wound Badge in Black.

Walking Wounded

A *Volkssturm* uniformed boy, perhaps a relative or acting as a volunteer caretaker, stands alongside a wounded soldier. The soldier's contorted upper body indicates some form of brace or further damage. Note the boy's clenched right hand, a sign of stress.

In the Service of the Fatherland
With their bandaged arms seemingly raised in half-salute, wounded soldiers pose with one of their doctors, the insignia visible on his uniform sleeve. All would soon be pinning Wound Badges to their uniforms before most being sent back to the front lines.

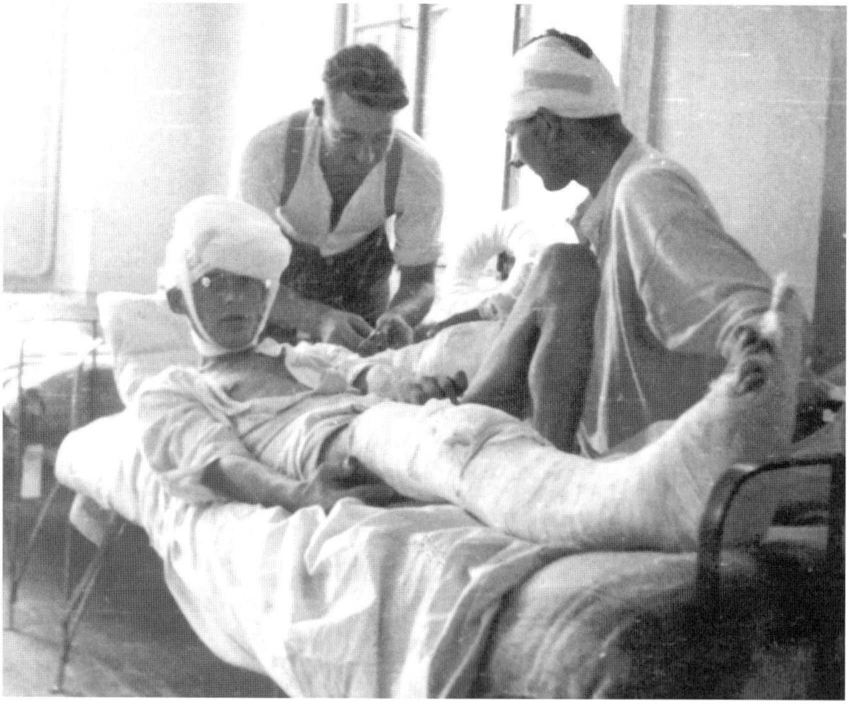

Bandaged Head to Foot
Two young soldiers seem crowded into one bed as a medical orderly tends to their bandages.

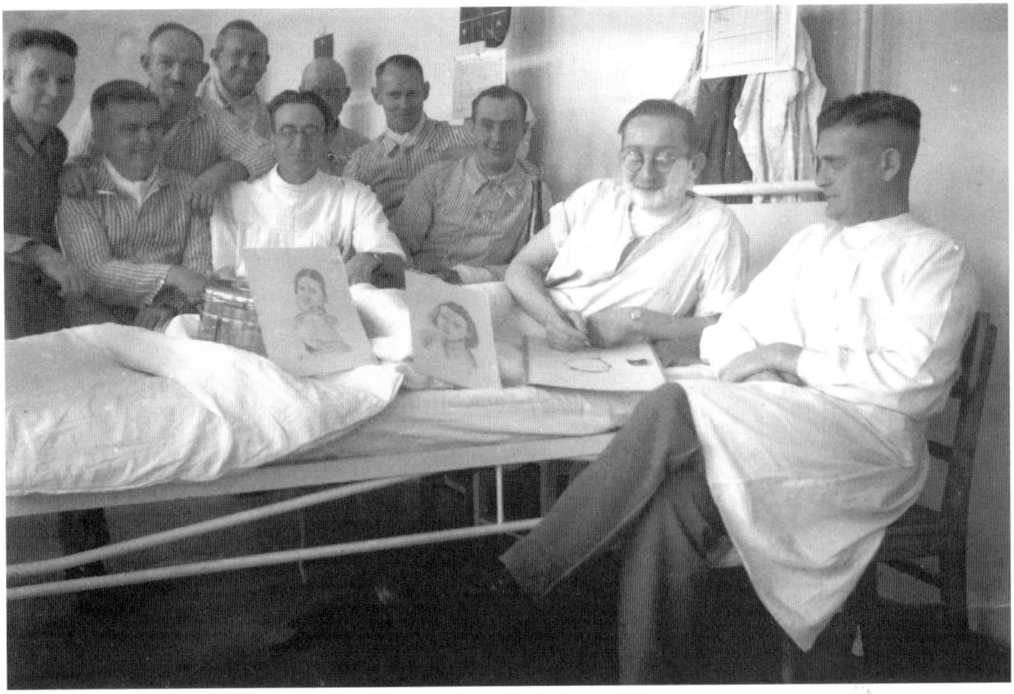

Recovery
Fellow patients and medical personnel gather round an amateur artist as he draws female portraits, his scarred left arm and the shaving cream-like ointment on his face indicating he was being treated for burns.

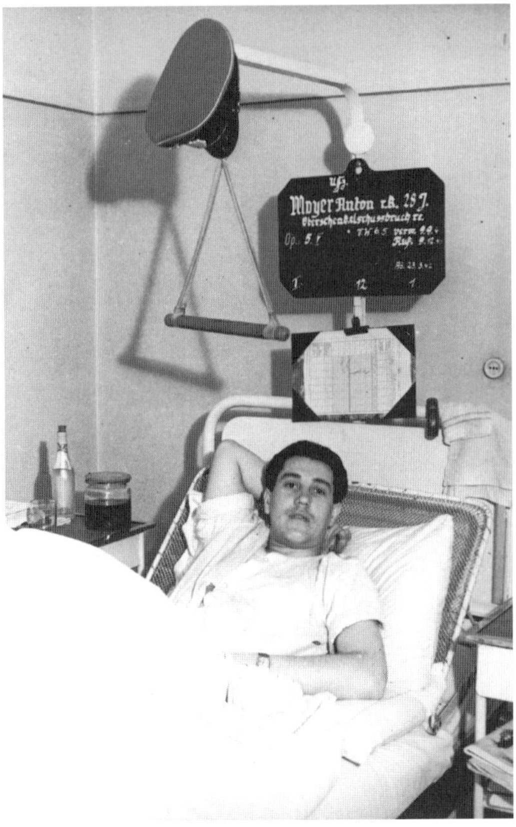

Sgt. Anton Moyer— "Shot through Upper Hip"— Admitted Sept. 9, 1941
Possibly a casualty incurred during the initial advance through the Soviet Union launched in June, the soldier could very likely return to the East upon his recovery. A large percentage of even seriously wounded German soldiers resumed their duties, for example during 1942–43, a reported 47.7 percent returned to combat.

Feldpostbriefe, die man – hören kann!

Auf Veranlassung des DRK. ist hier wie in vielen anderen Lazaretten ein Aufnahmeleiter erschienen und läßt den Patienten eine Grammophonplatte „besprechen". – Und alsbald vernehmen die dankbaren Lieben daheim immer auf's neue Vatis freudigen Gruß! Photos: Atlantic

"Now You Can Hear Your Fieldpost!"

According to the newspaper article appearing in the May 26, 1942 issue of the *Deutsche Illustrierte*, the German Red Cross provided a means by which soldiers recovering in military hospitals could record their voices via a gramophone, a record then sent to their families where "the grateful ones can, again and again, hear their father's joyful greetings."

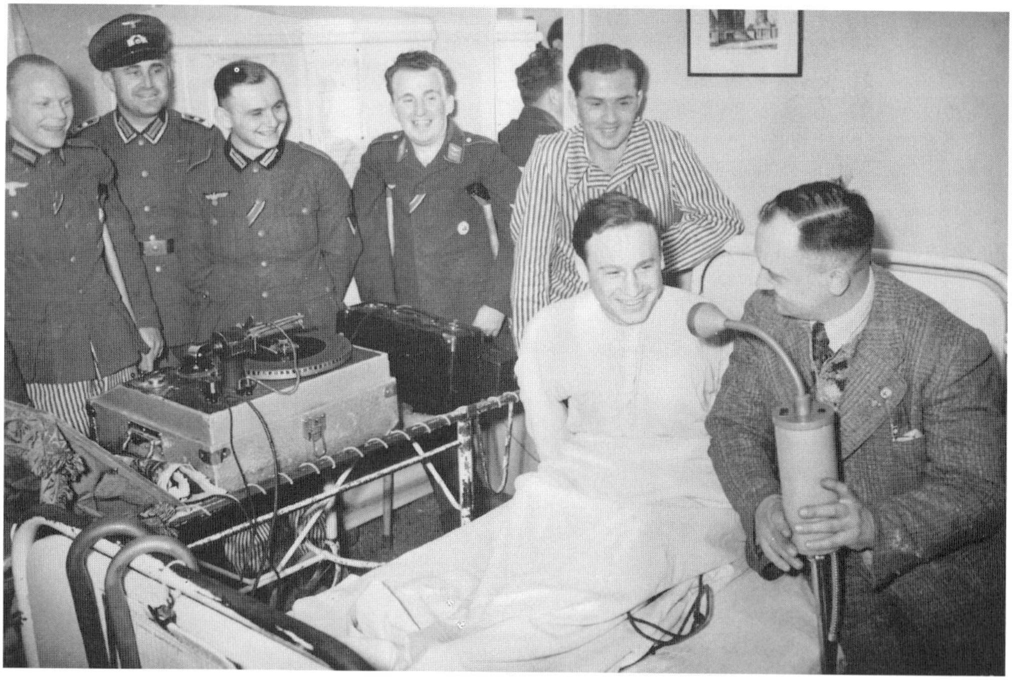

Speak into the Microphone

A photo op has been orchestrated by the Ministry of Propaganda showcasing a group of smiling wounded gathered around the bedside of a comrade being interviewed, the conversation recorded on a gramophone disk for later radio play. The same radio journalist who appeared in the previous newspaper photo is seen here holding the ungainly looking microphone, a Nazi party pin visible on his lapel. A closer look at the bed patient reveals he has lost one, perhaps both legs.

Returned to Duty …
The additional photo of Bernhard Antonius Tiemann accompanied his memorial card as it appeared in a family album. It shows him wearing his overseas insignia cap. The sterbebild announcing his death, states that he was born in Borghorst, the city situated north-west of Münster in the area of North Rhine-Westphalia. The "returned to duty" notation indicates he may have been wounded, recovered and sent back to the Front.

Zum frommen Andenken an den auf dem Felde der Ehre gefallenen

Bernhard Antonius Tiemann

Obergefr. in einem Inf.-Rgt,
Inh. des Inf.-Sturmabz.

Der liebe Verstorbene war geboren zu Borghorst am 13. März 1914. Bei Ausbruch d. Krieges wurde er zu den Waffen gerufen u. machte d. Feldzug in Holland, Belgien u. Frankreich mit. Bei Beginn des Ostfeldzuges gegen den Bolschewismus kämpfte er bis Ende Sept. 1941, wo er erkrankte. Nachdem er 2 Monate im Lazarett verbracht hatte, wurde er geheilt der Ersatztruppe überwiesen. Nach kurzem Erholungsurlaub wurde er am 21. Januar 1942 in Marsch nach seiner alten Kompanie gesetzt. Er traf am 15. Februar 1942 bei seinen alten Kameraden wieder ein. Am folgenden Tage wurde er als erster M.-G.-Schütze an der linken Schulter schwer verwundet. Obwohl er gleich von seinen Kameraden zurückgebracht wurde, starb er als echter Christ und Soldat auf dem Wege zum Verbandplatz. Er wurde am Nordausgang von Wiwino mit noch 3 Kameraden in die tief gefrorene Erde Rußlands zur letzten Ruhe gebettet.

Herr, gib ihm die ewige Ruhe!
Und das ewige Licht leuchte ihm!
Mein Jesus, Barmherzigkeit!

Anton Schmeken vorm. Victor badde, Borghorst

… and "Fell on the Field of Honor"
The brief biography states he was called to arms at the outbreak of war and served in the Dutch, Belgian and French campaigns and also took part in the beginning of the Eastern campaign, but in September 1941,became ill and was hospitalized for two months. After a short sick leave he rejoined his company on January 21, 1942 and met up with his old comrades on February 15, a month before his 28th birthday.

On the following day, after taking the position of first machine gunner, he suffered a severe wound to his left shoulder. Although his comrades went to his aid, he died on the way to the first-aid station. "He was a true Christian soldier and at the northern exit to Wiwino was buried by three comrades into the deeply frozen Russian earth for a lasting peace."

Crutches on Parade
Three convalescing soldiers with varying degrees of leg injuries practice their ambulatory techniques for the benefit of the camera. Several other wounded can be seen in the background, the location very likely at a large military hospital or *Lazarett*.

Til Death Do Us Part—A Wedding in Dresden
Newlyweds pose on the church steps after their marriage ceremony. The ribbon worn in the sergeant's second button hole denotes the Iron Cross 2nd Class while the Wound Badge in Silver indicates 3–5 wounds including the loss of his left arm. He appears to use his cap to cover his missing hand. The photo, turned into a postcard, was printed in Dresden, the famous city later in the war incinerated by Allied firebombing. On February 13–14, 1945 RAF and U.S. bombers rained bombs day and night in three successive waves. Estimates range from 60,000 to 200,000 civilian deaths.

The carnage was described by Hans Voight, then director of Dresden's Deceased Persons Department of the Central Bureau of Missing Persons. *Continued on next page.*

Never would I have thought that death could come to so many people in so many ways. Never had I expected to see people interred in that state: burnt, cremated, torn and crushed to death; sometimes the victims looked like ordinary people apparently peacefully sleeping; the faces of other were racked with pain, the bodies stripped almost naked by the tornado (firestorm); there were wretched refugees from the East clad only in rags, and people from the Opera in all their finery; here the victim was a shapeless slab, there a layer of ashes shoveled into a zinc tub. Across the city, along the streets wafted the unmistakable stench of decaying flesh.

Traumatic Amputation
A forest of crutches greets a cameraman who records his comrades' war wounds, the subjects wearing a wide spectrum of expressions. Some six million German soldiers suffered wounds. Of that number, who survived, at least 125,000 lost one leg, 400,000 one arm, 10,000 both legs, and 900 both arms.

Well-Composed Smiles
A trio of wounded and decorated NCO's stand together in soldierly solidarity, two missing legs above the knee, the third displaying a gloved prosthetic hand.

Rehabilitated (*above left*)

The German medical establishment developed an extensive rehabilitation program for the war wounded. In addition to repairing them sufficiently to return to combat or perform some military related occupation, those permanently disabled were given other opportunities to remain useful to the war effort.

A one-armed army corporal is seen assisting at a drill press operation. Injured soldiers were often paired together to offset their debilitating wounds, for example, a soldier missing a right arm or hand would be matched to another who had lost his left arm or hand and then the two trained together. A sighted soldier missing limbs would be assigned a blind companion who had use of his appendages and thus forming a work team.

Mask of War (*above right*)

A soldier wears his head wrapped in bandages and takes a defensive stance in his hospital slippers.

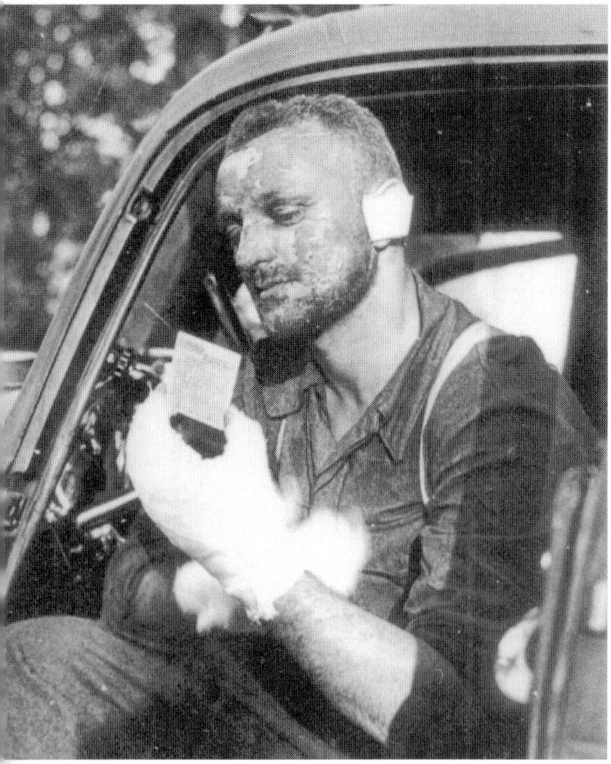

Burns (*above left*)

Scars of Battle and Grandmother (*above right*)
An army corporal has donned his *waffenrock* formal dress uniform on which he wears his Iron Cross 2nd Class ribbon as well as a Wound Badge likely relating to the head and facial wounds marked by scars.

Disfigurement (*right*)
A soldier with a facial wound still bandaged poses for his portrait in a Vienna photographer's studio in June 1941. His collar trim indicates his NCO rank while the button ribbon records his awarding of the Iron Cross 2nd Class.

The Merging of Crosses—SA "Brownshirts" Pretend to Throw Grenades (*above left*)
In 1929 the German Red Cross was officially recognized via the International Red Cross Geneva Agreement of 1864 as a "volunteer sanitary association."

Temporary Duty (*above right*)
In 1937 and now under the control of the Nazi authorities, the *Deutsches Rotes Kreuz* (DRK) was granted Third Reich legal status, its initial formal regulations established on January 1, 1938. Four years previously Hitler had violently purged the *Sturmabteilung* (SA) leadership including his longtime friend Ernst Roehm. The SA, seen as a potential threat to Hitler's power and at odds with Himmler's plans for the SS, was effectively neutralized. The regular army saw the SA as a dangerous revolutionary rabble and in order to gain their support Hitler effectively eliminated them. However, the SA was not formerly disbanded until the end of the war in 1945.

Hospital Convalescent (*left*)
As a Luftwaffe corporal watches from the sidelines, a *Heer* soldier, wearing his army longcoat over his hospital pajamas, samples a treat offered by a female volunteer who seems to be wearing stylish "cowboy" boots.

DRK Nurses on a River Cruise
The *Deutsches Rotes Kreuz* (DRK) was composed of both nursing and career administrative personnel. In addition to its civilian volunteer work, the DRK supplied the nursing staffs to all branches of the Wehrmacht. Extensive recruitment efforts called for women of 16–21 years to come to the aid of the country's soldiers by serving as nursing auxiliaries (*Schwesternhelferin*), the training beginning with first aid via the BdM (*Bund Deutscher Mädel*—League of German Girls). DRK personnel, including its nurses, swore an oath of allegiance to Hitler.

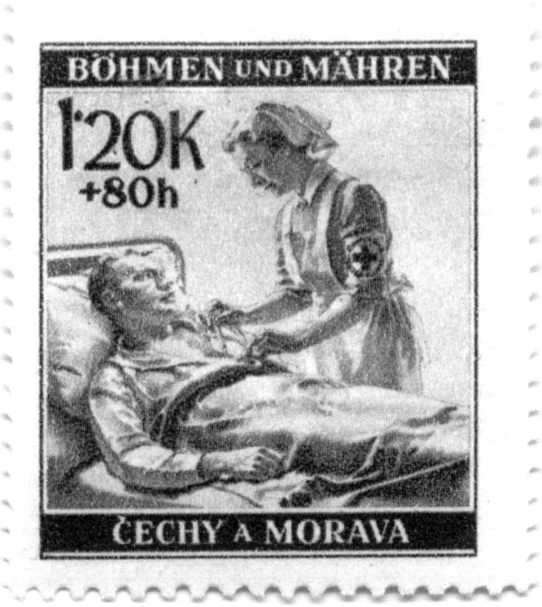

In Honor
A stamped issued in the Third Reich "protectorate" of Bohemia and Moravia, regions of occupied Czechoslovakia, depicts an DRK nurse administering to a patient.

* * * * *

A large percentage of German Red Cross affiliated nurses and hospital personal were affiliated with the Catholic religion and not prone to participating in the euthanasia programs or concentration camp medical activities of the Third Reich. To fill that need the Nazi regime recruited and trained the so-called *Brown Nurses*, some of whom were still carrying out the murder of "undesirables" into the last days of the war, and even beyond, until intervention by Allied authorities.

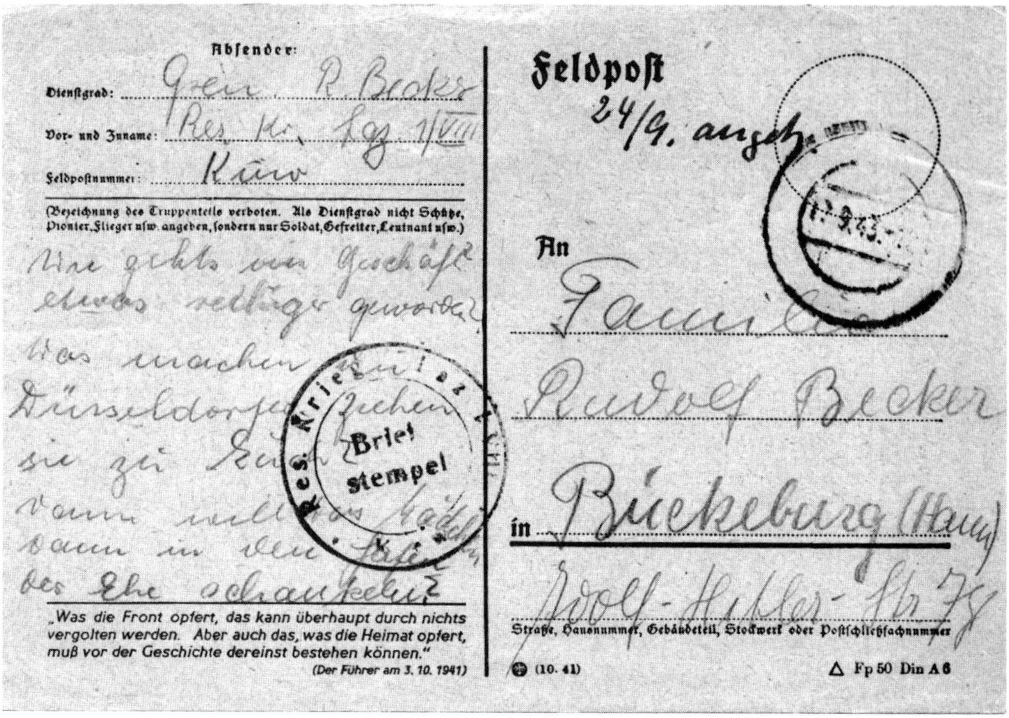
Absender:
Dienstgrad: Gren. R. Becker
Vor- und Zuname: Res. Kr. Laz. I/VIII
Feldpostnummer: Kuno
(Bezeichnung des Truppenteils verboten. Als Dienstgrad nicht Schütze, Pionier, Flieger usw. angeben, sondern nur Soldat, Gefreiter, Leutnant usw.)

„Was die Front opfert, das kann überhaupt durch nichts vergolten werden. Aber auch das, was die Heimat opfert, muß vor der Geschichte dereinst bestehen können."
(Der Führer am 3. 10. 1941)

Feldpost
24/9. angek.
Brief stempel
An Familie Rudolf Becker
in Bückeburg (Hann)
Adolf-Hitler-Str 78
Straße, Hausnummer, Gebäudeteil, Stockwerk oder Postschließfachnummer
(10. 41) Fp 50 Din A 6

Felpost—September 16, 1943—Wound Recovery on the Eastern Front

From: Pvt. 1st Class Rudi Becker at Reserve Hospital I/III in Kuno
To: The Rudolf Becker Family, Adolf Hitler Strasse 78, Bückeburg, Hannover

Dear Parents,

My treatment in the hospital will take another week and I shall be released in eight days. I am well and I hope you are, too. We have some entertainment, variety shows and movies, and it's not bad here.

Greetings,
Your Rudi

* * * * *

During September 1943 and the penning of this *Feldpost* card, German forces were in retreat from the Eastern Front as Soviet forces began sweeping the enemy from their country. The postcard also carries an October 3, 1940 quote by Hitler:

What sacrifices the Front makes, nothing can repay. But what the Home Front sacrifices, history may one day note.

Top of next page:

Front Row Seats
Wounded soldiers lie on stretchers in a theater filled with other convalescents, medical staff and nurses. By the facial expressions on several members of the audience, some form of entertainment is being performed on stage. However, on closer examination, a large portion of the audience apparently finds little to be amused about.

Official programs for improved health care, insistence on exercise and admonitions against smoking and drinking aided in preventing large scale epidemics among the German population and its foreign workers. However, some services remained relatively primitive, for instance, the practice of dangerous donor to patient blood transfusions and a lack of x-ray devices. In addition one of every 300 German medical practitioners took part in the infamous "experiments" carried out at concentration camps.

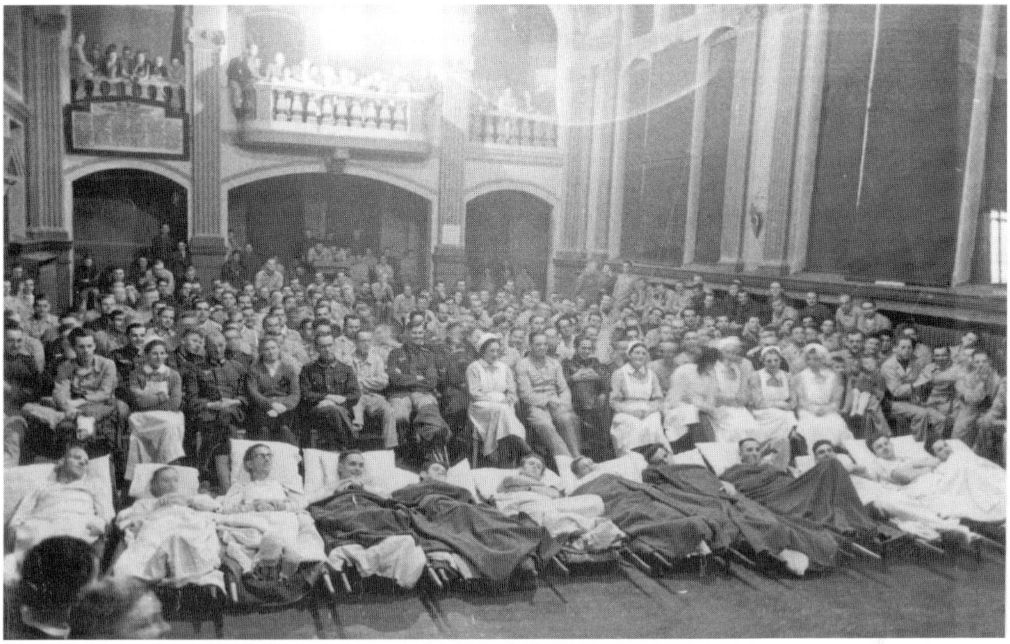

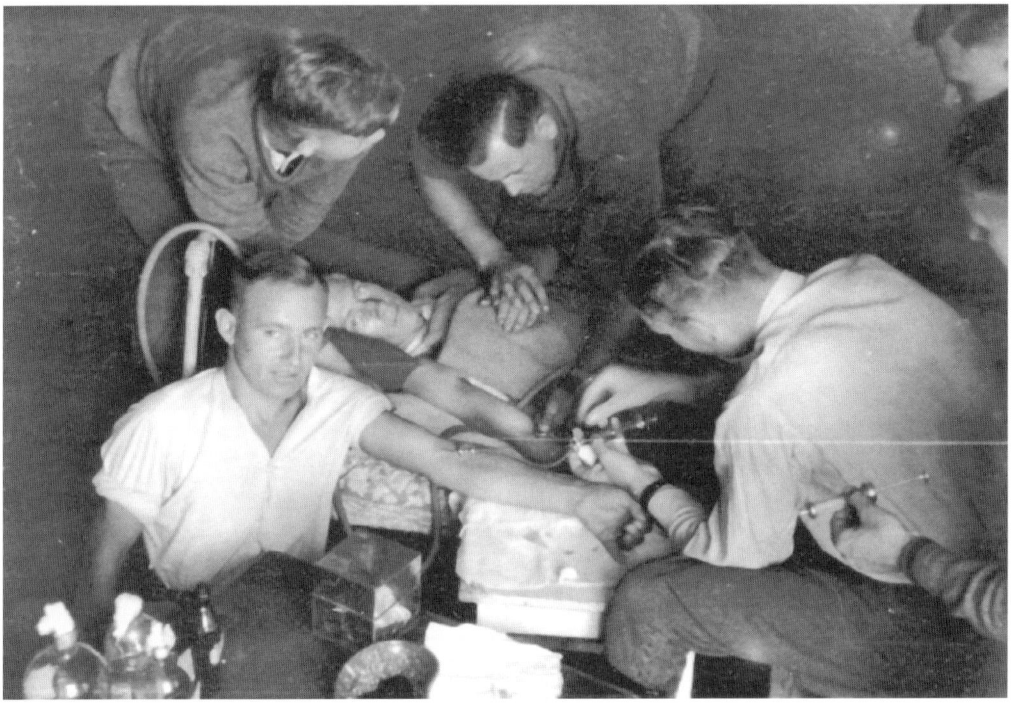

Transfusion
A soldier takes part in a direct blood transfusion for an injured comrade who is comforted by his brothers-in-arms.

SS men had their blood type tattooed on the upper inside of their left arm, a tell-tale sign that often proved their undoing when captured by the Allies and usually fatal when captured by the Russians. Many SS attempted to burn off or otherwise disguise the tattoo which in itself was literally a dead giveaway.

As the war ground on, blood supplies became increasingly critical giving rise to the practice of extracting blood from children in occupied countries and even from Jewish prisoners, apparently a moratorium placed on such acts of "blood defilement", the source kept secret.

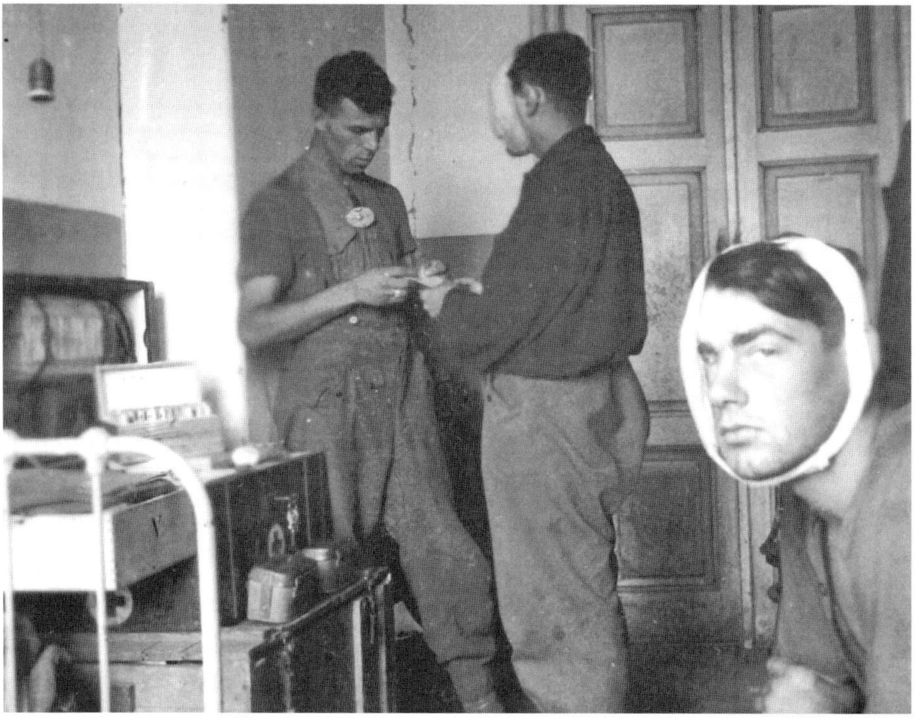

Facial Wounds
Two men with face wounds seem to be the focus of the cameraman's attention, one soldier viewing him with a rather jaundiced eye.

Berliner Illustrierte Zeitung 99

Volk, steh auf! Sturm, brich los!

Die Blutzeugen.

Während der großen Rede des Reichsministers Dr. Goebbels im Berliner Sportpalast, die ein Alarmruf für die Rettung der Zivilisation war, füllten die Verwundeten die ersten Reihen der Riesenhalle. Sie verkörperten die Front, an der in einem beispiellosen Heldenkampf der Ansturm der Steppe zerschellt.

People, Stand up! Break Loose the Storm! ***Die Blutzeugen*****—"The Martyrs"** (*continued on next page*)

The newspaper photo caption reads:

> During the great speech of the Reich Minister Dr. Goebbels in the Berlin Sports Palace that sounded a cry of alarm for the salvation of civilization, the wounded filled the first rows of the giant hall. You embodied the Front, injured during the unprecedented heroic struggle against the unprecented onslaught from the East.

Goebbels's infamous speech delivered on February 18, 1943 in response to the disaster at Stalingrad and during which he called for "total war" also contained the following:

> ... to this meeting today I invited a cross section, in the best sense of that word, of the German people. In front of me there sit, row on row, wounded soldiers from the Eastern Front, men with scarred bodies, with amputated legs or arms, men blinded in action who have come here with their Red Cross nurses, men in the prime of life whose crutches are standing in front of them. In between, I count as many as 50 wearers of the Oak Leaf Cluster and of the Knight's Cross, a splendid delegation from our fighting front.

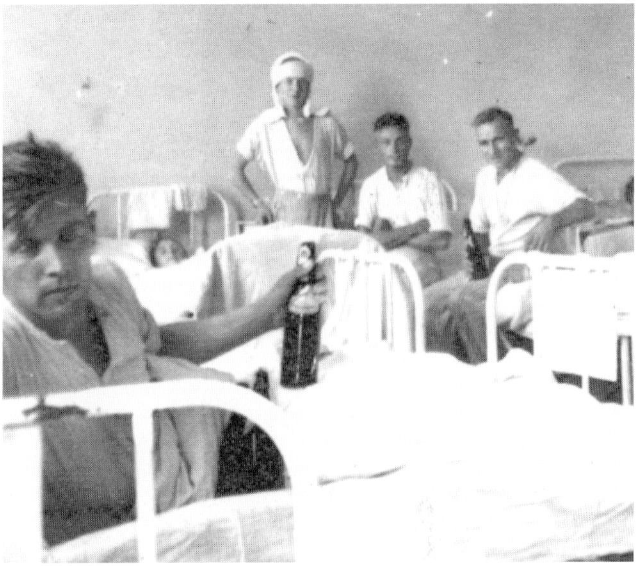

Recuperation
Members of the 37th Infantry Regiment recover in a military hospital with the help of beer. The man in the foreground with three botttles has lost both his legs. The two soldiers sitting in the background have each lost one leg.

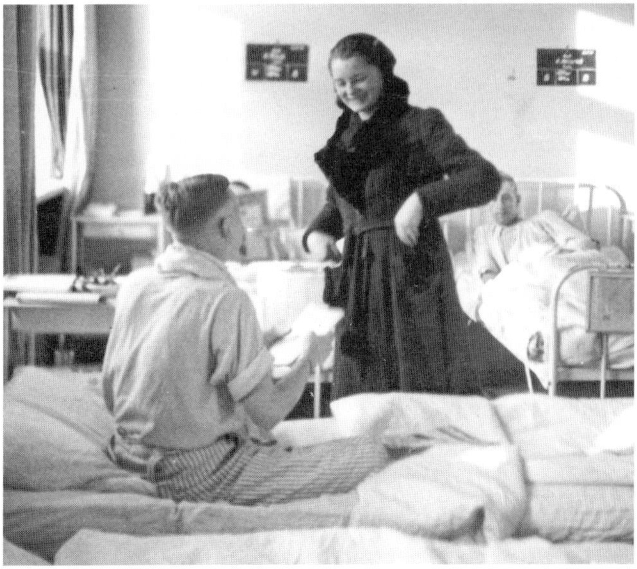

Visiting Hours
A pretty young girl, perhaps a film actress, brings a warm smile and perhaps some reading material for the same group of wounded 37th Regiment soldiers. It appears another soldier may have snapped the photo from an adjacent bed.

Country of the Crippled (*above left*)
A badly wounded young *Gebirgsjäger* or mountain trooper is aided by a Luftwaffe comrade. Due to its medical corp's penchant for amputations rather than repair, Germany achieved the post-war status of having the largest percentage of limbless people in Europe.

"War Stories for German Youth"—"Medic! Medic!" (*above right*)
The series of children's booklets extolling the virtues and heroics of the German soldier features a cover spotlighting the *Sanitäter* or German field medic..

Medical Corpsmen
While American troops when wounded in combat would call out "Medic!" German soldiers called out "Sani!" The term *sani* would include medical corpsmen, stretcher-bearers as well as doctors. They were identified by the uniform emblem of the traditional Aesculapius emblem with the addition of a Red Cross armband. In combat they also wore a more visible body tabard, a two-foot square cloth displaying a red cross on both the medic's back and chest since armbands could become obscured by dirt, snow, rain, smoke and blood. German medics and their patients also benefited from special sleds to carry stretchers and litters, pulled by a rope with one hand, and allowing the other hand to carry a large Red Cross flag, thus increasing their chances of survival, items much envied by their Allied counterparts.

Waffen-SS Medic
A Panzer medical attendant bandages a comrade's head wound, the photo appearing on a commercial postcard. While U.S. medics or "aidmen" were not permitted to carry weapons, this SS man appears to carry a sidearm. On the Eastern Front, the Soviets rarely showed leniency toward the German medical personel especially the SS.

Comrade-in-arms
A woodcut by German soldier artist Paul Weber speaks to the courage and sacrifice of the German soldier, the illustration appearing in a 1942 published book *Soldatengeist—Eine Deutung aus Bekentnissen der Front* ("Soldier Spirit—An Interpretation of Confessions from the Front.")

Combat Veteran—Field Hospital—Russia

A haggard, bearded, somewhat traumatized-appearing soldier stands outside a field hospital somewhere in the Ukraine. He uses a cane and his tunic carries a Wound Badge in Black as well as a Combat Assault badge. The Combat Assault Badge was awarded in bronze and silver, though which is difficult to determine in the photo. The bronze form was authorized in January 1940 specifically for members of the motorized infantry divisions. The requirements were one of the following: three or more infantry assaults; three or more motorized counter-attacks or combined with assaults; three or more reconnaissance actions. The silver version was also awarded for hand to hand combat in an assault situation. In regards to the psychological effects of warfare, "shell-shock" and other "nervous disorders" were given short shift by the German medical establishment. Music or a sudden shock was thought to be of benefit to reverse what was considered a "mental" condition although sanitariums also offered care.

Mit Gott fürs Vaterland hat sein Leben geopfert Jüngling

Fritz Meyer

Bauerssohn von Schweigersdorf
Sanitätssoldat i. einem-Gebirgsj.-Regt.
gefallen am 1. August 1942
bei Ausübung seiner Samariterdienste im lappländischen Kriegsgebiet im Alter von 19 Jahren 10½ Monaten.

Dein Grab im fernen Feindesland
ist uns wohl eine schwere Pein,
Doch nimm dies Wort zum Unterpfand,
Dein Grab soll nicht verlassen sein.
All' abends wenn die Glocken klingen,
Zieht liebend unser Geist dorthin
Und streut dir segnend Andachtsblumen
Auf's Heldengrab mit frommen Sinn.

M. W. Bauer Beilngries

A Medic's Death in Finnish Lapland—August 1, 1942

Fritz Meyer was a farmer's son from Schweigersdorf, a Bavarian village some 31 miles (51 km) from Nuremberg. As his family specifically stated on his deathcard, he died at age 19 and 10½ months while performing his medical services. At this point in the war, Finland was allied with Germany against the Soviet Union, Meyer dying in this conflict.

Top of next page:

Coming to the Aid

Sanitätsobergefreiter (Medical Corporal) Josef Borgel while tending to his comrades was killed in action somewhere on the Russian front on May 17, 1943 at the age of 27.

With the invasion of Poland in 1939, the German military counted some 7,798 doctors and 92,348 medical corpsmen serving with the troops. By 1943, and the fourth year of the war, that number had grown to 17,034 medical officers and 164,898 aids serving in the combat areas while thousands more cared for the wounded in military hospitals in Germany and the occupied countries.

Stalingrad—"He dies a Hero's Death for the Fatherland" (*below*)

Medical Staff Sergeant Josef Zierl, a veteran of actions in Austria, the Sudetenland, Czechoslovakia and campaigns in France had been awarded the War Service Cross with Swords, an award for bravery and courage beyond the call of duty but not quite meeting the criteria needed for an Iron Cross. He was killed in the East on December 7, 1942 during the height of the catastrophic battle of Stalingrad and three weeks before his 27 birthday.

Data on KIA medical personnel is incomplete, but by example, from September 1, 1939 and the beginning of the war until June 1, 1944, a few days before D-Day and the invasion of Fortress Europe by the Allies, German records stated that 1,777 of the 2,170 active doctors and 20,126 reserve doctors had been killed outright or died of wounds. Those figures indicate exceptional dedication as sell as a high fatality rate reflecting the 'no prisoners taken' policy of both German and Russian forces engaged in a war of mutual annihilation.

Wenn Liebe könnte Wunder tun
Und Tränen Tote wecken,
So würde Dich im Feindesland
Nicht fremde Erde decken.

Den Heldentod fürs
Vaterland starb

Josef Zierl

Sanitäts-Oberfeldwebel
Teilnehmer am Einsatz Oesterreich,
Sudetenland, Tschechei
und des Feldzuges in Frankreich
Inhaber des Kriegsverdienstkreuzes
mit Schwertern
geboren am 18. Januar 1915
gefallen am 7. Dezember 1942
im Osten

R. I. P.

Mein Jesus, Barmherzigkeit!
Süßes Herz Jesu, sei meine Liebe!
Süßes Herz Mariä, sei meine Rettung!
O Herr, gib ihm die ewige Ruhe!
Vater unser. — Ave Maria.

Georg Brand, Buchdruckerei, Regensburg

Graves, Grave Markers and Grave Makers

Practice Grave
A soldier sleeps in his freshly dug foxhole.

Heldentod in Russia
A lone German soldier's grave is marked by his rifle, his steel helmet and a decoration of spruce sprigs.

The Fallen
An airman's grave is marked with flowers and the shattered propeller and engine of his aircraft.

Sniper's work
Several Russian snipers have been credited with kills approaching and passing the 400 mark including Ivan Mikhailovich Sidorenko (500+), Nikolay Yakovlevich Ilyin (494), Ivan Nikolayevich Kulbertinov (489) and Vladimir N. Pchelintsev (456). The most famous Russian sniper was Vasily Zaitsev officially credited with 400 kills, half taken at Stalingrad; his exploits the focus of Soviet propaganda (and later by the modern film, *Enemy at the Gates*). The highest rated woman sniper was a Russian, Lyudmila Pavichencho with 309 confirmed German kills including thirty-six enemy snipers. Though wounded, Pavichencho survived and went on tour in the U.S., Canada and Britain. She was nicknamed "Lady Death."

Specialist (*above left*)

The soldier wears the arm patch identifying him as an Ordnance NCO (*Waffenfeldwebel*). The weapon is a lightened version of the standard Wehrmacht Mauser K98, a bolt-action 5-shot rifle in this case fitted with telescopic sights.

Top German sniper, Mathias Hetzenhauer, was credited with 352 kills while his comrade Sepp Allerberger of the Third Mountain Division was credited with 257 confirmed kills. Both served on the Eastern Front. Various sources mention unnamed German snipers with unconfirmed claims of over 500 personal kills.

However the top Second World War-era sniper was a Finnish soldier Simo Hayha with 542 confirmed kills against Red Army forces during the Russo–Finnish "Winter War" of 1939–1940. The total actually reaches 800 when adding his kills while armed with a machine gun in addition to his sniper rifle, and all "kills" recorded within 100 days of combat. He was eventually shot in the face himself, but survived, recovered and returned post-war to a hunter's life, living until the age of 96 in 2002. As to what he attributed his particular level of skill, Hayha once replied, "Practice."

April 11, 1941—The Balkans (*above right*)

A large rock has become a grave stone bearing the cryptic inscription: "Here lie eight foot soldiers who buried their hopes of holiday on April 11, 1941." On April 6, German forces, aided by their Hungarian allies, invaded the Balkan countries in the process also occupying Yugoslavia that was showing signs of detaching itself from German influence.

Coffin and Honor Guard

Den Heldentod starb im Osten
Leutnant
Heinrich Hauser,
Kompanie-Führer in einem Inf.-Regt.,
Inh. des Eisernen Kreuzes I. u. II. Kl.
und des Infanterie-Sturmabzeichens.
ᛉ 29. 11. 1913 ✠ ᛦ 15. 3. 1942

"A Hero's Death in the East"
An infantry company commander and holder of the Iron Cross 1st and 2nd Class, Lt Heinrich Hauser, 29, died on March 15, 1943 on the Russian front very likely during the German recapturing of Kharkov, the engagement resulting in some 11,500 dead or wounded. At this point in the war the Battle at Stalingrad had ended in disaster for German forces and Rommel was retreating in North Africa. (The symbols relating to Hauser's birth and death dates are pagan Runic, a Nazi preference over religious images, especially for the SS.)

Zur Erinnerung im Gebete an unseren lieben unvergeßlichen zweiten Sohn und Bruder
Obergefreiter
Franz Paul Landinger
Esterlechner-Sohn von Hemhof
Inh. des Infanterie-Sturmabzeichens, der Ost-Medaille u. d. Kriegsverdienstkreuzes m. Schwertern
welcher im Mai 1945 im Lazarett in russischer Gefangenschaft i. Ural i. 34. Lebensj. gestorben ist.
Als junger Bauer kraftvoll kühn u. stark / Gingst Du über den Acker hin — / Ein Sohn des Chiemgau's, den Pflug in der Hand, — / Nicht anders haben wir unseren Franz gekannt. / Jetzt decket russische Erde Dich zu / und Pflug u. Schwert hat beides Ruh'. / Du gabst Dein Leben für Heimat u. Brot / Auf dem Felde der Ehre u. das ist gut. / Oft hast Du den väterlichen Acker bebaut, / Jetzt gehörst Du der Erde, / die Dir so vertraut, / Unvergeßlich Deiner Heimat am Chiemseestrand, / Deinem geliebten Hemhof, Deiner Kampenwand, / Schlaf wohl lieber Franz, auf dem Felde d. Ehr' — / Du tapferer Krieger schlicht u. recht / Dich hat vom Kampfplatz Gott der Herr / Zur Ernte heim, Du treuer Knecht.

Zur Erinnerung im Gebete an meinen innigstgeliebten Gatten, besten Vater, guten Sohn und Bruder
Oberjäger
Karl Landinger
Esterlechner-Sohn von Hemhof
Inh. d. Kriegsverdienstkreuzes m. Schwertern, d. Ostmedaille, d. bronz. Tapferkeitsmedaille u. d. goldenen Verwundetenabzeichens
welcher am 17. Mai 1943 infolge schwerer Verwundung in Serbien im 30. Lebensjahr gestorben ist.
Auf fremder Erde schwer und müd',
Sank hin Dein Haupt zur letzten Ruh',
Für's Vaterland gabst Du Dein Leben,
Schlaf wohl Du tapfrer Krieger Du.
Vergebens ist nun unser Hoffen,
Auf eine frohe Wiederkehr.
Weil Du den Heldentod erlitten
Ist diese Hoffnung nun nicht mehr.
Wie gerne wären wir zusammen,
Doch ach das Schicksal wollt es nicht:
Du schriebst so oft „auf Wiedersehn'",
Doch nimmer soll nun dies' gescheh'n.
Und deckt auch fremde Erde Dich zu
Lieber Gatte, bester Vater, guter Sohn und Bruder Du.
Im Herzen bist Du uns geblieben
Es seh'n sich wieder, die sich lieben!

"Sleep Well Franz … and Karl"—Brothers-in-Arms and Death
A double deathcard memorializes the deaths of two brothers, Franz and Karl Landinger, both corporals in the German Army and from the Bavarian town of Hemhof near the shore of the Chiemsee. Karl, winner of the War Service medal with Swords, the East Medal and the Wound Medal in Gold indicating five or more wounds, died on May 17, 1943 at age 30 while fighting in Serbia. His older brother Franz, 34, holder of the Infantry Assault badge and War Service medal with Swords died at the very end of the war sometime in May, 1945 as a POW in the Russian Urals.

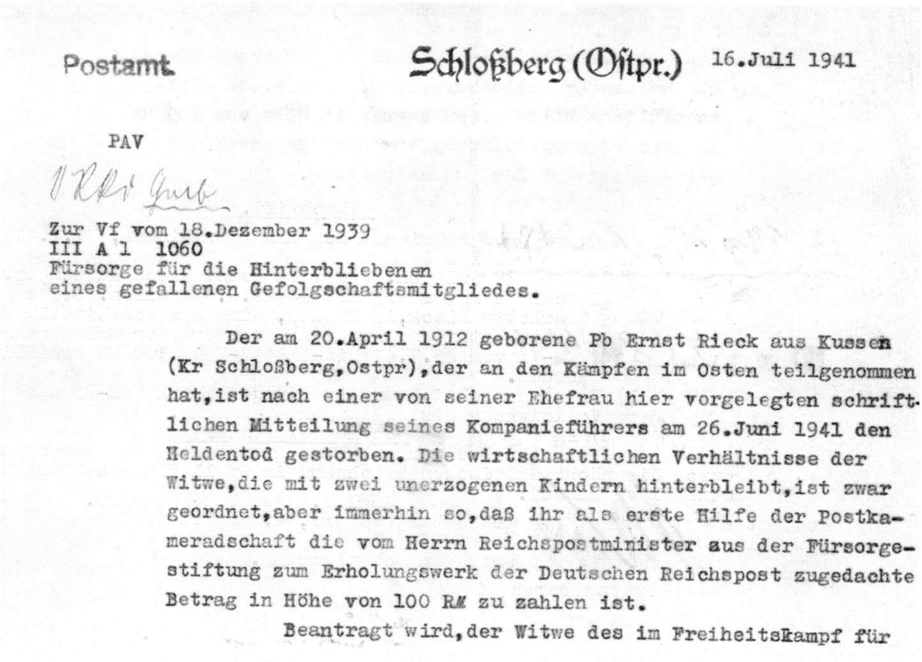

Postamt. Schloßberg (Ostpr.) 16.Juli 1941

PAV

Zur Vf vom 18.Dezember 1939
III A 1 1060
Fürsorge für die Hinterbliebenen
eines gefallenen Gefolgschaftsmitgliedes.

Der am 20.April 1912 geborene Pb Ernst Rieck aus Kussen (Kr Schloßberg,Ostpr),der an den Kämpfen im Osten teilgenommen hat,ist nach einer von seiner Ehefrau hier vorgelegten schriftlichen Mitteilung seines Kompanieführers am 26.Juni 1941 den Heldentod gestorben. Die wirtschaftlichen Verhältnisse der Witwe,die mit zwei unerzogenen Kindern hinterbleibt,ist zwar geordnet,aber immerhin so,daß ihr als erste Hilfe der Postkameradschaft die vom Herrn Reichspostminister aus der Fürsorgestiftung zum Erholungswerk der Deutschen Reichspost zugedachte Betrag in Höhe von 100 RM zu zahlen ist.

Beantragt wird,der Witwe des im Freiheitskampf für

***Heldentod* Recorded—Benefits Paid—KIA 4 Days after Invasion of USSR**

An official form dated July 16, 1941 contains information pertaining to an Ernst Rieck, born April 20, 1912. He served in the East and was killed in action on June 26, 1941, dying a hero's death (*Heldentod*) at age 29. As a former postal employee, his widow was eligible for financial support from the Care for the Survivors of the Fallen (*Gefolgschaftamtigliedes*). He died during the opening days of the invasion of the Soviet Union which began on June 21, the certification of his death supplied by the soldier's commanding officer. The document which continues on the reverse includes a statement by The President of the *Reichspost* Department, "Our former Comrade, Postal Worker Ernst Rieck, was killed in action on June 26th. His widow, Mrs. Charlotte Rieck in Kussen will receive 100 Marks from the Welfare Association of the Deutsche Reichs Post. Mrs. Rieck has two under-age children to support. Her living standard is sound, but nevertheless, first aid in the form of a payment of 100 Marks should be made to Mrs. Rieck. This payment is in line with the recommendation by the Reichs Minister for Postal Matters. The application for help was made by his widow. He died in the fight for freedom of the Greater German Reich and the sum of 100 Marks will paid out of the DRP."

Top of next page:

September 8, 1941—"20 German soldiers killed by terror attack" (*left*)

So states the photo's handwritten notation, referring to the aerial bombing (*Angriff)* as by the "*schweinhunde*." The bodies have been laid out along a river bank, the shadows of their comrades intruding into the photo. Rarely did soldiers take photographs of their comrades killed in battle; even less rarely were they seen by the German public as it was prohibited. At this point German forces had advanced into the Ukraine, about to capture its capital Kiev, thus the bombers inflicting the casualties were no doubt Soviet aircraft.

Feodosiya, Ukraine German Memorial—"Fallen in Battle for Greater Deutschland-132nd Infantry Division" (*right*)

A port and resort city in the Crimea, Feodosiya lies on the shore of the Black Sea. It is believed that here in 1347 the Black Death pandemic entered Europe for the first time via the entrance of Mongol invaders who hurled diseased corpses over the walls of the city during its siege. During the Second World War as German forces advanced into Russia after the June 22, 1941 invasion, the city came under siege again. The 132nd Infantry Division was among the first confronting the Soviet troops defending the city. The 132nd Infantry Division was destroyed later in the war by Soviet forces during fighting in the Kurland Pocket, some of the over 300,000 German and Soviet troops who died there.

After Feodosiya's occupation, and between November 16 and December 15, 1941, *Einsatzgruppe D* shot the Jewish population of 3,248. The memorial to their deaths erected post-war was eventually desecrated six times, including on April 7, 2012, the day of the Jewish Passover.

Pin with logo of the German War Graves Commission.
Founded in 1919 after the First World War, the German based *Volksbund Deutsche Kriegsgräberfürsorge* concerns its international efforts with the preservation of German war graves and also aids in providing information to the next of kin of those KIA. In 1954, the German chancellor Konrad Adenauer of the West German Federal Republic, tasked the Volksbund with the establishment, care and upkeep of German war cemeteries abroad. Its work led to the establishment of some 400 new war cemeteries in Germany and to burial sites in other countries. As of 2018 it was tending to 827 military cemeteries accounting for two million dead German soldiers interred within.

The organization's programs are carried out by some 500 employees and nearly 10,000 volunteers. After the fall of the Iron Curtain and the collapse of the Soviet Union, literally millions of German casualties have come within their province resulting in the building or reconstructing of 190 new First World War and 300 Second World War cemeteries in eastern, central and south-eastern Europe, a reclamation effort still ongoing.The GWGC provides an on-line service to help those searching for individuals via more than four million entries in their data base (www.volksbund.de).

A mission statement reads, "In establishing and maintaining these graves the aim of the *Volksbund* is to keep the memory of the war dead alive. The living are to be reminded of the past when they see these huge cemeteries and confronted with the consequences of war and violence."

Other Internet sites that aid in locating the burial places of German and Austrian soldiers include www.denkmalprojekt.org.

While individual efforts do take place, there is no such concerted effort by any of the affected countries to identify and rebury the estimate 1.5 million Jewish civilians shot to death by German execution squads and their collaborators, the bodies buried in countless graves across Eastern Europe, most still undiscovered.

Microcosms of Mayhem: Deathcards Chronicle the War

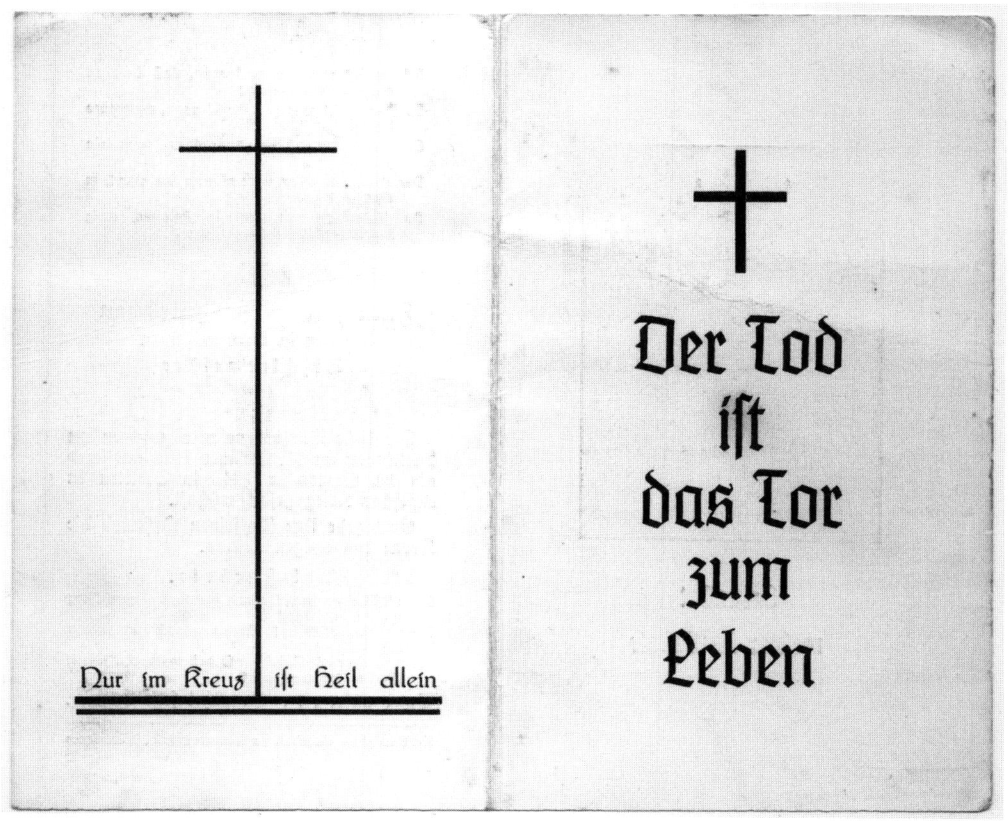

"Death is the Gateway to Life"—Memorial Inscription

Lives in Macrocosm: Deathcards

Between the war years 1939–45, hundreds of thousands of tissue thin rectangular slips of paper were printed, most measuring merely 60 mm × 105 mm (2.36 × 4.13 inches). The tiny missives conveyed the announcement of a death, praise for the deceased and often prayers for the departed spirit. These were the ubiquitous *sterbebild* or so-called deathcards handed out at funerals or sometimes mailed by the deceased's family to relatives and friends in homage to soldiers who had fallen on the field of battle for "Fatherland, Führer and Honor" but also for civilians killed during the conflict. It was a Catholic practice and thus issued principally from families in Austria, Bavaria and the Rhine-Moselle region.

"... Your Will Be Done ..."
One of several optional illustrations in black and white as well as color available from printers for the design of memorial cards.

Gateway to Heldentod

An inscription often found on memorial cards read "*Ich starb fur Dich, bête Du fur mich!*" translating "I died for you, remember me!

Death under the Nazi administration became not a gateway to spiritual rebirth but a mandate for the all-sacrificing warrior hero to be unflinching in his resolve, no greater glory than to die for the Fatherland. In the early war years, the memorial cards often bore the words "died for Volk, Fatherland and Führer." Later cards bore only references to dying for the Homeland.

A variety of stock prayers and invocations could be selected for inclusion on a memorial card. One such translated:

Plant a cross over me—that was my faith.
Lay a sword there, too; I always carried it with honor.
Then let me hear victory songs in sleep.
And grass should grow over my dust.
I had nothing than just my life
For the Fatherland I have given it to God.

Each of the memorial announcements usually carried a photograph of the deceased and a few words describing dates of birth and death and the location where he died. Often there was a list of his medals and awards and occasionally the manner in which he succumbed, for example a head wound or from "bandit" attack (a euphemism for partisan) or from *Terrorangriffs* (terror attacks) meaning death as the result of Allied bombings. Some deathcards took the form of small pamphlets that contained longer descriptions of service and accomplishments while the reverse surfaces carried religious imagery and prayers. Soldiers who were members of the SS or SA carried no such iconography.

A large percentage of the notations as to location of death listed the *Ost*, the East, referring to the Russian front. Sometimes a specific city or town was named, for example major battles at Leningrad and Stalingrad or foreign territories such as France, Italy, Croatia, Latvia or even areas like the Polar Seas.

While the war in Europe ended with the Third Reich's destruction and surrender in May of 1945, war-related deathcards occasionally appear for the year 1946 and beyond, sometimes the result of lingering wounds but most often attributed to Prisoner of War camp confinement, particularly in the Soviet Union.

The following memorial cards are for the most part listed in chronological order as the war ground on and casualties mounted, beginning with the invasion of Poland on September 1, 1939, of France on May 10, 1940, the Soviet Union on June 22, 1941 and continuing into the months following the war's end in May 1945 as deaths continued to be reported.

Family Album Entries
Two images of Corporal Walter Thiemann, his memorial card and the original photo, kept his memory alive. The inscription translates:

> Into the heavy mud of the Russian soil, sank your head at last to rest, sleep well! You brave fighter. You do not return to your loved ones, you stayed on the field of honor, rest gently in peace! Your loved ones weep.

The front of the *sterbebild* also contained the words:

> In all his letters he spoke of deep longing and care for his family. He was our joy and our hope. Our consolation is the reunion in the Beyond.

Previously awarded the Combat Assault medal and Wound Badge, he died on February 7, 1944 a month before his 25th birthday during heavy fighting in northwestern Welikiye Luki, a strategic rail point. He may have been a casualty of a major battle that raged in the Korsun-Cherkassy Pocket near the Dneiper River during January 24 through February 16 that resulted in some 55,000 Germans killed or wounded.

Condolences en Masse—Official State Printed Guidelines for the Bereaved

> A Word to the Grieving
>
> Many fathers, mothers and wives sacrifice their sons and husbands in this time of war. It would be unnatural if their hearts were not full of grief, for it is blood of their blood that has flowed. Who would not understand those who grieve. No one is so heartless that he does not feel with them and, if he could, would gladly help. But we are so powerless in this area. How do a few words of comfort help? Ultimately only one can help, the one who proclaimed to us the eternal truth for all time: I live and you shall live! They died, but see, they live!
>
> Certainly, it is not easy to understand these words, especially when the wound to the heart is still fresh. This realization must be won in difficult struggle with oneself. This is where our sympathy comes in. You mourners, once you get some rest, when you have a quiet hour, then read the contents of this book. Do not read it in one sitting! Reach for it again and again. Read the letters and the last words of the fallen! Your loved one could have written them as well.
>
> Then let God's words speak to you. They have been selected for you and they have shown who knows how many the right path. Try it and you will feel how an invigorating strength begins to flow through your heart—a strength not from men, rather from God. It demands nothing from you without immediately also giving to you. Surely, this certainly does not leap at us. We must want it. All mighty God helps you to want it.

Early Casualty—September 13, 1939—Poland (*above left*)
The comrades of Lt Haase, one of the first German casualties of the war, have fashioned an impromptu memorial propped against a truck that notes the death of their troop leader who "fell to a burst of Polish machine gun fire."

The German invasion of Poland had been launched twelve days previously and fighting was still intense. Overrun by the coordinated mechanized and airborne assault, the Polish government was forced to surrender in six weeks, the country then initially divided between Nazi Germany and Stalin's Soviet Union, the two dictators allied via their Non-Aggression Pact in order to occupy Poland, a temporary hold on their own cataclysmic clash to come some two years later.

"The First Three Fatalities in Miriampol"—Poland—September 17, 1939 (*above right*)
Neat handwriting on the back of the photo found in a soldier's album records the first KIA among his infantry company and lists their names … Albrecht, Gubitz and Tauber.

September 15, 1939—Letter of Condolence—To Wife of an Officer Killed During Polish Invasion

> On the morning after the forest battle where your husband fell, I went out to recover our dead. I was the first and only one to see him lying where he had fallen, surrounded by his company troop leader, his orderly and his messengers. He lay directly in front of the enemy nest that was to be assaulted. Based on the situation he certainly took with him the conviction that victory could be seized at that moment. His wound was such that, by human reckoning, he was killed instantly and could not have suffered any pain. He lay very quietly and peacefully in the forest in a clearing among birch trees. As expressed in his position, the bullet must have hit him at the moment of a brave charge.
>
> We gathered him and the men of his company and buried them somewhat to the rear. Each has his own grave, you husband on the right flank. The grave-site lies in the middle of a forest under pine trees and birch trees. We have placed a birch cross over each grave. When we recovered him, we officers buried him ourselves. First Lieutenant J. and I placed him into the grave. All of us together took leave from him and covered him with earth. Later the battalion assembled in an open square formation and the commander took leave, brief and serious, from the comrades we had to leave behind.
>
> I know that I cannot give much comfort. May it bring you some calm to know that your husband, whom we all valued so, fell in the most beautiful moment of struggle as an officer and leader, and that his burial could not have proceeded more honorably and soldierly. Be convinced that all of us, the whole regiment and especially the 2nd battalion and I personally, feel with you, wish to press your hand and tell you what a good comrade we have lost.

(Contained in the original Third Reich book "Fallen for the Fatherland" printed for family and friends of soldiers who had fallen in battle. The book contains poetry, letters from soldiers and their comrades and from their family members as well as religious quotes often Christian in origin and nature, much of the content taken from First World War sources. There is no mention of the Nazi Party in any way or any political comment.)

Some 6,000–10,000 German soldiers died in the invasion of Poland while Polish KIA exceeded 60,000.

Zur frommen Erinnerung im Gebete an

Josef Gebast

von Weinting bei Nittenau
Soldat bei einem Panzer-Reg.

geboren am 25. August 1904,
gefallen und begraben in Compie
am 15. Juni 1940.

Nun lieber Sohn, Du tapf'rer Soldat
Geh' heim in's himmlische Licht;
Deine Mutter, Deine Geschwister,
Führer u. Volk vergessen Dich nicht!

Karl Rieder, Nittenau

June 15, 1940—Death in France—and a Return to Compiègne

Josef Gebast, from the village of Weinting in Bavaria located on the Regen River, was a soldier in a Panzer Regiment when KIA at age 36 on June 15, 1940, the day after German forces entered Paris and six days before the French capitulation and armistice of June 21. He was buried in the town of Compiègne in northern France, the forest nearby noted for the signing in 1918 of the First World War armistice after the defeat of Germany and then again in 1940 the location for the signing of the new armistice after the German victory over France. Hitler required the French to sign the documents in the same railway train car in which the Germans had signed the surrender papers at the end of the preceding war.

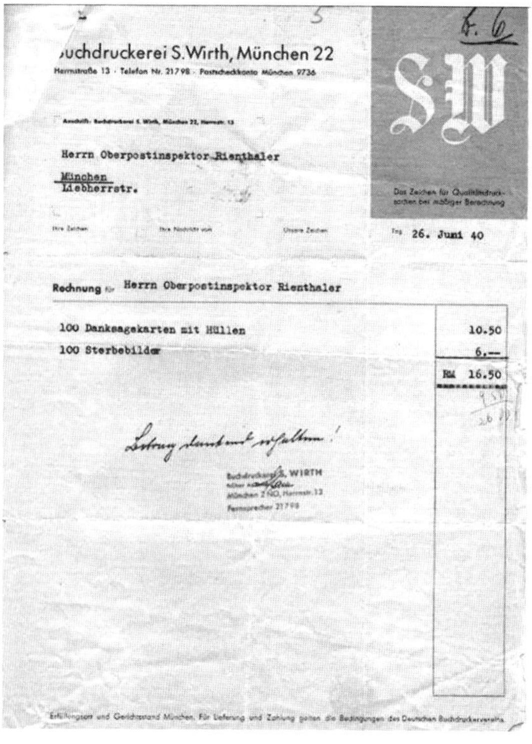

Buchdruckerei S.Wirth, München 22
Hermstraße 13 · Telefon Nr. 21798 · Postscheckkonto München 9736

Das Zeichen für Qualitätsdrucksachen bei mäßiger Berechnung

Herrn Oberpostinspektor Rienthaler
München
Liebherrstr.

26. Juni 40

Rechnung für Herrn Oberpostinspektor Rienthaler

100 Danksagekarten mit Hüllen	10.50
100 Sterbebilder	6.—
	RM 16.50

Buchdruckerei S. WIRTH
München 2 NO, Hermstr. 13
Fernsprecher 21798

Erfüllungsort und Gerichtsstand München. Für Lieferung und Zahlung gelten die Bedingungen des Deutschen Buchdruckervereins.

Order for 100 Deathcards—June 26, 1940

During the summer war against France, an order has been placed with a printer in Munich for memorial cards and a like number of thank you cards, with envelopes, the order placed by Chief Postal Inspector Rienthaler.

Das Liebste hat uns der Tod entrafft
Herr gib es zu trag uns Mut und Kraft.

**Zur frommen Erinnerung
im Gebete**
an unsern lieben unvergeßlichen
Gatten und Vater,
Sohn und Bruder

Max Heimhilger

**Friseur in Unterhaching
Obergefr. in einem Gebirgsjäger-Regt.**
Kriegsteilnehmer aller Feldzüge
welcher am 21. Mai 1941 auf Kreta
im Alter von 26 Jahren den Helden-
tod fürs Vaterland starb.

Er sinkt auf hoher See, es krampft sich die Hand
Es fordert sein Leben das Vaterland.
Dein Wille geschehe, ich bin bereit,
Mein Heiland, mein Jesus Barmherzigkeit.

Vater unser. Ave Maria.

Druck: A. Erdl, Trostberg

May 21, 1941—Death From Above—Crete—"Operation Undertaking Mercury"
A father, son, brother and uncle, Max Heimhilger, a *Gebirgsjäger* (mountain trooper) and veteran of many campaigns, was killed at age 26 during the second day of the nearly abortive assault on the British held island of Crete as German paratrooper forces fell into the defensive fire unleashed by an underestimated number of Allied troops.

Paratroopers Take Anti-Aircraft Defense Position
Using a comrade to support his light machine gun, a member of the *Fallschirmjäger* (elite airborne troops) fends off enemy aircraft in this training photo. While the Russians were the first to develop parachute units, the Germans enlarged on the strategy in the process creating perhaps its best fighting force.

Oberleutnant Götte—Fallschirmjäger-Strosstruppführer
Shown with the MP40 machinepistol, Shock Troop Squad Leader Götte has been rendered as a commercial German postcard adding to the luster of German wartime military personnel. The paratroopers had gained fame after their audacious and successful assault and capture of the purportedly invulnerable Belgian fortress of Eben-Emael on May 10, 1940.

Island Repose—Crete May 1941
A German graveyard on the island of Crete overlooks the island's walled citadel in the background. Crete, a British stronghold with airfields within striking distance of the strategic Romanian oil fields, was attacked on May 20, 1941 by the *Fallschirmjäger*. It subsequently has been called the graveyard of the German paratroopers as nearly 7,000 of the 17,500 taking part in the assault were killed although they eventually gained control of their target. As a result Hitler ordered the paratroopers to cease airborne actions and to function as ground troops. Later the elite soldiers were a major factor in the determined German resistance in Italy after the Allied landings of Operation Husky launched on July 13, 1943.

During the German occupation, the people of Crete mounted significant resistance and as a result suffered thousands of civilian executions. German forces also rounded up the island's total population of 206 Jews who were then sent to Auschwitz for extermination.

Into the Maelstrom—
Nazi Germany Invades Soviet Russia

The Germans named the invasion of the Soviet Union "Operation Barbarossa" after Emperor Frederick Barbarossa of the Holy Roman Empire, a leader of the 12th Century Third Crusade as the Nazi mindset saw it as a "holy war" against Bolshevism, the ultimate clash of Western culture, epitomized by the bulwark of Germany confronting the threat of the Eastern hordes as led by the Soviet Communists. On June 22, 1941 the attacking force numbered three million soldiers including Hungarian and Romanian allies, 3,580 tanks, 7,184 artillery guns, 1,830 planes and 750,000 horses.

Hitler had predicted the USSR would "fall like a house of cards" within a few months. So assured were the German generals that they failed to equip their troops with adequate clothing and equipment and tens of thousands, dressed in thin summer uniforms, would pay the price exacted by Russia's perennial ally "General Winter" that had historically conquered all invaders.

Fatal Mistake Fatally Induced?

Much discussion has focused around Hitler's pivotal decision to back off from invading Great Britain and instead invade the Soviet Union, its vast area, climate and the resolve of the Russian people as well as Hitler's irrational "not one step back" dictum eventually sealing the doom of the Thousand Year Reich and bringing death to millions of both Germans and Russians.

The destruction of Bolshevism/Jewry equated as one and the same in Nazi ideology and always Hitler's avowed primal and primary goal. But rather than wait to better prepare for the onslaught, it has been posited that he initiated the date of the attack when prompted by astrological signs. In addition the delay from a planned spring offensive and thus avoiding the Russian winter has been attributed to the time-consuming "bailing out" of Axis ally Mussolini when he became embroiled in military blunders while attacking Greece. However evidence mounts that the Nazi leader feared time was running out for him personally because of the rapid physical and mental deterioration caused by advanced Parkinson's disease, exacerbated by a host of drugs administered by his "quack" physician, which prompted him to advance his time schedule for world domination, a decision that proved fatal on all levels.

French Postcard

Three Army privates wearing their overseas caps, Fritz Senning, Heinrich Gergending and Walter Acus, while posted to France, have visited a photographer's studio for the purpose of producing souvenir postcards for friends and family. The card is dated April 1941. During this month German forces invade and occupy Yugoslavia and Greece while Rommel's Afrika Korps advances in North Africa. The lack of ribbons, medals or badges indicate these three young soldiers have not yet seen combat.

"Former Russian Border"

A cavalry trooper poses by a sign announcing the line separating Germany from Russia, the location somewhere on the Polish border. Behind him a long line of his comrades prepare for entry into the Soviet Union, the invasion having begun on June 21, 1942.

In the following mid-July, Hitler took up command at his Vinnitsa,Ukrainian headquarters known as "Werewolf" in order to direct the Sixth's Army's summer offensive targeting Stalingrad and the Caucasus oil fields.

Swallowed by Swamps

Two soldiers stand at the edge of a vast swamp, one of many such quagmires encountered by German forces as they penetrated the Soviet Union's vast landscape. In addition to the damage done to the machines of war, the swamps also served as refuge for fleeing Jews and for partisans, referred to by the Nazis as "bandits.' Notations on the reverse of the small contact print photo identifies the two men as NCO Lieber and Corporal Golbs sometime during the second summer of the invasion. The logs seen at their feet may be in the process of being used to construct the so-called "courdoroy" roadways in an effort to carry vehicles over the muddy terrain.

Frozen by Ice—First Winter in Russia

Notations on the back of the photo indicate it was taken on December 16, 1941, as a convoy of trucks winds its way through the Russian vastness apparently led by bicycle mounted troops. An MP40 machine-pistol hangs from the bicycle in the foreground. The soldiers have only their long summer coats for protection against the temperatures falling to -30 degree Fahrenheit. Lubricants froze in trucks and gun barrels were left unable to function while the German troops fell victim to frostbite and illness by the tens of thousands.

Whiteout—January 22, 1943 (*above left*)
A German soldier stands guard deep in Russia as documented by this official press photo taken by war correspondent Koltzenburg. The soldier wears the sheepskin winter coats made available during the second winter offensive. Nine days after the photo was dated, the 93,000 survivors of the German 6th Army at Stalingrad surrendered to Russian forces, a death knell that reverberated across the Third Reich.

"Are You Not the Standard—Especially at the Front!" (*above right*)
Postcard printed in Cracow (Krakau) on the occasion of the Day of the NSDAP (Nazi Party) as celebrated in the General Government (occupied Poland)—August 13–15, 1943.

The artwork titled "*Kameraden*" was created by approved Third Reich artist Wilhelm Tesch who painted the original in 1940 based on the fighting on the French coast when thousands of Allied British and French forces were pushed into the sea at Dunkirk, though most were rescued by the famous armada of large and small British naval and civilian vessels valiantly rallied across the English Channel to their rescue.

The soldier depicted in this particular artwork, though wounded himself, carries a more seriously injured comrade, but also retains his rifle indicating his fighting spirit is still intact. How much such imagery affected the millions who continued fighting when all was lost is a matter of debate.

War art was a major feature of the *Haus der Deutschen Kunst* (House of German Art) when the museum and galleries were opened in Munich on July 18, 1937. As an official showcase for "correct" Aryan art, the martial spirit portrayed in the imagery displayed was meant to encourage the readiness to fight and die for the Fatherland, emphasizing that sacrifice of the individual was valued as the highest virtue.

Most of the museum's artwork focused on fruits of glorious victory and very little on the pain and misery, thus leading people away from the reality of war into an emotionally charged dream world, moreover to create a communal experience that shared the same focal point, victory or glorious death. While the social engineers of National Socialism relied on the power of art to promote their ideology, they also required that it be kept under restraint that included a polished "photographic" style.

Third Reich artists were encouraged to create engaging representations of the archetypal Nazi soldier throughout the war. Tesch's "Kameraden" seeks to express and promote the warrior ideal as the Nazi mindset perceived it with the emphasis on self-sacrifice for the benefit of the German *Volk*.

Survivor?
A solid metal horseshoe-shaped frame bears an inscription commemorating Corporal Willi Watz as a veteran of service on the Russian front in 1941, the year of the German invasion of the Soviet Union.

Non-Mechanized Blitzkrieg
While the image of the German war machine focuses on the modern warfare of tanks and aircraft, much of it relied on horsepower with hooves. Of the 2,700,000 horses and mules utilized by the Wehrmacht, an estimated 750,000 died during the war from wounds, disease or starvation. Polish and French losses are unknown, while several million Russian animals are estimated to have perished.

Stalin Watches a Wedding Documentation
Stalin's paranoia knew no bounds and nearly resulted in the loss of the entire country when Germany first attacked. Prior to the invasion in 1941, and during spring 1937 to autumn 1938, Stalin decimated his own Red Army command structure. He ordered the execution of three of the five Russian marshals of the Army, all eleven deputy commissars of defense, all the commanders of the military districts, the heads of the Navy and Air Force, 13 out of 15 Army commanders, the head of the country's military academy as well as 80 percent of the Far Eastern forces. The success of the German invasion was almost guaranteed.

In Memory
Inscribed on the reverse: "For a long and good memory to dear Aunt Varja and to dear brothers Yurik and Borik from the sister Galochka."

But the Russian people rallied, spurred on by both their national spirit and the draconian methods initiated by Stalin and his secret police. As the war dragged on, the country coalesced, millions of soldiers gathering from all across the vast stretches of the USSR, dozens of diverse nationalities and ethnic groups rallying to the defense of the Motherland.

Over 800,000 women wore the uniform of the Red Army with 200,000 receiving commendations while serving as pilots, tank crew, medics, snipers and partisans.

Many such photos were carried to war by Russian fathers. *(above left)*

"June, 1941"—Liberator and Liberated *(above right)*
The date is handwritten on the reverse of the photo of a German NCO who has donned the traditional headdress of a Ukrainian girl who beams at the camera. Snapped just days into the invasion of Stalin's Russia, many like her saw the Germans as liberators from the terrors of the NKVD secret police and a means by which the Ukraine would regain its national identity and sovereignty … wishful thinking that would soon be buried in the mass graves created by the Nazi anti-Slavic policies geared toward annihilation rather than liberation.

***22 Juni 1941*—Death on the First Day of Operation Barbarossa** (*above left*)

The image of Paul Fuchsreiter has been cut from another photo and pasted on to his deathcard. He was killed on the very first day of the invasion of the Soviet Union … June 22, 1941 and therefore one of the earliest casualties of the conflict between the two monolithic dictatorships that would lead to millions of deaths on both sides.

June 22, 1941—A Second Death on the First Day—Brest-Litovsk (*above right*)

Infantryman Corporal Felix Daller, age 25, also fell on the first day of invasion of the USSR. The site of his death in battle with Red Army troops is noted as taking place in the city of Brest-Litovsk.

Previously, on September 22, 1939, both German and Soviet troops paraded together through Brest-Litovsk in mutual celebration of their successful joint invasion of Poland, the city having been transferred from Polish authority to Soviet control and assimilated into the Belarus region of western Russia. The German panzer General Heinz Guderian stood with Soviet Colonel Semyon Krivoshein as they reviewed their troops demonstrating the alliance of the two countries as a result of the Molotov–Ribbentrop Non-Aggression Pact.

General Konstanty Pilsowski, the commander of the Polish forces who defended Brest against the Germans, was arrested by the Soviet secret police and later executed in the Katyn massacre along with more than 20,000 other Polish military officers and members of the intelligentsia.

History's short-term memory, facilitated by Soviet efforts to fog over their perfidious treachery, often fails to recall that Nazi Germany and Stalinist Russia teamed up to destroy Poland. Members of the German Gestapo and the Soviet NKVD had convened four conferences in order to plan their joint subjugation of the Polish people. That partnership would end violently on June 22, 1941 when German forces swept into the Soviet Union, Brest-Litvosk falling back under the shadow of the Third Reich. An initial killing spree in June resulted in the murder of 5,000 Jews, and by the end of July 62,000 had been shot to death. Then in November 1941, the Germans established a Jewish ghetto in Brest-Litovsk as part of their more systematic approach to the Final Solution.

Gedenket im Gebete

an Jüngling

Vinzenz Schuster

Zeilersohn von Zeil

Obergefreiter in einem Inf.-Regiment

welcher am 22. Juni 1941 im 29. Lebensjahre bei Sokal in Rußland den Heldentod fürs Vaterland erlitten hat.

Die Pflicht rief mich zum Krieg hinaus,
Mit Gott ging ich vom Elternhaus,
Ich dachte euer fort und fort,
Wenn ich auch weilt am fremden Ort,
Und freute mich auf's Wiederseh'n.
O weinet nicht, ihr Teuren,
Mein junges Leben ist vollbracht.
Ich hab den Tod gefunden
In heißer, blutiger Schlacht.
Ich habe auch empfangen
Den größten Siegeslohn,
Der dem sterbenden Krieger ist verheißen,
Es ist die Himmelskron.
O tröstet euch, liebe Eltern und Brüder
Im fernen Heimattal [und Schwestern
Wir treffen uns ja wieder
Im schönen Himmelssaal.
Und klingt im Heimatskirchlein
Für mich der Glocken Trauerton,
So blickt mein Heldenauge
Auf euch hinab vom Himmelsthron.

Buchdruckerei Norbert Präbst, Dorfen

Im Kampf um die Verteidigung unseres Vaterlandes
haben ... den

am 1. ... odubje

am ... iza,

Gefreiter Kurt Sonnack
Zeche Robert Müser
am 2. 8. 1941 im Gefecht bei Swrdlikowo (Ukraine)

A Third Death—KIA Sokal—*den Heldentod*—June 22, 1941 (*above*)
Infantry Corporal Dinzenz Schuster died at age 29 in combat near the town of Sokal in the Ukraine on the first day of the invasion.

August 8, 1941—Homemade Deathcard (*left*)
The family of Kurt Sonnack has fashioned their own homemade memorial card from a larger obituary notice, perhaps clipped from a section of a newspaper. The Corporal's photograph eclipses the names of other local men who perished on the Russian Front. The young blue-eyed soldier who smiles for the camera in his new uniform died in the Ukraine, a few weeks after the June 22 invasion of the Soviet Union.

†

Zum frommen Gedenken im Gebete
an unseren
lieben Sohn und Bruder

Bankbeamter

Hermann Schäfer

Schütze in einem Inf.-Regt.

geboren am 3. April 1921 in Augsburg
gefallen am 19. Februar 1942 im Osten
bei Fetischteckewo (Orel)

Du hast ihn uns geliehen, o Herr, und er war unser Glück; du hast ihn wieder zurückgefordert und wir geben ihn dir ohne Murren, aber das Herz voll Wehmut.

St. Hieronymus

February 19, 1942—Orel, Russia

Infantry private Hermann Schäfer, age 20, a resident of Augsburg, died during the fighting around Orel, the city located some 220 miles south-west of Moscow. German occupation lasted from October 3, 1941 until August 5, 1943 at which point the end of the nearby battle of Kursk enabled its Soviet liberation.

Augsburg, a city in southwest Bavaria, is the second oldest city in Germany. During the Third Reich it was home to several sub-camps of Dachau from which slave labor was supplied to local industry. It was from the local Augsburg airfield that in 1941 Deputy Führer Rudolf Hess took off for his abortive flight to Scotland. Heavily bomb-damaged, it was occupied by U.S. Army forces in the last stages of the war.

Hart und unfaßbar ist für die Eltern diese Tatsache und eine Wunde hat ihr Herz zerrissen, die nicht mehr heilen wird. Aber gleichwie am Ostertag der Herr zu den beiden Jüngern sich gesellte und ihnen von seiner Auferstehung erzählte und sie aufrichtete mit den Worten: Mußte nicht Christus dies alles leiden, und so in seine Herrlichkeit eingehen? so möchte heute in dieser schweren Stunde auch Euch der Herr aufrichten und trösten mit seiner hl. Gegenwart und mit der Versicherung! Euer Josef ist nicht tot, er lebt und ist Euch nur vorausgegangen in ein besseres Jenseits, daß er nicht mehr vertauschen möchte mit dieser Welt. Auch er müßte dies alles leiden für Euch und für unser Volk, auf daß er so in seine Herrlichkeit eingehen konnte. Der Auferstehungsglaube kann und muß auch Eure wunden Seelen heilen und in ihm findet ihr den stärksten Halt, wenn auch die Finsternis des Lebens heute uns verzagt und mutlos machen möchte.

Wie jedem unserer lieben Gef. Helden versprechen wir auch ihm unser treues Gedenken und Gebet unsere Dankbarkeit übers Grab hinaus.

Die Pflicht rief ihn zum Krieg hinaus
Mit Gott ging er vom Vaterhaus
Und dachte Euer fort und fort.
Wenn er auch weilt an fremden Ort,
Er freute sich aufs Wiedersehn,
Wenn Krieg und Sturm zu Ende gehn.
Doch anders hats der Herr gewollt,
Und hat von hier ihn abgeholt.
Nun ruht in fremder Erd er aus,
Und ist in Gottes Vaterhaus. Amen.

Worte bei den Trauergottesdiensten
für den am 1. 2. 1942 im Osten
gef. Gefr.

Josef Geiger
von Rappendorf,
gespr. am 19. 4 1942 von H. H.
Pfarrer Schmid, Arnbruck.

Druck V. Oerler, Kötzting

KIA April 19, 1942—Complete Memorial Sermon Included

An especially detailed funeral notice chronicles the short life of Josef Geiger.

The translation of the invocation spoken by officiating Pastor H. H. Schmid of Arnbruck during the Christian Mourning Assembly held in his memory reads as follows:

It was the first day of Easter. With their hearts deeply saddened, two apostles left the city of Jerusalem and talked about the bitter suffering and death of their beloved master along the way. They mourned righteously and honestly, and they were especially tortured by the thought that not even the dead body of their lord was present anymore, as two pious women had come to inform them of the emptiness of his grave. This is the kind of mourning that permeates this hour today. An unfathomable pain and sincere suffering have visited the hearts of the Geiger family of Rappendorf; they've had to sacrifice their beloved son, Josef, out there on the Eastern front and now cannot even visit his grave. This young, blossoming life of the 21-year-old private in an infantry regiment, Josef Geiger of Rappendorf, has succumbed to a cruel death, and our parish once again mourns the loss of a good, hopeful young man and truly shares the agonizing pain of his inconsolable parents and siblings.

Born in the same year, on July 28, 1920, as his comrade Franz Gröller of Sinndorf, he, too, followed the call of his Fatherland on the same day, December 3, 1940, and joined the military. Soon thereafter, his probation period started with the short yet difficult campaign into the Balkans during the spring of last year. After being so fortunate and surviving it, an even more difficult task was awaiting him.

Already on the first day of the invasion into Russia, he faced the most unfathomable exertions and sacrifices, which we were to follow with bated breath. He saw battle in the southern part of the Crimean peninsula, a very embattled area still to this day. More than half a year he survived those hellish battles and was very hopeful of being relieved soon. But then, in the middle of March, the terrible news reached his worried parents and siblings that on February 1 a shell splinter had hit him and shattered his chest, injuring him fatally. His comrade, who had been at his side since the beginning of the campaign, described in words that trembled with pain the death of his friend:

"Some sad news I have to tell you, which you'll already have heard. By the time I returned from the military hospital, Josef had fallen, my only and best friend. He fell on February 1, when our house was directly hit; many were injured, but Josef had to die, with a shell splinter in his heart. He was just reading your letter, but wasn't able to finish it, unfortunately. Throughout Russia we had been together, even during our most difficult hours, and always managed to survive, but now our Lord has torn us apart. He is buried in Kojosan, just before the Strait of Kerch."

Difficult and unfathomable is this fact for many parents, and an injury has torn their hearts which will never heal. But just as the Lord joined the apostles that Easter Day and told them of his resurrection and encouraged them with these words: Did not Jesus have to suffer all this and thus enter into his splendor? Likewise may our Lord encourage you in this difficult hour and console you with His holy presence and His assurance! Your Josef is not dead, he lives and has only preceded you into a better beyond, which he does not want to exchange for this world. He, too, had to suffer for you and for our people so that he might enter into his splendor. This belief in resurrection can and must heal your grieving souls as well, and within him you will find the strongest support, even as the darkness of life discourages us today and wants to render us disheartened.

As we promise each of our dear departed heroes, so we promise him our faithful memory and prayer, our gratitude beyond the grave.

Duty called him into war
With God he left his father's house
And thought of you relentlessly
Even while he was far away
He anticipated seeing you again
When the war and storm would finally die
But the Lord had different plans
And has called him to His side
Now he's resting in foreign soil
And lives in God our father's house. Amen.

Flameweapon Forward!
The "War Stories for German Youth" booklet's cover focuses on a two-man flamethrower team as they target a French house. The larger units required three men, two to hold and direct the tube (up to 180 feet long) and a third to operate the tank's controls. The flamethrower system consisted of a mixture of pressurized nitrogen gas and Flammol contained in portable cylinders. Ignited by a magnesium triggering device, the weapon spewed a liquid flame that could easily gain entry into bunkers through their gun slits and incinerate the inhabitants. Soldiers equipped with the much-hated device bore a double indemnity as easily identifiable targets for snipers and subject to possible summary execution if captured.

Ach es ist ja kaum zu fassen,
daß Du nie mehr kehrst zurück,
So jung mußt Du dein Leben lassen,
vorbei ist unser aller Glück,
Ein jeder der Dich hat gekannt
und auch Dein gutes Herz,
Der drückt uns nur stumm die Hand
in diesem tiefen Schmerz.
Wenn Liebe könnten Wunder tun
und Tränen Tote wecken,
So würde Dich gewiß nicht dort
die fremde Erde decken.

Groß ist das Opfer das Du von uns gefordert,
O, Herr, Dein Wille geschehe.

Zum frommen Gedenken!

Hart und schwer traf uns die tieftraurige Nachricht, daß mein geliebter Sohn, unser lieber Bruder, Neffe und Vetter

Obergefr. Josef Neurohr

Flammenwerfer in einem Gren. Reg.

Inh. des Inf. Sturmabz. in Silber u. der Ostmedaille,

sein junges Leben am 5. Okt. 1943 in treuer Pflichterfüllung bei den schweren Kämpfen im Osten im Alter von nahezu 23 Jahren dahingegeben hat.

Wir bitten um ein inniges Gedenken im Gebete.

In tiefer Trauer:

Mutter, Geschwister und alle Anverwandten.

Schiffweiler, den 3. November 1943.

Ablaßgebete.

„Mein Jesus Barmherzigkeit"
„Heiligstes Herz Jesu ich vertraue auf Dich"
„Süßes Herz Maria sei meine Rettung"

Druck von M. Schnur, Schiffweiler

Flammenwerfer Fatality—October 5, 1942 (*above*)

Corporal Josef Neurohr carried the dreaded flamethrower in a grenadier regiment and so became a primary target. He was killed during "heavy fighting in the East" shortly before reaching his 23rd birthday. His memorial card notes that he was awarded the Infantry Assault badge in Silver, indicating close combat, as well as the East Medal. The funeral was held in the soldier's hometown of Schiffweiler, in the Saarland region of southwestern Germany on November 3, 1943.

"The Last Hand Grenade"—Commercial German postcard

An image drawn from the German First World War experience was incorporated into the Nazi propaganda machine as it sought to glorify the heroic stance of soldiers who fought to the last bullet, never giving ground, following Hitler's dictum.

Continued on next page

The original drawing was credited to Professor Elk Eber, a fanatical Nazi Party proponent and leading Third Reich approved artist, his work often appearing in the press, at exhibitions and reproduced on commercial postcards. His favorite subjects were depictions of soldiers and SA Men often in fierce profiles and brandishing their weapons. Elk died in August 1941 at the age of 48 while Germany's victory seemed certain. One of his colleagues contributing to his obituary, wrote, "*The Last Hand Grenade* was one of the most remarkable pictures in the Great German Art Exhibition, because it expressed the attitude of the Party and the whole Folk … Professor Elk Eber had basically only one theme: the soldierly, heroic masculinity of our time."

Gedenket im Gebete
an
Michael Wölfl
Landwirtssohn von Wies
Obergefr. in einem Geb.-Jäg.-Reg.
Teilnehmer am Feldzug in Polen u. Frankreich
Inhaber des Verwundeten-Abzeichens
gefallen am 29. August 1942 an der Leningraderfront durch Granatsplitter im 27. Lebensjahre.

Ich weiß, Ihr werdet bitter weinen,
Daß ich so ferne sank ins Grab:
Wo mir die stillen Sterne scheinen,
In meine dunkle Gruft hinab,
Doch einmal kommt der Tod zu allen,
Und bricht der Liebe zartes Band,
Wo wär ich herrlicher gefallen,
Als kämpfend treu für Gott u. Vaterland.

Barmherziger Jesus, gib ihm die ewige Ruhe! (7 Jahre Ablaß.)

Druck von Norbert Präbst, Dorfen

Grenade Splinter at the Russian Front—August 29, 1942 (*above*)
A corporal of the elite mountain troops (*Gebirgsjäger*), Michael Wölfl, a farmer's son, died at the end of August at Leningrad as the result of a "grenade splinter". The 29-year old veteran of the Polish and French invasions had also previously been wounded. Leningrad would survive a 900-day siege that by bombing or starvation brought death to over a million otf the city's civilians.

Stamp of Approval (*right*)
A Greater Reich issued postage features the image of a mountain trooper (*Gebirgsjäger*), his uniform showing a silver wound badge.

Directions to Disaster
A Luftwaffe flak corporal stands beside an optimistic road sign. German *panzers* would grind within 18 km of Moscow, but no further as Russian resistance stiffened. The road back in retreat to Berlin for him and his comrades would end in the destruction of the city and the Third Reich.

Top of next page:

Stalingrad Death Count Mounts—December 6, 1942 (*left*)
The deathcard tersely states that Michael Mühlbauer, a 36-year old Grenadier died on December 6, 1943 in "a battle in the East," most likely at Stalingrad where German forces had been encircled by Soviet forces since November 19. The inscription above his photograph reads: "Whoever falls bravely for his country builds himself an eternal monument," a quote by Karl Theodor Körner, a popular German writer of patriotic battle songs who himself died in battle in 1813 at age 21.

The ensuing disaster of Stalingrad convinced generals in the Wehrmacht leadership that the war was lost and that Hitler and his Nazi regime had to be deposed to prevent further catastrophe.

Col. Gen. Ludwig Beck led one coup effort termed the "Stalingrad Putsch." Beck called upon General Friedrich von Paulus to initiate a revolt with his 6th Army then encircled in Stalingrad, but von Paulus faltered when Hitler suddenly awarded him the position of *Feldmarschall* knowing that no previous German Field Marshal had ever surrendered. While von Paulus did not call for the intended uprising within the army as Beck had hoped, he did make history by surrendering himself and his surviving troops to Soviet forces. Beck, after later taking part in the failed July 20, 1944 bomb plot against Hitler, committed suicide. Von Paulus survived Soviet captivity and returned in 1953 to Soviet-controlled East Germany, dying there in 1957 at the age of 67. Only some 5,000 of the 93,000 German POWs of Stalingrad survived to return home.

Stalingrad—December 20, 1942—The Beginning of the End (*right*)
This funeral card also represents the loss of the entire 300,000 man German Sixth Army. 22-year old Franz Holzbauer, a farmer's son from "the good farm meadows" of Bruck in the Austrian parish of Andorf, died for the "German Fatherland" during the pivotal battle of Stalingrad on December 20, 1942. The loss considered the turning point, both militarily and psychologically, for the war in the East and signaling the ultimate defeat of the Third Reich.

After von Paulus surrendered the remnants of the 6th Army in early January 1943, the Soviets reportedly collected the corpses of 250,000 German and Romanian troops. Soviet dead is estimated at over 1,000,000. The term 'war of attrition' was adding up.

Stalingrad Still Life—Postcard—Death of the 6th Army
"In Memory of Stalingrad" is the title of the drawing by Franz Eichorst as seen on a commercial postcard, the original artwork placed on display in the Munich House of German Art. The illustration shows white camouflage added to the beleaguered soldiers' helmets in an attempt to blend in with the winter snow and thus limit their visibility to snipers. Considered "defeatist," the postcard was pulled from circulation.

Zum Gebetsandenken
an Pionier
Johann Liebl
von Burglengenfeld
gefallen am 31. Januar 1943 im Osten
im Alter von 31 Jahren.

Mit Gott ging ich von Frau und Kind,
Der Abschied fiel mir schwer.
Doch dacht' ich immer fort und fort,
Wo ich auch weilt' an fremdem Ort,
Es gibt ja doch ein Wiederseh'n,
Wenn Krieg und Sturm zu Ende geh'n
Doch anders hat's der Herr gewollt
Und hat von hier mich abgeholt.
Nun ruh' in fremder Erd' mich aus
Und bin bei Gott im Vaterhaus.

Mein Jesus Barmherzigkeit!
Vater unser! Ave Maria.

Buchdruckerei Gg. Nußstein, Burglengenfeld

Zum frommen Gedenken
im Gebete
an den am 6. Febr. 1943 im Osten gefallenen
Oberschützen in einem Pionier-Regiment
Michael Liebl
von Burglengenfeld
im Alter von 33 1/2 Jahren.

Wissen nicht, warum zerschlagen
Unser reiches und sonniges Glück,
Wissen nicht, wie sollen wir's tragen
Weil Du nicht mehr kehrst zurück.
Können nur in Händen halten
Dein Bild und drücken an's Herz,
Können nur die Hände falten,
Herr, heile Du doch unseren Schmerz.

Mein Jesus Barmherzigkeit!
Vater unser — Ave Maria!

Buchdruckerei Gg. Nußstein, Burglengenfeld

A Deadly Week—January 30–February 6, 1943—Combat Engineer Brothers
The Bavarian-born Liebl brothers died just one week apart. Johann Liebl fell in battle on January 31, 1943 in the Eastern Front at age 31. A member of a *Pionier* battalion (combat engineers), he died near Wassiljewka am Olym where his remains still lie, the information recorded in the German Graves Registry.

His older brother Michael, an *Oberschutzen* or private 1st class and also serving in a Pioneer Regiment was 33½ when killed the following week. According to records, he died near the strategic port of Novorossiysk in southern Russia on the eastern side of the Black Sea.

Soviet Sailors Fought on Land—Novorossiysk
A little known but important and fiercely contested battle was fought at the port of Novorossiysk, the location of Michael Liebl's death, he likely taking part in its siege. In 1942 Novorossiysk was occupied by German forces. However a small unit of Soviet sailors defended a pivotal section of the town for 225 days until the area was liberated by the Red Army on September 16, 1943. The heroic defense allowed the Russians to retain possession of the city's bay, strategically important because it was the only year-round ice-free port in the southern Russian basin. The defense also prevented the Germans from using the port for their own desperately needed supply shipments. Novorossiysk was awarded the title Hero City in 1973. In 2005 the seaport celebrated its 160th anniversary and remains a major shipping center.

O Herr, gib ihm die ewige Ruhe und das ewige Licht leuchte ihm, Herr lasse ihn ruhen im Frieden. Amen.

Zur frommen Erinnerung
im Gebete
an meinen lieben, unvergeßlichen, herzensguten Gatten, meinen guten Sohn, Schwiegersohn und Bruder

Johann Lankl

Feldwebel in einem Grenad.-Regt.
Teilnehmer am Einmarsch Österreich, Sudetenland, Tschechei und Frankreichfeldzug, Inhaber des EK II und Verwundeten-Abz.
geboren am 24. März 1916,
gefallen den Heldentod für seine geliebte Heimat am 4. Febr. 1943 bei Kursk in Osten.

Nicht wir allein, die um dich weinen
Nein, wer dich kannte, liebte dich,
Der Herr auch kennt u. liebt die Seinen
Drum nahm er frühe dich zu sich.
Du warst so gut, starbst viel zu früh,
Solch braves Herz vergißt man nie

Mein Jesus Barmherzigkeit
Süßes Herz Maria sei meine Liebe
Vater unser . . . Ave Maria.

Druck von Jg. Forstner, Oberviechtach

Killed in Kursk—Corporal Lankl—KIA February 4, 1943
"In memory of my loving, unforgettably good-hearted spouse, a good son, son-in-law and brother." So reads the inscription describing Grenadier 1st Sergeant Johann Lankl, a veteran of the Austrian *Anschluss*, the taking of the Sudetenland and Czechoslovakia and the French campaign. A recipient of the Iron Cross 2nd Class and a previous Wound Badge, he was killed on February 4, 1943, a few weeks before his 27th birthday. One day prior to Lankl's death, German forces had begun the first of three official days of mourning for the loss of the Sixth Army at Stalingrad.

A few months later the area of Kursk north of Kharkov erupted in the greatest tank battle in history. Code named by the Germans as Operation Citadel, the Battle of Kursk raged on from July 4–20, 1943. Fifty German divisions, some 900,000 infantry including nineteen armored (2,700 tanks and assault guns, 2,600 aircraft) clashed with 3,600 Soviet tanks, 2,400 aircraft and well over one million Soviets troops with another 500,000 in reserve. The German forces found themselves entangled within a massive network of defensive positions including 26,000 anti-tank guns and artillery batteries plus millions of mines. Military historians argue Kursk was even more significant than Stalingrad.

The Germans, still reeling from the loss at Stalingrad, sought to strike at the Red Army forces with a pincher movement, but due to the miles-deep defensive positions, the Soviets were able to thwart the blitzkrieg efforts. Over 6,000 mines were laid for every mile while 300,000 Soviet civilians had dug thousands of miles of anti-tank trenches and other fortifications. While many consider it a total victory for the Soviets, others call it a draw although all can agree that the attrition level of man and machine was unmatched, that the German war effort had been permanently blunted and that the monumental battle marked the last German offensive initiative in the East.

Casualty estimates of German dead and wounded vary widely, at least 60,000 killed and missing with some 150,000 wounded while Soviet casualty figures were more recently estimated as 70,330 KIA and 107,517 wounded and missing. Both sides lost over 300 tanks.

Today near the Kursk village of Besedino is the largest German cemetery in Russia, primarily filled by the dead of the Battle of Kursk.

Unser Herr
JESUS CHRISTUS
dem der Vater alles Leben anvertraut hat, rief am 15. 2. 1943 bei Demjansk unseren lieben Bruder, Schwager und Onkel

Hermann Ammann

Unteroffizier in e. Pion.-Batl. im Alter von 34 Jahren zu sich in das Reich seiner Herrlichkeit.

Gar früh stiegst Du ins kühle Grab,
Im heißen Kampf sankst Du hinab,
Betrauert von uns allen.
Doch gabst Du gern Dein Leben hin,
Fürs Vaterland mit treuem Sinn
Bist Du als Held gefallen.

Demjansk—February 15, 1943—Sergeant Hermann Ammann—Combat Engineer (*above*)
The town of Demjansk stood in the path of Soviet forces as they sought to relieve the German siege of Leningrad.

At Demjansk some 90,000 German troops of the Second Army Corps and elements of RAD labor youth and OT construction workers, police, Russian volunteers and SS, were encircled during February 1942, but due to the efforts of Waffen-SS troops, they were able to make a break-out on April 1st through a narrow 800 meter access route. The fighting in the area lasted fourteen months tying down eighteen Russian divisions. The Germans sustained some 13,000 casualties, the survivors eligible for the special issue Demjansk Shield award; a silver-washed zinc decoration worn on the uniform sleeve. As Sgt. Ammann was KIA on Feb. 15, 1943, his death was probably associated with the battle of Stalingrad, German forces having surrendered on the previous 2nd, followed by Russian troops quickly taking control of the so-called Demjansk Pocket.

Waffen-SS—March 12, 1943—Rudi Ellmayer (*Top of next page*)
"While in the bloom of the age of 17½, he gave his brave life for the Fatherland … during the hard struggle in the East." Such is the brief epitaph for the young member of a Waffen- SS pioneer battalion (combat engineers).

Separate from the traditional Germany Army, the Waffen-SS were the Third Reich's so-called "political soldiers" steeped in Nazi indoctrination and fanatically committed to Hitler and his racial policies. The armed and largest branch of the SS, they were initially looked down upon by the regular Army leadership, but gained repute during the invasion of the Soviet Union and infamy for their treatment of civilians, especially Jews. Eventually the SS expanded to thirty-nine divisions, the "elitism" of its selection requirements substantially lowered allowing in some 1,000,000 members. Originally SS recruit acceptance was based on strict criteria of physique and Aryan ancestry, but as the war ground on, members were recruited from fifteen nationalities including volunteers from conquered lands, even from among Russian ethnic groups. The desperate programs proved relatively inconsequential to the war effort, some members even turning against their brutal German overseers. The original three SS groups: Hitler's bodyguard (*Leibstandarte*-SS Adolf Hitler), the SS-*Totenkopfverbande* (concentration camp personnel), and the *Verfugnungstruppe* (military units) were combined in 1939 under one banner, the Waffen-SS.

Excerpt from an article published in an SS magazine:

> Bitter weeks lie behind me, weeks full of horrible experience. But we soldiers here in the East learn a tremendous self-consciousness and sobriety over ourselves. Here we become cleaner, better, harder, healthier. The soldiers who have already held out for over three years in Russia, those are the best men of our folk, by far the best. It is so: one should no longer train recruits in German barracks with shower rooms, beds, lockers etc., rather in filthy nests on the East. One should no longer assemble German divisions in Western Europe, rather in the occupied East.
>
> The homeland is too beautiful for us; it makes us sick, slack, soft. *Contined on next page.*

After the war, the Regular Army endeavored to cast off the onus of all war crimes on the SS, although their complicity and cooperation was finally exposed. Meanwhile members of the Waffen-SS tried to create their own post-war image as elite fighting troops combating Communism rather than appearing as war criminals, another self-serving posture that proved without foundation.

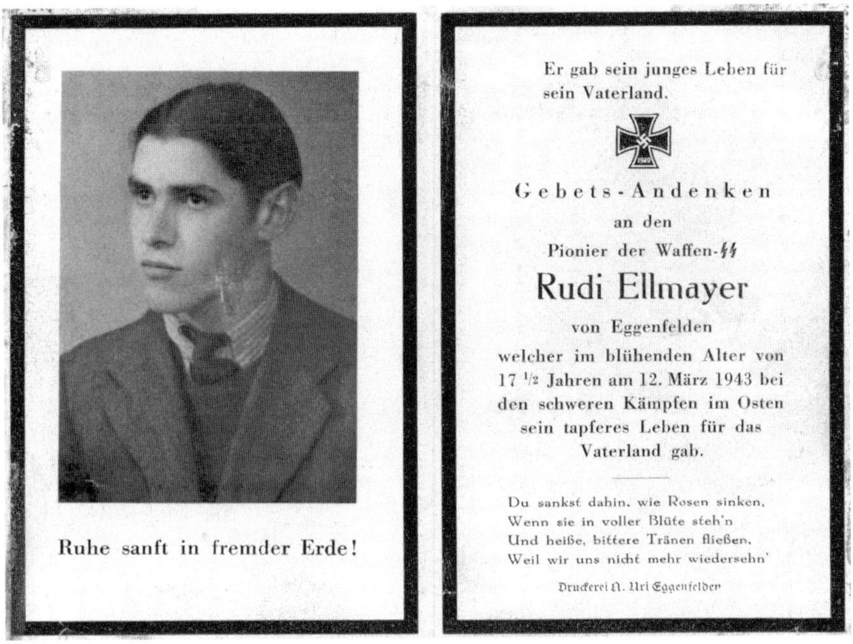
Ruhe sanft in fremder Erde!

Er gab sein junges Leben für sein Vaterland.

Gebets-Andenken
an den
Pionier der Waffen-SS
Rudi Ellmayer
von Eggenfelden
welcher im blühenden Alter von 17 1/2 Jahren am 12. März 1943 bei den schweren Kämpfen im Osten sein tapferes Leben für das Vaterland gab.

Du sankst dahin, wie Rosen sinken,
Wenn sie in voller Blüte steh'n
Und heiße, bittere Tränen fließen,
Weil wir uns nicht mehr wiedersehn'

Druckerei A. Uri Eggenfelden

Kuban Bridgehead—July 26, 1943—Georg Zitzelsberger (*right*)

A farmer's son from the Black Forest town of Oberried and a corporal in an anti-tank regiment, he was awarded the Iron Cross 2nd Class, Infantry Assault and Wound Badge. His family received the specially issued Kuban Shield honoring the battle and their son's death posthumously, the metal emblem worn on the upper uniform sleeve although too late for the memorial card photo.

The confrontation with Soviet forces pursuing their massive offensive after the fall of Stalingrad further pushed German and Romanian troops toward the Crimean Peninsula, trapping them in a bottleneck connected to a defensive line between the Sea of Azov and the Soviet naval base at Novorossiysk. A battle ensued when on February 12, 1943 Soviet troops poured in along the Kuban River. The defensive line held for several months against increasing odds and allowed for a retreat into the Crimea of large numbers of the trapped Germans. The award for the Kuban Bridgehead defensive was announced on September 20, 1943 by Hitler. Soviet forces eventually took control of the area on October 9, 1943.

Den Heldentod im Osten starb unser einziger lieber Sohn u guter Bruder
Georg Zitzelsberger
Bauers-Sohn von Oberried
Obergefr. in einem Panz.-Jäg.-Rgt.
Jnh.: E.K. II, Jnf.-Sturmabz. Verw.-Abz.
gefallen 26. Juli 1943 im Blütenalter v. 22 Jahren am Kuban-Brückenkopf.

O, gute Eltern u. liebe Schwester Marie mein
Ich kehre nicht mehr zu Euch heim
Mein letzter Gedanke, der letzte Blick
Eilte noch zu Euch zurück.
Als ich starb im Feindesland
Reichte niemand mir die Hand,
Doch als mein Auge war gebrochen
Sah den Himmel ich schon offen.

Es ist so schwer, dies zu versteh'n
Daß wir uns niemals Wiederseh'n!

Druckerei A. Lackerbauer, Regen, Tel. 78

Zitzelsberger's hometown of Oberried in southern Germany, (population 2800), affords spectacular scenic views and is currently the location of the *Barbarastollen* (Barbara Caves), the tunnels dug into the Schauinsland mountain. The installation serves as Germany's central safekeeping archive, a repository of some 28,000 km. of microfilm containing millions of images from German archives and museums, copies of German cultural, historical, political and social assets from the past 1,500 years. In that ocean of documents is the writ of appointment of Adolf Hitler as Chancellor.

This national archiving effort in great part resulted from the massive loss of books, paintings and historic documents during the bombing of German cities during the Second World War. First created in 1970, the German government's stated purpose was to preserve "reading material" for the survivors of a nuclear cataclysm. As a post-apocalypse world may not have computers or electricity, microfilm was chosen as it can be read without highly technical equipment.

The tunnel and repository are accessible only once a year, limited to a group of twenty visitors having made advance reservations. To insure the sanctuary, the rules dictate that no military vehicles are permitted in the vicinity and uniformed soldiers must remain at least three kilometers distant while aircraft are forbidden to fly over the site.

So schlaf denn wohl, du Liebster unseres Lebens
Kein Kampfgetöse stört mehr deine Ruh,
All unser Hoffen, ach es war vergebens,
Nun deckt in Feindesland dich fremde Erde zu.
Du warst so jung, so brav und starbst so früh,
Wer Dich gekannt vergißt Dich nie.

Für die innige Teilnahme beim Heldentod unseres lb. Sohnes, Bruders und Bräutigams danken wir herzlich.

FAM. HEINRICH NELLEN
KUNIGUNDE SCHMITZ

Jüchen, im Okt. 1943.

Heinrich Schüller
gefallen am 28. 8. 1943
bei Duchowschtschina

Betrothed—KIA August 28, 1943 (*above*)

An unusually large memorial card printed on thick paper has been chosen for Heinrich Schüller, killed at Dukhovshchina near Smolensk on the Russian front. At this point Soviet forces had sent the German Army into general retreat and the city of Orel was captured on August 4. Hamburg had just been devastated by a 1000-bomber raid and a few weeks earlier Italian dictator Mussolini was overthrown by his countrymen.

Absent from the card are mention of Schüller's military rank or service attachment, rather the words extend appreciation to others for expressing their sympathy for the loss of their "loving son, brother and fiancé" indicating he was betrothed. His hometown of Jüchen is located in the North Rhine-Westphalia area near Düsseldorf. Instead of a marriage, the memorial ceremony was held in October, 1943.

Lebt wohl — ein hartes Abschiedswort,
Doch frohen Mutes zog ich fort.
Im fernen Land, in heißer Schlacht,
Da hab ich oft an Euch gedacht.
Auf Wiedersehn! Da rief mich Gott,
Mein Los war der Soldatentod.
So tröstet Euch, schaut himmelan,
Was Gott tut, das ist wohlgetan.

Gebets- Andenken
an meinen herzensguten Mann, unseren lieben Sohn und Bruder

Hans Lankes

Stabsfeldwebel in einem Gren.-Regt. — Inhaber mehrerer Militär- und Kriegsauszeichnungen
Teilnehmer an den Feldzügen in Frankreich und Rußland, sowie beim Einsatz in Österreich und der Tschecho-Slowakei
geboren am 10. Juni 1911, gestorben am 8. Okt. 1943 nach 13jähriger Dienstzeit in Zwiahel.

Du hast ihn uns geliehen, o Herr,
Und er war unsere Freude,
Du hast ihn zurückgefordert,
Und wir übergeben ihn Dir ohne Murren,
Aber das Herz voll Wehmut.

Kuban Casualty—Joined by Three Family Members KIA (*previous page, below left*)
Army *Gefreiter* Philipp Harth, serving with a Grenadier Regiment, "fell in the difficult fighting on Kuban" on September 17, 1943 at age 36. He joined his brother and both in-laws in death, leaving behind a wife and daughter. The German Graves Office lists him as killed in Kertsch and buried in Sevastopol, Ukraine. The notation accompanying his photo reads "Lived Well—A Difficult Farewell."

October 8, 1943—Staff Sgt. Hans Lankes—13 Years of Service (*previous page, below right*)
A veteran *Landser* or German foot soldier and member of a grenadier infantry troop, he took part in the French and Russian campaigns as well as the pre-war Austrian Anschluss and takeovers in Czechoslovakia. He died with the rank of *Stabsfeldwebel*, equivalent to a staff sergeant, and as in any army, a leading force among front line troops. He had entered the pre-Nazi *Reichswehr* military in 1930 as a 19-year old and died in the uniform of the Third Reich at age 32.

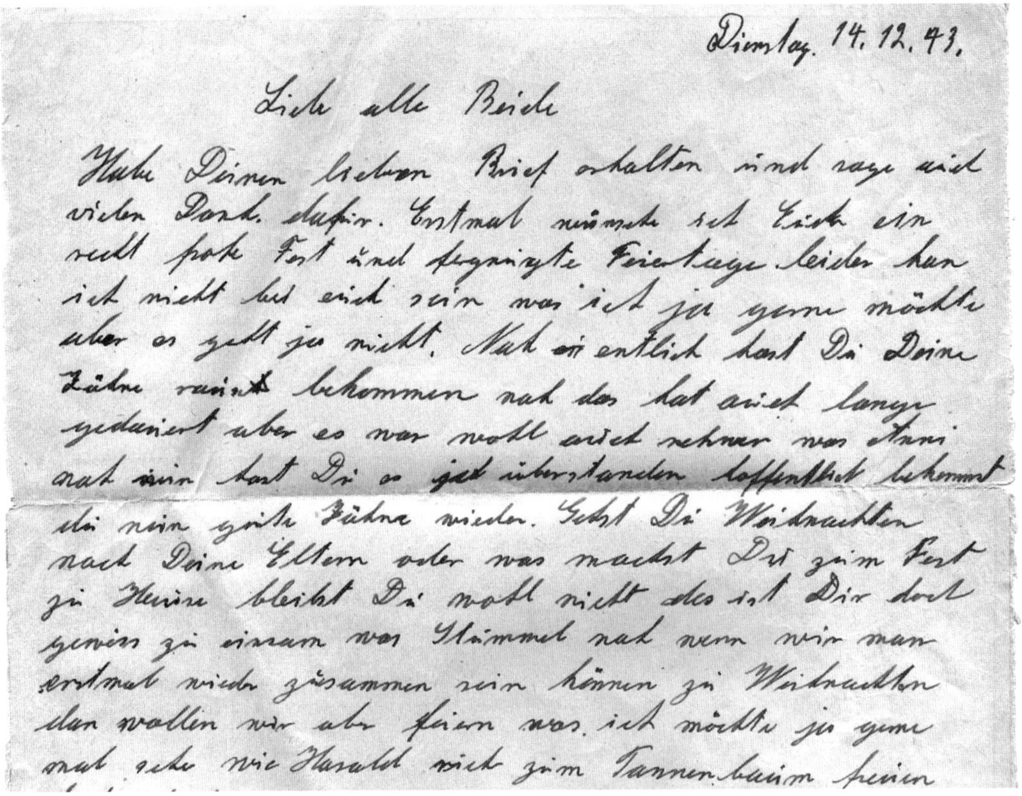
Dienstag. 14. 12. 43.

Liebe alle Beide

Habe Deinen lieben Brief erhalten und sage dir vielen Dank dafür. Erstmal wünsche ich Euch ein recht frohe Fest und gesegnete Feiertage leider kann ich nicht bei euch sein was ich ja gerne möchte aber es geht ja nicht. Nah endlich hast Du Deine Zähne raus bekommen nah das hat auch lange gedauert aber es war wohl auch schwer was Anni nah nun hast Du es jetzt überstanden hoffentlich bekommst du nun gute Zähne wieder. Gehst Du Weihnachten nach Deine Eltern oder was machst Du zum Fest zu Hause bleibst Du wohl nicht das ist Dir doch gewiss zu einsam was Schimmel nah wenn wir man erstmal wieder zusammen sein können zu Weihnachten dann wollen wir aber feiern was. ich möchte ja gerne mal sehe wie Harald sich zum Tannenbaum freuen

Tuesday December 14, 1943—Christmas Letter from the East
From: Private 1st Class Autzen, FP#0294 E—Staff Company Infantry Battalion 235
To: Mrs Anni Autzen, Apenarder Strasse 29. Flensburg, Germany

Dear Both of You,

Thank you very much for the letter. For a start, I am wishing you a very merry Christmas and I am sorry I cannot be with you as I would love to be there. At last you had the teeth pulled. It has taken a while before you decided. Well, that problem is solved now, and let's hope you get good ones now. What are you doing for Christmas? Are you going to your parents or do you stay at home? And home it will be lonely for you, but once we are together again it will be a better Christmas for both of us. I would love to see Haral's face when he sees the Christmas tree. I can see him grinning when he sees the lit tree.

I think that grinning he has from his Dad or was it from you? He will be a real boy I think. In two days is my birthday and it looks bleak already for me. Thank you for the congratulations and I am glad you received some presents for the boy for Christmas. Don't give him too much, he would not know what to grab first. Not very nice to hear about Walter Wonser. I hope it is not bad, but at least he is safe now. You don't know where Karl Heinz is?

Do you get the whole house redecorated or only the kitchen and bedroom? Let's hope you have no more air raids over Christmas. It is no fun to sit in an air raid shelter at Christmas. I suppose we will get drunk over Christmas so we can forget about home for a while. But nevertheless I shall think about my beloved wife and my boy. After bad times there always will be a good time. I will close now. Greetings from your Papa. A very merry Christmas and all the best … have some good dreams.

Private Autzen's hometown Flensburg is in the northernmost town in Germany, and served as seaport for the *Kriegsmarine*. Then at the war's end in May 1945 it was designated as the last government seat of Nazi Germany as led by Grand Admiral Karl Dönitz. While Flensburg escaped most bombing, on March 23, 1943, twenty nursery school children died when twenty-eight British Halifax bombers dropped their bomb loads on the city.

"They Come"—the First World War Re-Visited in 1944—Grasping at Straws
In one of the many efforts to draw on First World War heroism of its soldiers, Nazi propagandists published this postcard with an illustration of a machine gunner and grenade thrower in First World War trenches. This card was stamped September 9, 1944 in Nuremberg, a major center for Nazi fanaticism. The reverse of the card calls for "Victory! Germany wins a new era for Europe!" In reality, most realized the war was lost at this point although many still imagined a last minute victory through new "wonder weapons" inflamed by their messianic faith in Hitler although an attempt was made to assassinate him on the preceding July 20 by members of the military.

Augsburg Civilian Casualty—February 25–26, 1942

The German city of Augsburg, located 40 miles northwest of Munich, was first established in 15 B.C. as a Roman settlement. During the war, some 50 percent was destroyed by Allied bombing raids. Among the civilian casualties of the so-called *Terrorangriffs* or "terror bombings" were Maria Johanna Windholz, 37 and her two children Maria, age 8 and Josef age 3.

The first bombing of the city took place a week earlier on February 17, 1942 composed of two squadrons of British Lancaster bombers sent out from England to attack war manufacturing plants. One target of the daring daylight raid into the heart of Germany was a submarine diesel engine plant subsequently damaged to the point of being put out of action for several weeks before being repaired. Of the twelve RAF aircraft that took part, only five returned.

The second mass bombing in which the Windholz family died was a two-part, day and night operation on February 25–26 conducted in daylight by the USAAF Eighth Air Force tasked with destroying the Messerschmitt aircraft facilities. Following up with a night raid, the RAF Bomber Command sent 594 aircraft whose combined incendiaries and high explosives effectively destroyed the center of the city. Firefighting was hampered by the frozen condition of the city's river. Twenty-one British bombers were lost.

Bertolt Brecht, Germany's most important playwright and one of the literary world's most influential writers, was born in Augsburg on February 10, 1898. While he served in the First World War, his politically themed work targeted him for Nazi persecution causing him to first emigrate to Scandinavia in 1933 then to the U.S. in 1941 where he composed anti-Nazi plays. Post-war he returned to Germany and died in East Berlin in 1956. In 1985 his hometown of Augsburg celebrated its 2000th birthday. In 1964 Augsburg and Dayton, Ohio became sister cities and in 2014 celebrated their 50th anniversary.

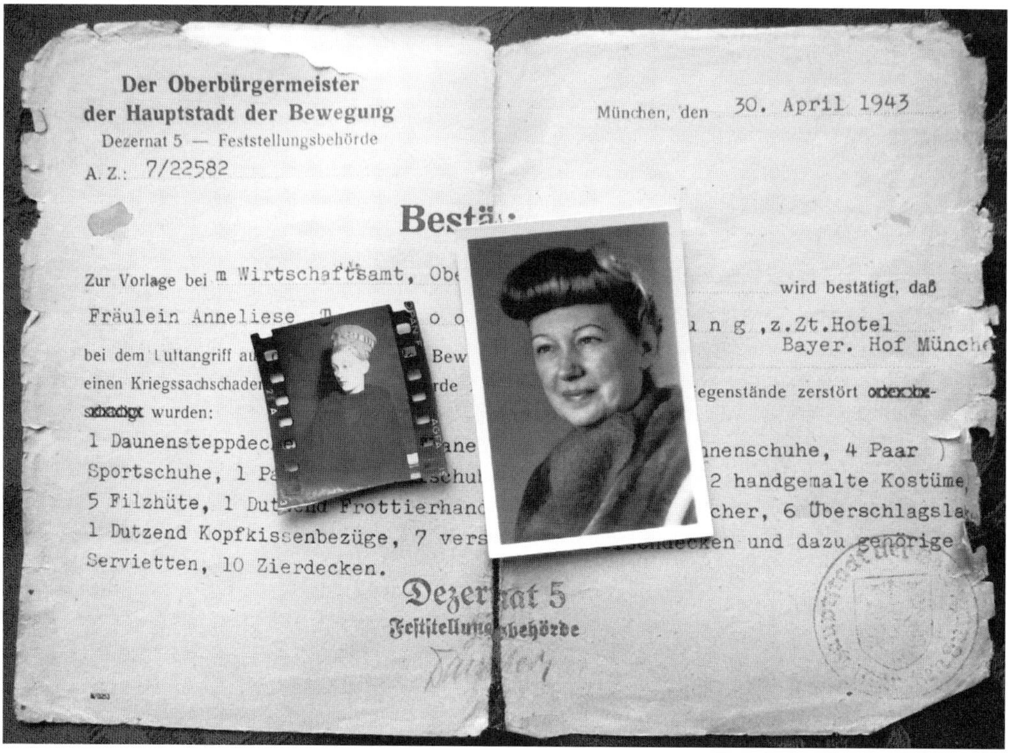
Der Oberbürgermeister
der Hauptstadt der Bewegung
Dezernat 5 — Feststellungsbehörde
A. Z.: 7/22582

München, den 30. April 1943

Bestä...

Zur Vorlage bei m Wirtschaftsamt, Ob... wird bestätigt, daß
Fräulein Anneliese ... ng ,z.Zt.Hotel Bayer. Hof Münch...
bei dem Luftangriff a... Bew...
einen Kriegssachschade... rde ... egenstände zerstört ~~oder be-schädigt~~ wurden:
1 Daunensteppdec... ane... nenschuhe, 4 Paar
Sportschuhe, 1 P... schu... 2 handgemalte Kostüme,
5 Filzhüte, 1 Dut... Frottierhand... cher, 6 Überschlagsla...
1 Dutzend Kopfkissenbezüge, 7 vers... ...en und dazu gehörige
Servietten, 10 Zierdecken.

Dezernat 5
Feststellungsbehörde

Celebrity Seeking Bomb Damages—April 30, 1943
The mayor of Munich, Karl Fiehler, has signed an official letter certifying the damages claimed by the film actress Anneliese Te Klodt von Fladung. The text states:

> It is hereby attested that Fräulein Anneliese Te Klodt von Fladung, current residence in the Bavarian Hof Hotel in Munich, suffered war damages on 10 March 1943 during an air raid attack on the city. It is attested that following items had been destroyed:
>
> 1 comforter, 1 white flannel quilt, 4 pairs of film stage shoes, 4 pairs sports shoes, 1 pair of new ski boots, 1 sports coat, 2 hand painted costumes, 5 felt hats, 1 dozen terry towels, 6 linen sheets, 6 bed linen, 1 dozen pillow cases, 7 table clothes and napkins, 10 doilies.

The March 10, 1943 bombing of Munich as mentioned in the document was one of seventy-three sorties flown against the city, targeted as a major industrial center and transportation hub and also known as the cradle of the Nazi movement. While it was heavily damaged, especially late in the war, deaths were rather light when compared to other cities such as Hamburg and Dresden which suffered the effects of massive fire-bombing. Attacking Munich on this date was a flight of British bombers (142 Lancasters, 81 Halifaxes, 41 Stirlings). While a major target was the BMW aircraft engine factory, several hundred structures were destroyed including 294 military buildings, among them the headquarters of the local flak brigade.

According to Munich official reports, 208 people were killed and 425 injured including two party officials, ten soldiers, one Hitler youth boy and two policemen. Seven of the 264 British bombers were lost. Von Fladung, despite the loss of her bed linen, survived unscathed, living another 22 years before passing away at age 86 in 1965.

After three years of attacking military targets, and a focus on supporting Stalin's drive against German forces on the Eastern front, the massive aerial bombing campaigns by Anglo-American aircraft shifted to Germany's civilian centers in an effort to break enemy morale. By March 1945, RAF Bomber Command's Air Marshal Sir Arthur "Bomber" Harris announced, "Bomber Command has virtually destroyed 45 of the leading 60 German cities. So far we have managed to keep up, and even to exceed our average of two and a half cities devastated a month. There are very few industrial centers left intact." At this point some 500,000 German civilians had been killed by the bombing. While devastating, the constant day and night attacks failed to significantly slow German war production that had been diversified and sent underground, nor did it apparently break morale among German civilians or military forces who continued to fight even after Hitler's death.

Altenburg, den 8. 12. 42.

An die

Wehrmachtsauskunftstelle,

B e r l i n W.30.
Hohenstaufenstr. 47/48.

Wehrmacht - Gräberoffizier 56.

Ich habe mich am 19.6.42 an den Wehrmachtsoffizier für Gräberfürsorge Nr. 56, unter Feldpostnummer 44 345 betreffs eines Bildes des Grabes für meinen Sohn Kurt, der am 4. Oktober 1941 im Feldlazarett zu Belik den Heldentod fand, gewandt. Mir wurde der Bescheid, dass darüber schon Vormerkung in der Bildkartei erfolgt ist und ich mich im Spätherbst nochmals an Ihre werte Adresse wenden solle.

ist
Unser Sohn, Kurt Eidam,/am 4.Oktober 1941 im Feld - lazarett zu Belik den Heldentod gestorben,

wurde auf dem Ehrenfriedhof V der Division in Belik, etwa 30 km südwestlich Jelna bestattet,

Die Grabstätte ist Nr. 102, (7.Reihe, 4.von links.)

Die o.a. Bitte habe ich schon an den Evangel.Kriegspfarrer gerichtet, dieser hatte mich an den Wehrmachtsgräberoffizier Nr. 56 verwiesen.

In der Hoffnung, dass meine Bitte Gehör findet, zeichne ich mit

Heil Hitler!

Father Seeking Photo from Poland—Grave No. 102, 7th Row, 4th from the Left

Fritz Eiden has written (December 8, 1942) seeking a photo of his son Kurt's grave. According to the letter he died "a hero's death" while in a field hospital on October 4, 1941 in the town of Belik, some 30 km south-west of Jelna, Poland. He received the following reply:

Evangelical War Priests
Office fieldpost no. 15626

On 7 June 1942

Mr. Fritz Eidam
Altenburg / Thuringia
Hermann Köhler strasse 82

Dear Mr. Eidam
Unfortunately, we cannot fulfill your request because we are no longer in the East. However, we advise you to send your request to the Wehrmacht Graves Officer 56, who is now in charge of our memorial cemetery at Belik.

Yours Truly,
Wehrmacht Head Priest

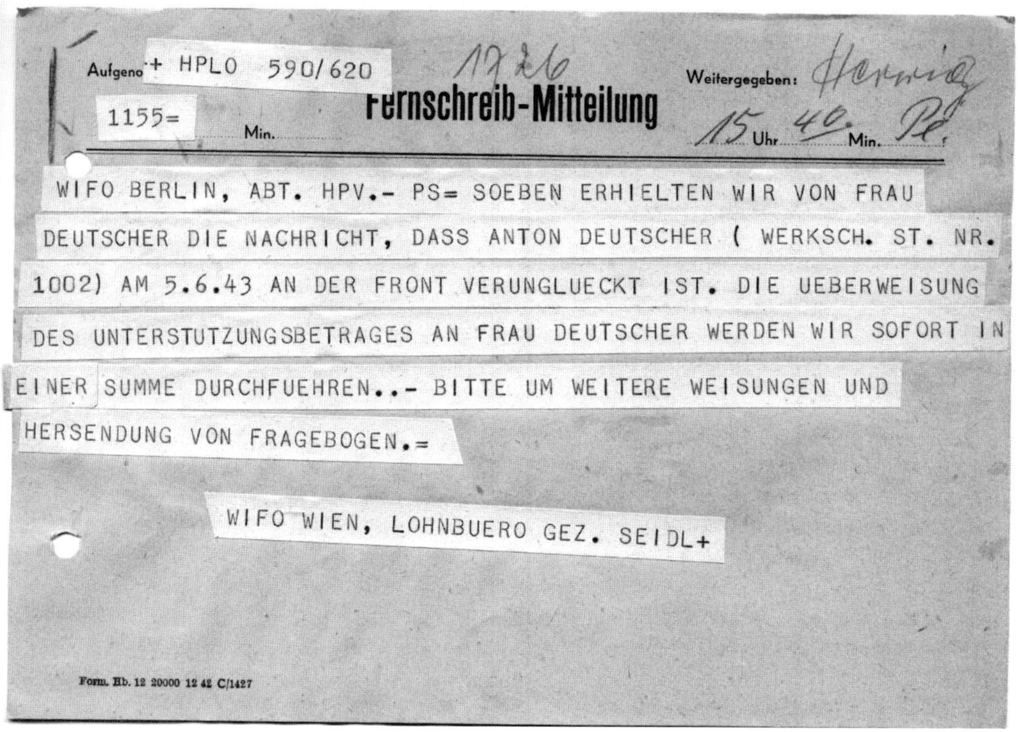

Aufgeno + HPLO 590/620

1155= Min.

Fernschreib-Mitteilung

Weitergegeben: 15 Uhr 40 Min.

WIFO BERLIN, ABT. HPV.- PS= SOEBEN ERHIELTEN WIR VON FRAU DEUTSCHER DIE NACHRICHT, DASS ANTON DEUTSCHER (WERKSCH. ST. NR. 1002) AM 5.6.43 AN DER FRONT VERUNGLUECKT IST. DIE UEBERWEISUNG DES UNTERSTUTZUNGSBETRAGES AN FRAU DEUTSCHER WERDEN WIR SOFORT IN EINER SUMME DURCHFUEHREN..- BITTE UM WEITERE WEISUNGEN UND HERSENDUNG VON FRAGEBOGEN.=

WIFO WIEN, LOHNBUERO GEZ. SEIDL+

Form. Hb. 12 20000 12 42 C/1427

Telegram—June 5, 1943—Transfer of Death Benefits—WIFO Secret Installation

A message sent from the Berlin offices of WIFO to its offices in Vienna gives instructions for the disbursement of benefit funds to the wife of a soldier named Anton Deutscher, a name that as "A. Deutscher" translates to "A German."

Deutscher was apparently at one time a guard at the WIFO installation. According to records at the German Graves Registration, he was drafted into the artillery and killed in action on June 5, 1943 in Merefa, buried in the Kharkov city area of the Ukraine.

The text of the telegram reads:

> WIFO Berlin—We just received the message by Mrs Deutscher, that Anton Deutscher (plant security no 1002) was killed in action at the frontline on 5.6.1943. We will immediately transfer the benefit amount to Mrs Deutscher. We request further instructions and transfer of the questionnaire.

WIFO refers to the Third Reich operated *Wirtschaftliche Forschungsgesellschaft* (Economic Research Company) engaged in, among other projects, the construction and operation of solid fuel (natural and synthetic) storage depots. Initial work began in the summer of 1935 under the auspices of the IG Farben conglomerate toward construction of an underground research center and storage depot located at the existing Kohnstein mine facility near the town of Nordhausen at the southern border of the Harz Mountains.

Located two kilometers south-west of the village of Niedersachswerfen and three kilometers north-west of the center of Nordhausen, is the Kohnstein Hill, historically a source of gypsum since 1917. Its series of tunnels were incorporated by WIFO into the plans to store strategic petroleum reserves. By mid-1943, this complex was Germany's largest storage area for fuel and oil and later poison chemicals.

Adjacent to Nordhausen was the infamous Dora-Mittlebau concentration camp, its brutally treated slave laborers forced to construct the underground V-1 and V-2 missile manufacturing sites, thousands dying in the process. In September1943 work had begun to restructure the tunnels for V-2 rocket production as scientists from Peenemunde on the French coast sought protection from Allied bombing, thus relocating to the subterranean research center. In April 1945 U.S. forces occupied the area. In 1948, after the area came under Soviet control, the entrances to the mine were closed by demolition. In 1995 a section was reopened for tourists. Official reports of extensive looting estimated seventy tons of material had already been removed.

Könnten Tränen Dich erwecken,
würd' Dich nicht die Erde decken.
Du warst so gut und starbst so früh,
wer Dich gekannt, vergißt Dich nie.

Jesus! Maria! Josef!

†

Zum frommen Andenken
an meinen lieben Mann, unsern guten,
treusorgenden Vater, Großvater, Schwieger-
sohn, Sohn, Bruder, Schwager, Neffen,
Vetter und Onkel, Herrn

Franz Klein

Er verschied plötzlich und unerwartet in-
folge eines Dienstunfalles am 29. April
1944 im Alter von 54 Jahren.

In tiefer Trauer
Wwe. Rosa Klein u. Kinder
und alle Anverwandten.

Oberkirchen, Nohfelden, Nentershausen.
Kleinhofshüz O.Schl, im Juni 1944.

"Died Suddenly"—Party Member Franz Klein, age 54—April 29, 1944

Klein appears in the photo wearing his Nazi Party pin. While he died on April 29th, the memorial service was not held until June perhaps due to the time required to return the body home to his wife Rosa. He is described as a good, faithful and caring father, grandfather, cousin, brother, uncle.… While no military connection is mentioned, the notation states he "died suddenly as the result of a service-related accident."

On the day of Klein's death, the Soviet air force dropped its largest bomb, an 11,000 pounder, on the city center of the east Prussian city of Königsberg. After repeated bombing, 90 percent of the city was reduced to rubble, and then occupied in April 1945 at which point the entire German population was expelled and the city renamed Kaliningrad.

Death Delivering
Shadowed by death, a soldier negotiates a muddly, shell-cratered battlefield while carrying hot meals and water for his comrades. The illustration by Paul Weber is one of several found in the 1942 Third Reich printed book *Goldatengeist—Eine Deutung aus Bekentnissen der Front* ("Soldier Spirit—An Interpretation of Confessions from the Front.")

Luftwaffe Kitchen Unit
Eventually, as the war swallowed the main line troops, support personnel, office workers and cooks would find themselves thrust into combat.

Baker's Dozens

A crew of German Army bakers prepares loaves of freshly rolled dough ready for baking in the commercial-sized ovens producing some 6,000 loaves daily.

Along with the various rations of meat, a soldier's roster of breads included *Knackebrot*, a hard, crisp whole wheat cracker-like product; *Hartzweiback,* a hard biscuit more like bread than crackers and *Hartkeks*, a hard biscuit/cracker combination produced in several shapes. The bread and meat was sealed in a paper sack, a label listing contents and manufacturer, in effect the Wehrmacht version of the sandwich. On the whole, the regular German Army foot soldier (*Landser*) received scientifically designed, hi-calorie/protein rich rations. Typically each soldier carried a daily emergency supply of the so-called "*Halbieserne*" or "Iron Ration" that contained one 300-gram tin of meat and one 125- or 150-grams of hard bread.

Den Heldentod im Osten starb mein
lieber Sohn unser guter Bruder

Karl Frank von Gotteszell

Bäcker in D a ch a u
Grenadier einer schweren Granatw.-Abt.
gefallen 1. Sept. 1943 bei den schweren Kämpfen im Alter von 19 Jahren 6 Monaten.

Mein guter K a r l lebt nicht mehr
Nach Russland zog er mit dem Heer
Eine feindl. Kugel brach dein gutes Herz
O, wie bitter ist fur mich der Schmerz
Zu kurz war unsere Freud' und Glück
Niemals kehrest du zurück

Druckerei A. Lackerbauer. Regen. Tel. 78

The Baker of Dachau—KIA September 1, 1943

Serving in a mortar battalion, Karl Frank von Gotteszell, fell during heavy fighting at the age of 19 years and six months. The photo shows evidence of photo-retouching including a sketched in uniform. His family added the following commemoration: "My good Karl lives no more, drawn to Russia with the Army. A hostile bullet broke your heart. Oh, how bitter is the sorrow. Too short our Joy and Happiness. Never will it return."

Karl had been a baker back in his home town of Dachau, site of the first Nazi concentration camp established in 1933.

Butchering
As one man perched on a beer truck holds the meat hook, a pig is being prepared to feed the troops.

In der Reife Deiner schönsten Jahre
Mit dem Bewußtsein Deiner Kraft
In der schönsten Lebensspanne
Hat Dich der Tod dahingerafft!
Zwar bist Du manchen Leid entgangen
Gar mancher Kummer blieb Dir erspart
Wer weiß, wie viele bittre Schmerzen,
Hätten hienieden Dein noch geharrt.
Doch für jene, die Dich liebten,
War Dein Scheiden viel zu früh,
Die im Leben Dir ergeben
Vergessen Dich im Tode nie.

May 31, 1944—Corporal Peter Hartman—Butcher Detachment
Hartmann died in a German military hospital from severe wounds suffered on the Eastern Front at age 39. During early May 1944, Germany had lost 100,000 men in the Crimea as Soviet troops recaptured the area including Sevastopol. Hartmann was likely one of those casualties.

DEN MÜTTERN UND
FRAUEN UNSERER
GEFALLENEN ZUM
MUTTERTAG 1944

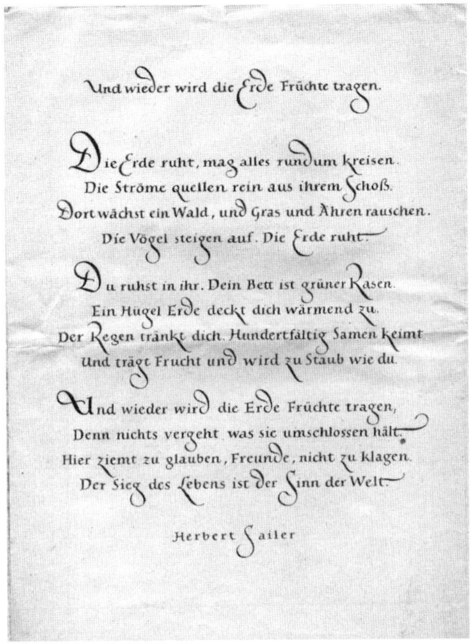
Und wieder wird die Erde Früchte tragen.

Die Erde ruht, mag alles rundum kreisen.
Die Ströme quellen rein aus ihrem Schoß.
Dort wächst ein Wald, und Gras und Ähren rauschen.
Die Vögel steigen auf. Die Erde ruht.

Du ruhst in ihr. Dein Bett ist grüner Rasen.
Ein Hügel Erde deckt dich wärmend zu.
Der Regen tränkt dich. Hundertfältig Samen keimt
Und trägt Frucht und wird zu Staub wie du.

Und wieder wird die Erde Früchte tragen,
Denn nichts vergeht was sie umschlossen hält.
Hier ziemt zu glauben, Freunde, nicht zu klagen.
Der Sieg des Lebens ist der Sinn der Welt.

Herbert Sailer

Mother's Day May 1944—*For the Mothers and Wives of Our Fallen* (*above left*)
An illustrated pamphlet produced by the Reichs Ministry of Propaganda contained quotes from Hitler and Goebbels and verse by Herbert Sailer as well as a monologue *Worten einer Deutschen Mutter* coping with the loss of German sons to the war as written by a D.H.

Words of a German Mother—The Dead are Alive
Today is mother's day and our thoughts first of all belong to grieving mothers who have lost sons … The German people however must say thanks to those mothers for whom the war has made a lonely life. More and more Mothers are missing their sons every year, sons who once upon a time showed their appreciation this day. But many a mother is silent on this day …

There is only one thing that is worth living for in this world, and that is our own Folk and for us Germans, it is Germany. We stand with this Folk, we live with it and we are committed to it, for better or worse. It is our holiest desire to keep our Folk together and no sacrifice is too great.

Adolf Hitler

"And the Earth Will Bear Fruit" by Herbert Sailer (*above right*)

The Earth will bear fruit. The Earth is resting.
Everything revolves around her,
Rivers flow from her bosom,
There a forest grows, grass and corn is growing,
Birds alight… the Earth is resting.

You rest inside it, your bed green grass,
a mound of earth keeps you warm, rain will drench you,
seeds will grow bringing forth fruit and then will
turn into dust like you….

Then once again the Earth will bring forth fruit.
Nothing can take away what the Earth has held close.
Please believe me, friends, do not despair.
Life's victory is the world's purpose

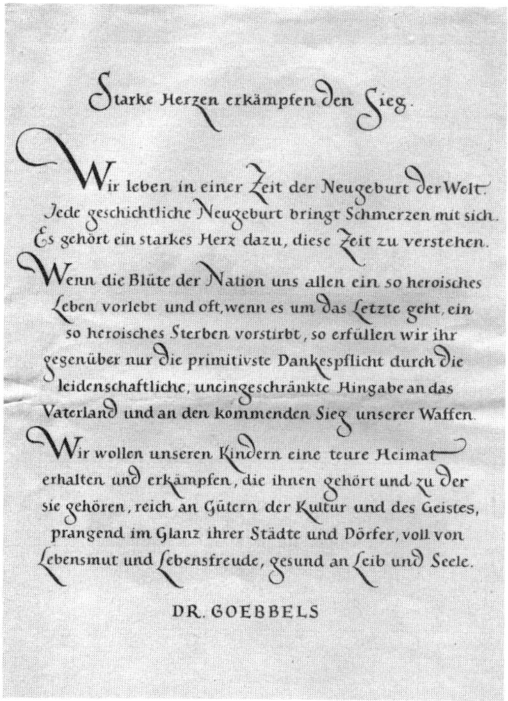

Starke Herzen erkämpfen den Sieg.

Wir leben in einer Zeit der Neugeburt der Welt.
Jede geschichtliche Neugeburt bringt Schmerzen mit sich.
Es gehört ein starkes Herz dazu, diese Zeit zu verstehen.
Wenn die Blüte der Nation uns allen ein so heroisches
Leben vorlebt und oft, wenn es um das Letzte geht, ein
so heroisches Sterben vorstirbt, so erfüllen wir ihr
gegenüber nur die primitivste Dankespflicht durch die
leidenschaftliche, uneingeschränkte Hingabe an das
Vaterland und an den kommenden Sieg unserer Waffen.
Wir wollen unseren Kindern eine teure Heimat
erhalten und erkämpfen, die ihnen gehört und zu der
sie gehören, reich an Gütern der Kultur und des Geistes,
prangend im Glanz ihrer Städte und Dörfer, voll von
Lebensmut und Lebensfreude, gesund an Leib und Seele.

DR. GOEBBELS

Propaganda Poetry by Goebbels
Goebbels placed his signature to everything "creative" as produced by the Third Reich, including the following words of praise and consolation for the soldiers who died the Hero's Death.

Strong Hearts will be Victorious—A Heroic Death

> Strong hearts will be victorious. Every new birth will bring pain; one needs a strong heart to understand the signs of this time. The flower of our Nation gave us an example of heroic life, and often, died a heroic death. We then fulfill our duty by our unaltered commitment to our Fatherland and the victory of our weapons. We want to give our children a true home, to fight for it, and one belonging to them rich in Culture and showing the wealth of her cities and villages, full of livelihood and healthy in soul and body.

Goebbels as Third Reich Art Connoisseur
The occasion was the grand opening of the Great German Art Exhibition 1942. *Contined on next page.*

The caption for the photo that appeared in the *Munich Illustrated Press* stated:

> The most representative show of German artistic creation to date was Doctor Goebbels' exhibition this year, which was officially opened at the House of German Art in Munich, and which is a high-quality expression of strong creative power. Our picture shows Dr Goebbels on tour of the exhibition, on the right, Director Kolb, on the left, Frau Professor Troost and Professor Adolf Ziegler.

"Gerdy" Troost was the wife of Hitler's once favorite architect Paul Ludwig Troost who designed the House of German Art. After her husband's death in 1934 Frau Troost then oversaw its construction as well as other Third Reich building projects. Known for disagreeing with Hitler, post-war she was declared by the de-Nazification process as "less responsible" and resumed her architectural work. She died in 2003 at the age of 98.

des Mittelstandes, der Hypothek, haben solche Ueberlegungen aktuellen Charakter bekommen. Ein führendes Institut, die Bay-

einen Kamm gesch
heute nicht der Ze
Schreibarbeit zu en

KfA

Starke Staaten und große Männer bewahren in allen Wechselfällen des Schicksals den gleichen Mut und die gleiche Würde

NICCOLO MACHIAVELLI (1469-1527)
Aus „Machiavelli: Gedanken über Politik und Staatsführung"
Kröners Taschenausgabe Bd.173

Barrese
a) Kass
disch
b) Guth
Post
Fällige
Scheck
Wechse
und
die
Hier
sel,
setz
ents
Abs.
Kred
Schatzw
anwe
Hier

Machiavelli Quote—May 7, 1944 issue of *Das Reich* newspaper
"Great men and powerful republics preserve an equal dignity and courage in prosperity and adversity."—Niccoló Machiavelli—*The Discourses.* 1517. The advertisement was posted by a Berlin bookseller, Kröners, in reference to Machiavelli's *Thoughts Concerning Politics and State Management.*

The choice of quotes may be a plea for solidarity because at this point Germany's war is coming home with a vengeance, the Eastern Front turning into a vast Third Reich graveyard.

Very influential, with a circulation of 14 million readers, *Das Reich* aka "The German Empire" was founded by Propaganda chief Joseph Goebbels. Publication began in May 1940, the features covering a wide spectrum of subjects including features about the U.S., the battlefront, but overall with an anti-Jewish focus, often publishing lurid photos other German newspapers would not feature. In the last issues Goebbels, who some compared to Machiavelli, called for unrelenting resistance even as Germany collapsed around itself.

Bicycle Bugler
Despite the early German optimism surrounding large scale use of bicycle troops as a result of their success in the Western campaigns, the rainy seasons (*Rasputitsa*)—which occurs twice a year—in the spring and autumn—turned the Russian unpaved roadways into quagmires effectively immobilizing all vehicular traffic. As a result, thousands of German bicycles were left abandoned across the vastness of the Soviet Union.

Deathcard for a Bicyclist—"I have fought the good fight"
Andreas Hummer, a farmer's son from Wildstein serving in a bicycle squadron, was killed "like his brother Josef" on the Russian Front, so notes the inscription on the reverse of the memorial card. He was 20 and had served for 18 months when KIA on August 21, 1943 perhaps as a result of the fighting raging around the city of Orel which the Red Army had recaptured on August 4th, the Germany army in retreat from the Soviet Union and suffering massive losses.

The caption reads:

> I have fought the good fight, kept the faith, finished the race, now for me the crown of righteousness is bestowed, given me by the Lord, the righteous judge.
> Lord, grant him eternal rest

Frontliners

Carried aboard *Kraftwagen mit Beiwagen*, sidecar-equipped BMW 750 cc motorcycles, a line of *Kraftradschütze*, motorcycle riflemen, stretches into the distance.

Companies of Motorcycle Rifle were established in 1935 and designed to transport three fully equipped soldiers into action as quickly as possible. The Armored Division alone counted 4,400 motorcycle troops. Tactically considered the "fastest earthbound weapon," the Rifle Troop went through rigorous motorcycle training at special schools.

"Sniper Magnets"

A motorcycle messenger (*Kradmelder*) was a moving target in the vast emptiness of the East. His life depended on his skill, his Mauser Kar.7.92 mm bolt action rifle and in this case his DKW NZ350. Note the headlamp shrouded for "black-out" conditions. The canister across his chest contains the standard issue gas mask.

The cycle soldiers rode exposed without the armor plating of the Panzers, without the safety of hundreds of foot soldiers beside them. They faced minefields, artillery fire, and strafing aircraft. The enemy, including partisans, often stretched a virtually invisible wire or cable across a road. Pulled to neck height, a speeding motorcyclist could literally lose his head. Eventually, the bikes were outfitted with metal bars or rails above the handlebars in an effort to counter those lethal ambushes.

Death of a Motorcycle Company Commander—"A Hero is one who sacrifices his life for the Greater"
So reads the deathcard for Lt Ludwig Schlander, company commander of a motorcycle troop battalion who took part in the Western, Polish and Eastern campaigns during which he was awarded both the 2nd and 1st Class Iron Cross, the Infantry Combat badge, the Wound Badge and the East Medal. He was killed in action on February 26, 1943 in Russia, his hero's grave in the vicinity of Kolejkowo near Bolekhov/Bolechow.

Battalions of the Axis allied Hungarian–Slovakian army first entered the Ukrainian town of Bolechow on July 6, 1941 after the retreat of Red Army forces. The Jewish residents, numbering over 5,000 were first stripped of their valuables then forced into hard labor. Ukrainian militia continued to rob and abuse them prior to their execution.

The first *Aktion* took place on October 28, 1941, when a number of Jewish men and women were driven into a building, its chimney blocked to produce fumes. The women were stripped and forced to dance while the men were beaten. Members of the German police and the Ukrainian militia took part in the action ending at a mass grave in the nearby Tenyava forest. Because of the shortage of bullets, the wounded were buried alive. A second *Aktion* followed on August 20, 1942 that involved 60 hours of torture upon a large group of Jews assembled by Germans and Ukrainians. Those that survived, approximately 4,000, were packed into cattle cars and sent to their deaths at the Belzec Death Camp. Bolechow was just one of thousands of such towns and villages destroyed, their residents murdered by German forces and their collaborators.

A Kill for a Flak Team

A 20 mm anti-aircraft gun crew celebrates an apparent success with a "hats off" salute for the camera. Seen around the bare-chested man's neck is a chain holding his German version of dog tags. Both sections of the two-part disc contain the same i.d. information. In case of death, the tags were snapped in two, one staying with the body to aid in recognition, the second section collected by the medics for record keeping.

No amount of German anti-aircraft defense could stem the waves of American and British bombers raining high explosives and incendiaries over German military targets and metropolitan centers. Some 300,000–600,000 civilians perished at the expense of the Nazi leadership's refusal to end the war until Berlin was a smoking rubble heap and Hitler dead. Moreover, Admiral Dönitz, now in charge of German forces, delayed signing the surrender documents for ten days so that German soldiers could make their way to American and British forces in order to surrender rather than fall into the hands of the Russians who regarded all German soldiers as war criminals.

Flakman Home on Leave

An NCO anti-aircraft soldier sits on his bed while on furlough from his military service.

Flakman—KIA January 25, 1944—"In the East" (*above left*)
Corporal Johann Ernst, a farmer's son from the Rhineland town of Katzenbach, winner of the Iron Cross 2nd Class, the Infantry Combat badge and West Wall Service medal, died in the East at age 26 years 6 months as specified by his deathcard that described him as a "beloved son and brother."

Flakman—October 18, 1944—Closer to Home (*above right*)
Named after a 6th century German hermit, Army Corporal Wendelin Gaus, died at the age of 36, while serving with a flak battalion in East Prussia. The German Graves Office listed the location as Wersele with burial in Garbas, Poland. As Germany sought to stave off the intense Allied bombing, its flak defenses also came under heavy fire incurring mounting casualties.

East Prussia was a region along the southeastern Baltic Coast and home to 2.5 million inhabitants, mostly ethnic Germans. The area, annexed by Nazi Germany in 1939, remained mostly unscathed by war until Allied air raids devastated the historic city of Königsberg. Then when Soviet forces launched an offensive, some 2,000,000, of its ethnic Germans attempted to escape in what is considered to be the largest mass exodus of people in history. Caught in the war chaos and the frigid cold of winter, an estimated 300,000 civilians died.

Gebets- Andenken

an

Josef Hartl

Obergefr. in einer Flak-Abtlg.

Inh. d. Kriegsverdienstkreuzes m. Schw.

Landwirt von Weiherhaus

welcher am 2. Jan. 1945 in Uriupinsk
bei Stalingrad im Alter von 39
Jahren gestorben ist.

Ehre seinem Andenken!

Druck von Jos. Nothhaft, Deggendorf

Stalingrad Flakman Casualty (*above left*)
According to the card's inscription, Josef Hartl, a 39-year old corporal in a flak battalion, died at the Russian town of Uryupinsk located some 200 miles north-west of Stalingrad. It was late in the war on January 2, 1945 since German forces had by this time been pushed back out of the Soviet Union, so he may have died as a POW, perhaps one of the 93,000 men of the 6th Army captured at Stalingrad. Before the war, he had been a farmer in the town of Wiherhaus near Nuremberg.

Alter Flak Kameraden (*above right*)
In the latter stages of the war, boys as young as 14 and men in their 60s were pressed into military service. Here an older man wears the uniform of a corporal in the Luftwaffe, a 37 mm anti-aircraft cannon visible behind the earthen wall guarding what appears to be an electric power station.

Musical Artillery (*left*)
A young soldier carries his tuba slung like a rifle, both essential instruments for a German military band. As the war grew more desperate, especially on the Eastern Front, musicians found themselves thrust into the cacophony of battle.

July 7, 1942—Musician Georg Pantoulier—Deathcard for a Birthday (*below*)
Seen wearing his musician's shoulder insignia, Georg Pantoulier, an Army corporal, was killed "in the East" just one day short of his 35th birthday.

Bands were an integral part of the Third Reich military. All but the German Navy uniform displayed the distinctive "swallows nest" shoulder insignia including the Hitler Youth, SA and SS. Of various patterns and colors, some also included braiding and fringe that further indentified the individual's instrument, for example drum and fife band members, trumpeters and buglers.

O Herr gib ihm die ewige Ruhe
und das ewige Licht leuchte ihm!

Herzliche Bitte
um ein Gebetsgedenken an
Gefreiten
Georg Pantoulier
geboren am 18. Juli 1907
gefallen am 17. Juli 1942
im Oſten

Unſer guter Gatte und Vater lebt
nicht mehr,
Der Platz in unſerm Heim iſt leer,
Er reicht uns nicht mehr ſeine Hand
Er ſtarb den Heldentod in Feindes-
land,
Wir konnten ihn nicht ſterben ſehen,
Auch nicht an ſeinem Grabe ſtehen.
Du ſtarbſt ſo jung und ach ſo früh,
Vergeſſen werden wir Dich nie.
Mein Jeſus, Barmherzigkeit!
Vater unſer! — Ave Maria!

Beziehbar durch Karl Rieder, Nittenau

The Soundtrack of the Third Reich

A group of BdM girls parade while playing the strange looking *Schalmei* (Shawm) or Tyrolean Many-Belled Reed Trumpet, the instrument originating in the 12th century, but eventually its use in classical music faded with the appearance of the oboe family of instruments.

Musical parades were a common and constant sight on the boulevards and streets of German cities, towns and villages as the Third Reich kept up a steady barrage of music of one kind or another, from the constant thump of marching boots and drumming of military bands, to street recitals to radio broadcasts of German classical to light romantic fare, all part of the "emotion over intellect" campaign that Party ideology promoted. The incessant soundtrack engulfed citizens and soldiers within a litany of songs designed to promote morale and infuse martial spirit as well as to drum in Nazi political and racist propaganda. Everyone sang, from school children to the SS.

"Jazz Band"—The Melody of Mayhem

Eleven Luftwaffe musicians make up a predominantly brass band.

A popular German "jazz song," a commentary on the mortal battle between National Socialism and Soviet Communism was based on a revised version of a popular British tune and contained the following lyrics sung in English:

> "Red Front, Red Front, Red Front … atty zacky … want some Communism …
> I like murder … I like the smell of blood … murder and vice … it's very nice!"

And the Band Plays On
German musicians march along a rubble strewn city street.

Requiem for a German Orchestra
A first-hand report by a Russian soldier describes the fate of a group of German military musicians sent to the battle front near Kiev:

> Next the Germans resolved to break the defenses at Boayrka station south of Kiev. The strike was as powerful as it could be, but the 5th airborne brigade of Colonel Rodimtsev was one of the smartest. Colonel Rodimtsev was later made General and Two Times Hero of the Soviet Union. His brigade was formed from border guards right before the war. The border guards were used to close battle but the Germans didn't know that. The enemy brought three motor divisions, several tank regiments and then put a 100-member orchestra out in front, all this on a narrow strip of land. They counted on psychological attack. And as they came closer, the (Soviet) paratroopers shot them all—the orchestra, the tanks and the divisions. The battle lasted for an hour or half an hour. The Germans got the bulldozers and for the next two weeks were removing bodies. We thought then that the enemy would never capture Kiev.

Top of next page:

Trumpets of Doom
Dwarfed by field artillery cannons, band members await their turn to perform at a military review.

German state-of-the-art artillery included a wide range of weapons from light weight to medium to heavy to massive in the case of siege mortars and train-mounted guns. The range included anti-tank (37 mm–120 mm), field (75 mm–340 mm), railroad mounted (150 mm–800 mm), coastal (150 mm–300 mm), and anti-aircraft (20 mm–120 mm) as well as the iconic all-purpose 88 mm effectively used for anti-aircraft, anti-tank and anti-personnel use, even deployed on submarines. The weapons were produced in Germany as well as occupied territories, particularly Czechoslovakia via its extensive Skoda munitions facilities.

However as America ramped up its war production, the Axis forces were outgunned by the Allies as evidenced by the total number of artillery pieces produced: the Axis 180,141 versus the Allies 914,682.

November 10, 1943—Artillery Lt Andreas Daffner (*right*)
Daffner at 22 had attained officer's rank at a young age and his tunic displays both assault and wound badges. His memorial card information is sparse and only mentions he was from the Bavarian town of St Gilla. The date indicates he may have died during the successful November 6th Soviet assault to recapture Kiev. The Bible inscription reads, "He has no greater love, than he who gives his life for his friends."

Eine größere Liebe hat niemand,
als wer ſein Leben hingibt
für ſeine Freunde
Joh. 15, 13

100th Year of the German Railroad—Commemorative Postal Stamp 1935

Potsdam Train Station—1939 Architectural Drawing

While Allied aerial bombing reached virtually around the clock intensity, in reality it was mostly inaccurate, most bombs falling a half mile or more from the intended target thus the reliance on "saturation" bombing. While the strategic railway network was a prime focus of attack, damaged sections were virtually repaired overnight. Meanwhile Armaments Minister Albert Speer, Hitler's chief architect, had redirected war time production underground and diversified to innumerable small workshops, production actually increasing as the war ground on.

Shower Stop in Yugoslavia
With the advent of war, the *Reichsbahn* expanded throughout conquered territories and occupied countries. More than 50,000 miles of track were operating for the purpose of moving troops, civilian passengers, military hardware, munitions, raw materials, agricultural and manufacturing materials. This made the *Reichsbahn* one of the largest railroad networks in Europe. It was also the prime mover of victims to the Death Camps and without it The Third Reich's Final Solution could not have been conceived or achieved.

Signs of the Times—Arrival in Ohrdruf at High Noon 1936
A contingent of soldiers have either just arrived or preparing to depart the train station at Ohrdruf, the town located south of Gotha in Thuringia central Germany. In 1944 a sub-camp of the Buchenwald concentration camp system was erected nearby. Initially a forced labor camp and eventually taking on some 20,000 prisoners who worked on road and train construction as well as underground bunkers and tunnels, and some suggest a facility for the German nuclear bomb research. As the allies advanced, the prisoners were led away on death marches, 1,000 killed by members of the Hitler Youth and the Volkssturm while the SS shot many remaining in the camp, the corpses left where they lay. A total of some 7,000 prisoners died. It gave notice to U.S. troops what lay in store as it was the first such camp liberated by American forces, the date April 4, 1945.

Railway Police
An estimated 100,000 individuals kept the German train system functioning at Herculean levels even during the last months of the war when under constant bombing. Part-time police officers served as guardians of the rail system via the *Bahnschutzpolizei* tasked also with anti-sabotage duties as well as guarding POW and concentration camp transport trains.

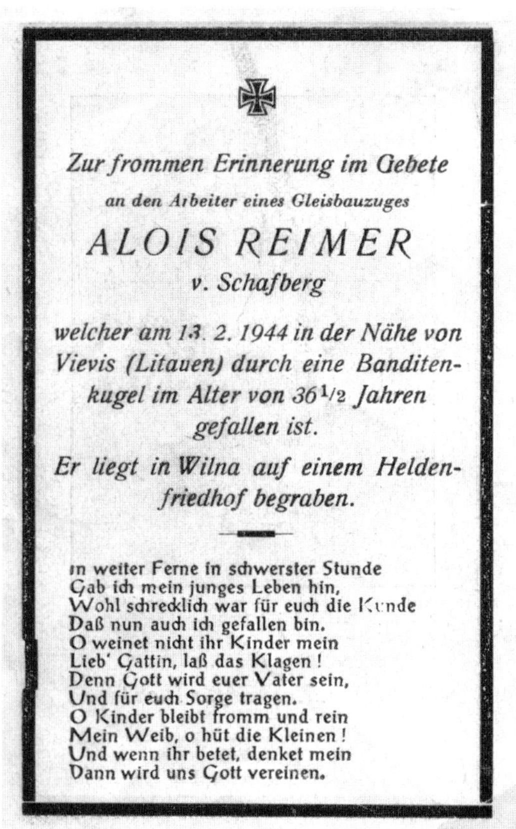

Zur frommen Erinnerung im Gebete
an den Arbeiter eines Gleisbauzuges
ALOIS REIMER
v. Schafberg

welcher am 13. 2. 1944 in der Nähe von Vievis (Litauen) durch eine Banditenkugel im Alter von 36 1/2 Jahren gefallen ist.

Er liegt in Wilna auf einem Heldenfriedhof begraben.

In weiter Ferne in schwerster Stunde
Gab ich mein junges Leben hin,
Wohl schrecklich war für euch die Kunde
Daß nun auch ich gefallen bin.
O weinet nicht ihr Kinder mein
Lieb' Gattin, laß das Klagen !
Denn Gott wird euer Vater sein,
Und für euch Sorge tragen.
O Kinder bleibt fromm und rein
Mein Weib, o hüt die Kleinen !
Und wenn ihr betet, denket mein
Dann wird uns Gott vereinen.

Trainman Alois Reimer—Killed by Bandits in Latvia—February 13, 1944
The 36½ year-old track construction worker died during an attack by "bandits," the German euphemism for partisans. The card notes that "He remains in Vilna buried in a Hero's Cemetery."

Death in the Lands of Germany's Allies

The Italian Non-Connection (*above left*)
An Italian soldier and German Luftwaffe corporal take a stroll somewhere in Italy, their caps slanted at opposing angles.

Tourists (*above right*)
German soldiers consult a map as they sit amongst Roman ruins.

The Germans often looked upon the Italian soldier as more of a hindrance and detriment than of any military benefit. However, Hitler continuously honored his agreements to Mussolini, often coming to his aid and bailing him out of one military blunder after the other. In gratitude for Hitler's support, Mussolini sent 229,000 Italian troops to the Russian front. Some 21,000 died in battle, another 64,000 taken prisoners by the Soviets who reported that 28,000 died in captivity. Italian soldiers suffered further after Italy overthrew Mussolini's dictatorship and sided with the Allies. Thousands of Italian soldiers were murdered by the Germans or sent into slave labor.

Death in Italy—November 4, 1943 (*right*)
Described on his deathcard simply as "A Soldier," 19-year old Johann Gierl was KIA while serving in Italy, the former ally country which a month earlier had declared war on Germany after the ouster of *il Duce* by his own people. Anglo-American forces under Britain's Field Marshal Bernard Montgomery and America's Gen. George Patton, after an amphibious landing in Sicily on July 10, 1944, had made progress, though slow, up the boot of Italy as German forces still occupied the upper half of Italy, Hitler ordering his command to hold the line south of Rome.

Gebets-Andenken
an Soldat
Johann Gierl
Landwirtssohn von Taffnern
welcher am 4. 11. 43 bei den Kämpfen
in Italien im Alter von 19 Jahren
sein junges Leben für d. Vaterland opferte.

Es kam ein Brief von fremder Hand geschrieben
Es gab nicht viel was darin zu lesen war
Der Eltern Blick ist starr darauf geblieben
Vom Schlachtfeld kam die Nachricht furchtbar klar
Für uns, ein herber Schlag in alten Tagen
Denn unser HANNS liegt im Paradies
Nur der liebe Gott allein kann es nur sagen
Was jedem Menschenkind beschieden ist.

Zum Andenken
an den tapferen Helden
Nepomuk Stödkl
von Vilshofen
Unteroff. in einem Gren.-Regt.
Inh. d. EK. 2, d. Panzerkampfabz.,
der Ostmed. u. des Verwund.-Abz.
welcher am 29. Febr. 1944
bei den Kämpfen in Italien
im 33. Lebensjahre den Heldentod fürs Vaterland starb.

Erdl Vilshofen.

Death in Italy of an Unusual Name—February 29, 1944
Awarded the Iron Cross 2nd Class, Tank Combat medal and East Medal, 33-year old Grenadier Sergeant Nepomuk Stöckl hailing from the 1200-year old Bavarian town of Vilshofen, died on February 29, 1944 in Italy. The name Nepomuk is of Czech origin and is derived from the name of the patron saint of Bohemia (part of Czechoslovakia). However, in Germany, "Nepomuk" was also employed as a derogatory term for Czechs.

Two weeks prior to his death, on February 15th, German troops in Italy counterattacked American forces at the Anzio bridgehead, but in fierce fighting were in turn stopped by U.S. troops. However the Wehrmacht was able to seal and contain the bridgehead for another two months before U.S. Gen. Truscott broke their hold on May 23rd.

Romania—German Ally/Enemy
Wearing a traditional embroidered shirt, a Romanian civilian has been brought into a souvenir photo joining a decorated Luftwaffe flak corporal taking center stage.

Romania was a strategic target for both Axis and Allied control due to its large oil refineries which Hitler needed to fuel his blitzkrieg. As a German ally, its fascist Iron Guard was led by the dictator Ion Antonescu. In June of 1940, Romanian forces joined in the invasion of the Soviet Union. However, Germans held their Romanian allies in low repute as soldiers while Soviet forces would often target what they also considered weaker Romanian defensive lines in order to breach German positions.

As the war turned against the Third Reich, on August 23, 1944 Antonescu was overthrown and then in conjunction with Soviet forces, some 538,000 Romanians turned their arms against the Axis. A total of 370,000 Romanian soldiers died including those killed both fighting with Nazi forces against the Soviets and then alongside Russian troops battling the Germans. In addition, Romania was enthusiastic about the ethnic cleansing of its Jewish population, second only to Nazi Germany in the number of Jews killed.

Zum frommen Gedenken

an unseren lieben, unvergeßlichen Sohn und Bruder

Ludwig Straßer

Obergefr. in einem Gebirgsjäger-Regt.

Geboren 31. Januar 1915 in Leitheim, seiner schweren Verwundung erlegen am 13. Juni 1944 in einem Kriegslazarett in Rumänien.

Im heißen Kampf im Feindesland
Traf Dich die Todeswunde.
Die Lieben Dein im Heimatland
Traf schwer die bittre Kunde.
Den Heldentod fürs Vaterland
Bist Bester Du gestorben,
Hast mutig Dir mit tapfrer Hand
Den Himmelslohn erworben.

Bete für mich, ich starb auch für Dich.
Vater unser... Ave Maria

N 1129

KIA Romania—June 13, 1944—Coinciding Deaths
29-year old mountain trooper Corp. Ludwig Strasser's home was the Bavarian village of Leitheim located 27 miles (43 km) north of Augsburg. He died of severe wounds while in a field hospital. Coincidentally, on that same June 13th of Strasser's death, the Romanian partisan leader Stefan Plavat, after being betrayed, was killed by Romanian fascist troops and German field police.

In that same month of June 1944 Soviet forces launched *Operation Bagration* having previously recaptured Sevastopol and forced German troops from the Crimea. The offensive effectively destroyed the German Army Group Center with the Soviet momentum steamrolling on to Warsaw. On June 6th, the Allies also launched their D-Day landings at Normandy, establishing the long sought Second Front in the European war.

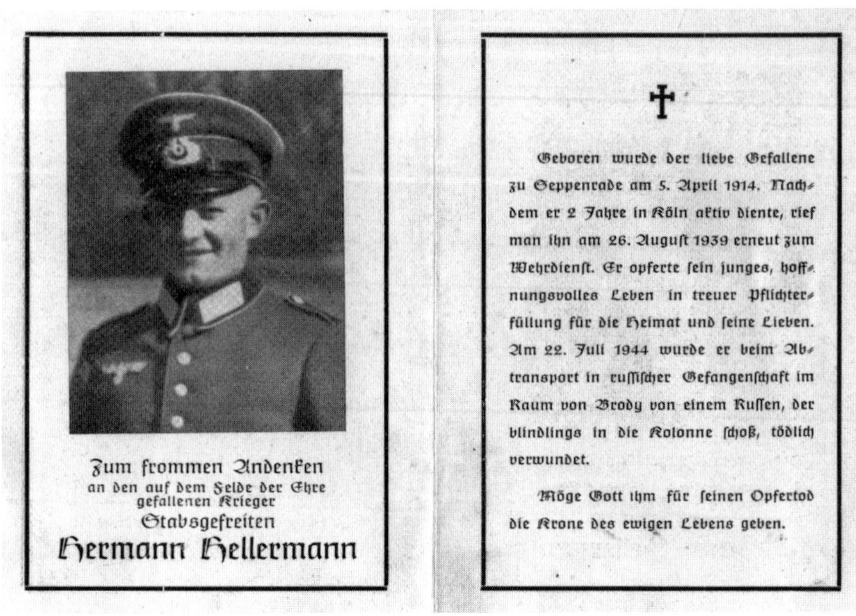

Zum frommen Andenken
an den auf dem Felde der Ehre gefallenen Krieger
Stabsgefreiten
Hermann Hellermann

†

Geboren wurde der liebe Gefallene zu Seppenrade am 5. April 1914. Nachdem er 2 Jahre in Köln aktiv diente, rief man ihn am 26. August 1939 erneut zum Wehrdienst. Er opferte sein junges, hoffnungsvolles Leben in treuer Pflichterfüllung für die Heimat und seine Lieben. Am 22. Juli 1944 wurde er beim Abtransport in russischer Gefangenschaft im Raum von Brody von einem Russen, der blindlings in die Kolonne schoß, tödlich verwundet.

Möge Gott ihm für seinen Opfertod die Krone des ewigen Lebens geben.

Poland—July 22, 1944—Killed in POW Transport
The deathcard notation states that 30-year Lance Corporal Hermann Hellermann began his military service on August 26, 1939, just a few days prior to Germany's invasion of Poland and that he served his country faithfully. His death reportedly occurred while being transported to a Soviet POW camp in Raum near Brody in Poland. The card's text reports that a Russian guard shot randomly into the crowd of prisoners, fatally wounding Hellermann.

He may have been among the thousands captured in July by the Soviets as Minsk was liberated, the German Army Group Centre virtually destroyed with losses of over 200,000 men. The Polish cities of Vilna and Lvov were also liberated as Russian forces approached East Prussia. Two days prior to Kellerman's death, on July 20th, German military officers led by Colonel Claus von Stauffenberg failed in their attempt to assassinate Hitler at his Rastenberg East Prussian headquarters, the so-called Wolf's Lair.

Lithuania—August 9, 1944—"Shot in the Throat"—"Honor his Memory!" (*above left*)
Ludwig Traurig, a farmer's son from the Bavarian town of Prünst was killed in action at age 24. According to the notes supplied on his memorial card, he had been shot in the throat and "buried in the street" near Schacken in Lithuania. Schacken was the German name for the Lithuanian city of Saiki located 45 miles west of Kaunas. It is also the location of a mass grave of 4,000 Jews executed after Lithuania was invaded in 1941. By the summer of 1944, Soviet forces had begun their assault on the area.

A week earlier, on August 1st, Polish Army and resistance fighters began the 63-day Warsaw uprising which failed when Stalin deliberately withheld Soviet military support. As a result, 18,000 Polish soldiers and more than 150,000 civilians were killed by German forces.

Finland—Enemies at Both Gates (*above right*)
Soviet invaders during the 1939–1940 100-day "Winter War" preceded the German invasion of the USSR in 1941. The Russians found the outnumbered Finns steadfast in their resistance, thwarting the aggressors in great part. In the early phase of the war, the Russians suffered 27,000 KIA contrasting to the 2,700 Finnish casualties, a ratio of ten to one. The government, to avoid further deaths, capitulated to Russian demands for the annexation of Finish territory.

Top of next page:

German Ski Trooper and Finland's Quota Unfilled
During the infamous Wannsee Conference of January 20, 1942 in which the Final Solution was articulated by Heydrich and Eichmann, Nazi officials examined the problem of disposing of 11,000,000 European Jews. They meticulously listed each country and their Jewish population. Finland was found to have 2,300 Jews. Although an ally of Germany in its war against the Soviets, the Finns protected their small Jewish population. At the end of the war, the death count was 17. The remainder of Finnish Jews survived the Holocaust.

Unwanted War

The Sami people for thousands of years led a peaceful, nomadic existence traveling with their herds through remote areas of Finland, Sweden, Norway and Russia. Though they never sought a separate homeland, the war caused cross-national border warfare that found them fighting against their own people depending where they happened to be, Axis or Allied territory. Adapted to the extreme landscape and expert skiers they were recruited by all sides for long distance reconnaissance.

After fighting the Russians, the Norwegian Sami found themselves fighting the Germans who invaded the country in April 1940, eventually forcing the Sami to serve them. The Finns, now allied with the Germans, fought the Russians who previously extracted territory from them. At this point Russian Sami were fighting Finnish Sami. Sami POWs in German prison camps suffered harsh treatment and their culture felt the effects of the German scorched earth policy directed against their lands, herds and villages. 60,000 Sami remained as refugees in Sweden unable return to their homelands until after the war.

Zum Gedenken

an unseren zweiten unvergeßlichen Sohn, bzw. Bruder, Schwager und Onkel

Leopold Schiel

Obergefreiter in einem Grenadierregiment, Inhaber des Inftr.-Sturmabzeichens in Silber und des Verwundetenabzeichens in Schwarz,

gefallen am 14. September 1944 im Kandalakscha-Abschnitt in Nordfinnland, im 22. Lebensjahre.

So plötzlich kam die Trauerkunde,
Gebrochen sei Dein gutes Herz.
Mein Gott, wie schwer war diese Stunde,
Wie unaussprechlich, groß der Schmerz.
Auf Wiedersehn! so stand in jedem Briefe,
Auf jeder Karte, die Du schriebst,
Du bist zu früh von uns geschieden,
Und läßt im Schmerz uns nun allein zurück.

M. F. Lenk, Znaim

Finland—Leopold Schiel—September 14, 1944—Reversal of Fortunes

Corporal Schiel, a grenadier, had earned the Infantry Combat Award in Silver and the Wound Badge in Black before he was KIA at the age of 21 in northern Finland. After Soviet troops, driving toward Berlin, incurred heavy casualties fighting the Finns, Moscow opted for a ceasefire on September 4, 1944, followed by an armistice on September 19. The agreement called for Finland to expel its previous German allies resulting in the so-called Lapland War. Therefore it is possible Schiel was killed not by Red soldiers but by the Finns.

Yugoslavia/Croatia/Serbia—Saluting the Occupiers

Civilians in national dress parade before their fellow citizens at an early point in the German invasion and occupation that began on April 6, 1941. The country was divided, often violently, between ethnic, religious, pro-fascist, pro-national and pro-communist forces. Pro-fascist Croatia had joined the Axis on June 15, 1941, a week before the invasion of the Soviet Union. As a satellite state ruled by the brutal *Ustaša* (Ustasha), its leadership and members were responsible for the murder of half a million people, another 200,000 forced to convert to Catholicism.

Zum Andenken
an meinen lieben Gatten und Vater

Franz Herlt
Jungbauer
Uffz. u. Troßführer in einem Infant.-Reg.
geboren am 11. 9. 1906
gefallen am 29. 7. 1944
in einem Gefecht bei Leskovač (Serbien).

Du gabst dein junges Leben,
Und ich mein ganzes Glück.

Serbia—"In Memory of My Dear Husband and Father"—KIA July 29, 1944 (*above left*)

Some six weeks before his 38th birthday, and serving as an infantry sergeant and troop leader, farmer Franz Herlt was killed in battle. According to the German graves reclamation organization, he still lies buried near Leskovac, the town located in southern Serbia with a history traced back to the 8th century BC.

By 1944, Partisan attacks had pushed German forces from the Leskovac area, but not before some 300 Roma civilians were executed in reprisal for the anti-German guerrilla warfare. American Allied forces, in an operation called "Operation Ratweek" attempted to use air-strikes against the fleeing German divisions thought to be hiding in Leskovac. On September 6th, 1944, some 50 American B-29 aircraft bombed the city. While some German forces were destroyed, reports estimate that some 2,500–4,000 Leskovac civilians were unintentionally killed, with over 1,840 of the city's buildings leveled.

Croatia—SS Leader Artur Gustav Martin-Phleps—KIA September 1944 (*above right*)

Phleps, born in Romania, served in the First World War and the Second World War in the Austro-Hungarian, Romanian and German armies, eventually becoming a lieutenant general in the Waffen-SS. He led elements of motorized and mountain troops including the SS Handschar Division made up of Croatian volunteers. While in Yugoslavia Phleps and his 7th SS Prinz Eugen and V SS commands committed atrocities against civilians of Croatia, Serbia and Montenegro as well against partisans. He was eventually killed by Red Army troops in September 1944.

Gedenket im Gebete

an den Obergefreiten

Johann Grabner

welcher am 16. Dezember 1944
in Kroatien im 31. Lebens-
jahre gefallen ist.

Die Kugel, die dich niederwarf,
Sie traf auch mich ins Herz;
Doch eines Helden Gattin darf
Nicht untergehn im Schmerz.
Die Kraft, die dich im Kampf gestählt,
Sie sei mein Halt in Not,
Der Trost des Wiedersehens hält
Mich aufrecht bis zum Tod.

Druck: H. Zauner Lambach

Croatia—Saturday December 16, 1944

A few terse few words record the death of Corporal Johann Grabner. At this point in the war, tens of thousands of German soldiers are dying weekly, the printing presses running overtime to produce deathcards.

On this same Saturday, hundreds of miles distant, Hitler launched his last ditch effort through the Ardennes (the Battle of the Bulge) in an attempt to split British and American forces. Employing two panzer armies and 300,000 troops, the surprise attack was initially successful but faltered and failed, due in part to lack of fuel and the clearing of the weather allowing for Allied aircraft to take action. It was effectively the last large offensive action taken by the Germany military. On the day, December 16, 1944, George Marshall became the first American general to be promoted to 5-star rank, assuming the newly created position of General of the Army.

Hungary—German and Hungarian Soldiers at Railyard—September 1944

The *Reichsbahn* cattle car behind them bears stamps indicating its original point of origin was Posen/Pozen, Poland.

In the West, four months after the D-Day landings at Normandy, the Allies thrust forward having established a solid front from the English Channel to Switzerland, much of France liberated and Allied forces now targeting the German "Siegfried Line" aka The West Wall with its miles of "dragon's teeth" anti-tank obstacles and some 16,000 bunkers and pill boxes.

Six months previously, on March 19, 1944 German forces had occupied their former Hungarian ally, to prevent collaboration with Soviet forces, and also intent on a primary target, its 725,000 Jewish inhabitants, the last large population left in Europe. By mid-July, under SS Colonel Eichmann's orchestration, 430,000 men, women and children had been transported by cattle cars to Auschwitz, 75 percent gassed immediately upon arrival, the crematoria working non-stop.

Gebetsandenken
an meinen lieben
Gatten unsern lieb.
Sohn u. Bruder
Unteroffizier
i. e. Geb.-Jäg.-Regt.

Martin Auerhammer

Inh. d. E. K. 2 u. verschied. Auszeich.

geb. am 19. 6. 1916 in Walleshausen
gef. a. 12. 12. 44. i. Losak | Ungarn

Er zog von uns mit leichtem Herzen
Er hoffte auf ein Wiederseh'n,
Doch größer sind nun uns're Schmerzen
Da dieses kann nicht mehr gescheh'n.
Die Kugel die dich hat getroffen,
Die traf auch uns ins Herz.
Du warst so gut, starbst viel zu früh
Solch braves Herz vergißt man nie.
So schlaf denn wohl in fremder Erde
Bis zu dem großen Aufersteh'n.
Hier sollst Du nicht vergessen werden
Bis wir uns droben wiederseh'n.

Vater unser. Ave Maria.

Heinz Blank

* 22. April 1927 + 13. Oktober 1944

Ein junges Leben geht dahin –
Herr, gib ihm die ewige Ruhe!

Hungary—12.12.44—Warsaw within Sight (*above left*)
A sergeant in the Mountain Troops (*Gebirgsjäger*), Martin Auerhammer, awarded the Iron Cross 2nd Class, was killed in action in Losak, Hungary. On this same day, December 12th, Soviet forces captured the strategic railway junction and town of Gödöllő, only ten miles north of Budapest and announced the imminent fall of the Hungarian capital. On the Western Front, the U.S. 1st Army was engaged in the fierce fighting taking place in the Hürtgen Forest near the strategic German city of Aachen.

Location Unknown (*above right*)
Blank translates from the German into "bright or clean." The 17-year old's memorial card shows only his name, birth date, day of death, October 13, 1944 and a short invocation: "A young life is given-God, please give eternal peace."

The omission of cause of death, by illness, Allied bombing or military service or even the location makes it both highly personal as well as a universal statement about the war is in its final months of mounting attrition, the old and young relentlessly thrown into the maw of death.

Kriegsmariners—Photo dated November 19, 1942
Ten days prior to the taking of the snapshot, the Russian counter-attack at Stalingrad had begun sealing the fate of the vaunted German 6th Army. Earlier on September 12, some 500 miles off the coast of West Africa, *Unterseeboot* 156 fired two torpedoes into what was thought to be a British troopship. It was indeed a converted ex-Cunard Star ocean liner, the RMS *Laconia*, and now fitted with deck guns and depth charges, thus a legitimate military target. However, among the 2,732 passengers were some 1,800 Italian prisoners of war on their way to POW camps in Canada, as well as 285 British troops, 160 Polish guards, 138 crew and 80 civilians including women and children. After the ship had fallen beneath the waves, the U-boat's commander Captain Werner Hartenstein, guided by the then current practice of rescuing survivors of sinkings, and having realized he had sunk a ship full of Italian allies, set a rescue effort in motion. In plain English language, he broadcasted messages seeking aid from any other vessels in the area. He also announced a cessation of hostilities, and eventually remained in the area for two and half days. Two more German submarines (U-506 and 507) along with an Italian submarine (the *Cappelini*) rallied to the cause, arriving on September 15. Towing 200 survivors in several lifeboats with hundreds more standing on their decks as well as many civilians crammed inside the submarines, they headed for the African coast to rendezvous with Vichy French rescue ships. However on the next morning, the flotilla, draped with Red Cross banners, was spotted by a U.S. Air Force B-24 Liberator bomber. The survivors waved and the U-boats signaled for help. The pilot flew off and reported the scene, but returned after being ordered to attack. The survivors thought the plane has returned with supplies. Instead they were met with bombs and depth-charges. Hundreds died when one bomb landed amidst the lifeboats. Forced to submerge, the survivors riding the decks were thrown into the sea. The death toll was lessened when the Vichy ships arrived on the scene the next day and plucked survivors from the waters.

While 1,111 of the Laconia passengers were rescued, another 1,619, mostly Italian POWs, died. As a result of the attack, German submariners were thereafter ordered not to engage in rescue attempts. Hartenstein would eventually be credited with 19 ships sunk and awarded the Knights Cross on September 17, 1942. It was on the U-156's fourth sea tour that the "Laconia Incident" occurred. On March 8, 1943 during her next mission, the U-156 was sunk east of Barbados by a U.S. Navy aircraft with all hands lost.

River of Coffins—Kriegsmarine Mass Grave

Hundreds of German naval personnel from the heavy cruiser *Blücher* are buried in the earth far from their fate in Norwegian waters. Mourners arrange memorial wreaths along with the Kriegsmarine battle flag.

In many ways, the loss of the heavy cruiser *Blücher*, just six months after its commission, was due to German arrogance. Showing disdain for the Norwegian shore defenses when entering the fiord at Drøbak Sound on April, 9, 1940 during the first day of the invasion of Norway, the ship kept its heavy guns pointed fore and aft and therefore unable to fire on the Norwegian coastal installations that then fired, disabling the *Blücher*'s main guns. The Norwegian artillery consisted of obsolete 11-inch guns installed in 1893, and ironically of German Krupp manufacture. There were three guns—ironic also in their nicknames—Joshua, Moses and Josva—but only two were manned when the Germans attacked, and those by 30 young, untrained recruits, but enough to help seal the fate of the *Blücher* which they severely damaged. When struck by other coastal guns and torpedoes, she sank following the explosion of its munitions resulting in the tremendous loss of life.

The *Blücher* was the flagship of the Kriegsmarine flotilla *Marine Gruppen 5* and had led the naval invasion of Norway. In addition to its 1202 member crew, the *Blücher* carried 1000 troops scheduled for landing on shore. Some 500 of the troops died in the flaming oil or by drowning, another 320 sailors perishing. It was a standing order for the seamen to relinquish their life preservers to the land troops who might not be able to swim.

The unexpected loss of the *Blücher* and damage to other German naval ships caused a delay in the occupation of Oslo which in turn provided time for the Norwegian Royal family and parliament members to escape as well as to transport Norway's gold reserves safe from German grasp.

Downed Flyer—Floating Gravesite

Aboard a motor launch, a contingent of Luftwaffe personnel salutes a comrade, apparently his plane lost at sea and thus a watery grave.

Frozen Land and Sea
German soldiers, their rifles stacked, huddle in a group by the ice bound seashore.
Accurately forecasting weather patterns were strategic to German military operations especially during the late war period as the Allies pushed toward Germany's borders. The source of meteorological information relative to Europe were weather stations near Greenland in the Polar Seas. U.S. Coast Guard patrols destroyed several of the weather stations.

In early September 1944 three new German weather expedition groups were sent into the area but encountered the new class of U.S. "icebreakers" which captured the German scientists and support teams in their camps as well as an entire German ship thought by its crew to be permanently stuck in the ice. However the Americans were able to free it as a war prize, all accomplished with no casualties on either side.

Landlocked Soldiers—German Naval Marines in Training—June 1939

Gebets- ✠ Andenken

an meinen lieben, unvergeßl. Gatten, unſerer guten Vater, Sohn und Bruder

Josef Biebl

Obergefr. in einer Marine-Einheit,
Schneider von Mietraching,

welcher am 9. Febr. 1945 bei den ſchweren Kämpfen in Oſtpreußen nach 4jähriger treuer ſold. Pflichterfüllung im Alter von 37 Jahren ſein Leben für ſeine geliebte Heimat opferte

Heiß beweint von deinen Lieben,
Die gebeugt von Leid und Gram,
Biſt du in der Schlacht geblieben,
Die dich in den Himmel nahm.

Ach, es iſt ja kaum zu faſſen,
Daß Du nicht mehr kehrſt zurück;
So jung mußteſt Du Dein Leben laſſen
Zerſtört iſt unſer aller Glück.

February 9, 1945—German Marine

During the very last weeks of the war, Naval Marine Corporal Josef Biebl, 37, a tailor from the small village of Mietraching, was killed in action in East Prussia, after four years of "faithful" service to his homeland. It is possible that he was involved in the Kriegsmarine efforts to evacuate German troops from the area as they had been surrounded in the Baltic ports of Danzig by Soviet forces.

Lazarett-schiff »Wilhelm Gustloff«

Links: **Kamerad aus Nord und Süd,** beide verdiente Narvik-Kämpfer mit dem EK, kehren an Bord des Lazarettschiffs heim

Die Reise geht weiter. Ganz in der Nähe des Lazarettschiffs wartet der Zug, der die verwundeten Kämpfer aus dem Norden weiterbefördern wird

Links: **Im deutschen Hafen** wurden die Verwundeten durch Sanitätssoldaten behutsam von Bord gebracht. Schon auf der Seereise unter bester Betreuung durch Ärzte und Pfleger begann die Genesung

Rechts: **Der Geschwaderarzt** geht noch einmal persönlich durch den Lazarettzug, ehe dieser dem Ziel entgegenrollt

Links: **Die Bordschwester** als die treue Helferin der Verwundeten auf der Überfahrt erhält den letzten Händedruck ihres Schützlings

The Hospital Ship *Wilhelm Gustloff*—Greatest Ever Loss of Life at Sea

As profiled in the July 31, 1940 issue of the weekly news magazine *Die Woche*, the ship is portrayed as administering to German troops wounded in the Western campaigns including the invasion of France begun in June of that year.

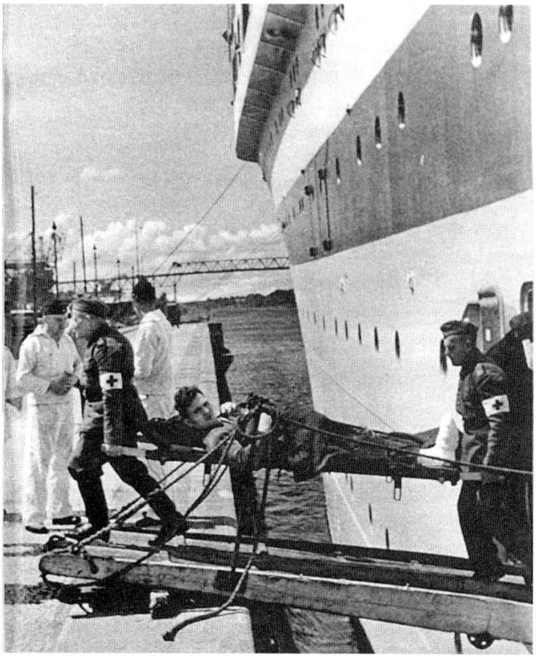

Disembarking

A converted luxury cruise ship, the *Wilhelm Gustloff* had been named for an assassinated Nazi official in Switzerland. While transporting as many as 8–10,000 civilian refugees and wounded German soldiers fleeing the Red Army's advance on East Prussia, it was sailing toward Kiel when sunk 20 miles offshore by a Soviet submarine on the night of January 30, 1945. In less than an hour it disappeared beneath the frigid 150 foot-deep waters. An estimated 9,400 died, mostly women and children. Later, on April 17, 1945, another transport ship, the *Goya*, also carrying many women and children as well as German troops, was also sunk by a Soviet submarine off the Baltic coast. Sinking in four minutes, it claimed some 7,000 lives, thus, along with the *Wilhelm Gustloff*, the two greatest losses of life at sea.

FROZEN DEATHS

Burial without Burial

A German soldier, his uniform sleeve showing a cuff-title indicating membership in an elite group, lies frozen in death on a snow-covered Russian field, more bodies scattered in the background. 80 percent of all Third Reich troops killed during the entire war fell to the Soviets.

By war's end an estimated 4,932,000 German soldiers had made the ultimate sacrifice for the Fatherland. Of some 3,000,000 Germans and Axis allies who became Soviet POWs in the NKVD-administered camps, the Russians themselves stated that 381,067 died.

Russia's Icy Graveyard

Beneath a "Greater Germany" Iron Cross lies the body of a Corporal Grochol, a member of the Regimental Staff for Infantry Regiment 82. He was killed in action on a summer day August 13, 1942, months before the snows fell on his grave in Russia. It is possible that he died during the German Sixth's Army advance into the Stalingrad area that took place in that month.

Darum still, darum still,
füg ich mich wie Gott es will.

Nun ruhe sanft Du tapf'rer Held,
Geblieben auf dem Feld der Ehre,
Dein Lohn sei in der bess'ren Welt,
Inmitten aller Engel Chöre.
Wir alle zum Lenker der Schlachten flehn,
O, gib uns Herr ein Wiedersehen!

Führ mich zum Berg der Herrlichkeit,
Zu Deiner Heilgen Zahl,
Wo ewig, ewig ist bereit,
Des Lammes Hochzeitsmahl.

Zum steten Andenken
an unsern lieben, immer frohen

Fritz.

Er war geboren am 16. 2. 1914 in Hackenheim. Am 21. 3. 42 schloß er vor dem Altare seiner Heimatkirche den Bund fürs Leben. Hier sprach er das inhaltsschwere Wort: „Ich gelobe Dir Treue und schützende Liebe bis der Tod uns scheidet." Nur ganz kurz währte unser junges Eheglück. An unserem 4. Hochzeitstage am 21. 3. 45 ließ er im Kampfe um Deutsche Heimaterde sein junges Leben für uns alle.
Seine junge Gattin und alle, die ihn lieb haben, finden Trost in dem Gedanken, daß der junge Kämpfer den ewigen Frieden gefunden und der Herrgott ihn gerufen habe zum ewigen Hochzeitsmahle.
Um ein stilles Gebet für den lieben Gefallenen bittet im Namen aller:

Frau Johanna Theos
geb. Bubach.

March 1942–March 1945—"Fritz"

His wife, Frau Johanna Theos, has simply placed her husband's first name on the memorial card. She also writes that he spoke the following words to her. "I vow you loyalty, protection and love until death do us part." The occasion was their wedding on March 3, 1942, in their Rhineland city of Hackenheim's church. It would be the last time she would see him. Four days after the ceremony, Fritz Theos returned to the battle front and remained there. Almost three years to the day of his marriage, he was killed near the end of the war on March 21, 1945. Two weeks earlier, on March 7th, the pivotal crossing of the Rhine into Germany took place when the bridge at Remagen was discovered intact, allowing U.S. forces entry into the Third Reich.

Old Graves Re-Visited—Sierpów—1943

At a grave site in the central Poland village of Sierpów, near Łódź, German soldiers who had died fighting Polish troops during the 1939 invasion were exhumed for reburial. A German policeman, cigarette in hand, ponders one of the corpses, its uniform insignia indicating the individual was a corporal. The civilian standing man wears an armband identifying him as a Polish volunteer.

The village of Sierpów, located some four miles north of Ozorków, was renamed Brunnstadt during the1943–45 German occupation. A third of its population was Jewish, its two historic synagogues were burnt by German troops who then forced the surviving Jews to demolish the remaining walls. Over 5,000 were eventually killed or sent to death camps, including all children below the age of ten.

Götterdämmerung:
The Funeral Pyres of the Third Reich

The Lost Seeking the Lost

The rubble of a destroyed German city serves as a message board for lost family members seeking each other amidst the devastation. Some names are chalked in the form of memorials, others indicate new addresses of refuge, for example "the family Stolz has relocated to Potsdam." (The collectible card published post-war in West Germany in a series titled, *The Second World War in Pictures*).

An estimated 410,000 (perhaps as many as 600,000) German civilians died as the result of American and British carpet bombing of German cities, towns and villages in effort to break the will of the population and the German military machine.

The statistics on the bombing of Germany as recorded by the RAF during the period of October 1939–May 1945 included 500,000 tons of high explosives, incendiary and fragmentation ordinance directed against 61 German towns and cities with a population of 100,000 or more, in total some 25 million people or 32 percent of the country's population. This includes low level attacks on an unknown number of smaller towns and villages.

The statistics of one raid that took place on February 25, 1945 against Munich was summed up in a local German police report: In the two-and-a-half hour attack, 5,000–6,000 heavy bombs, 250,000 incendiary bombs and also some 20,000 leaflets fell on the city.

On March 21, 1945 Berlin was bombed for the 30th night in a row, on that occasion some 1,300 aircraft attacked the city's airfields. As Soviet forces completed their ground assault on Berlin in the last week of April 1945, Hitler ordered the flooding of the city's underground railway tunnels through which the Red Army troops were advancing, but also where thousands of German civilians and wounded soldiers had sought shelter, a fact well-known to Hitler and his subordinates. The locks of the River Spree were opened, the waters rushing through the tunnels with fatal results.

According to the U.S. Bombing Survey prepared in September 1945, the operation of Allied air forces in the European theater involved 28,000 aircraft and 1,335,000 personnel. They took part in more than 1,440,000 bombing runs and 2,680,000 fighter sorties; numbers difficult to grasp. The air war against Germany cost the U.S. 18,000 aircraft and 79,625 deaths while British losses were chillingly very similar, some 22,000 aircraft and 79,281 men lost.

NAZI HANGED— Three Yanks stand around the body of a German who was hanged in a side street of Aschaffenburg, supposedly because he wanted to surrender to the Seventh American Army units attacking the town. A placard pasted on the wall (center), states: "Cowards and traitors hanged! Yesterday an officer candidate from Alsace Lorraine died a hero's death while destroying an enemy tank. He lives on! Today, a coward in officer's garb is hanged because he betrayed the Fuehrer and the people . . . he is dead forever." The Yank at center looks up at spot from which the Nazi was hanged.

Associated Press Wirephoto via Signal Corps Radio.

April 1945—U.S. Newspapers Carry Image of Executed German Soldier

Special punitive squads scoured German cities for deserters and "defeatists" then conducted summary executions, bodies left hanging from lamp posts and balconies as a warning to others.

This execution took place in the city of Aschaffenburg, the largest Bavarian city on the lower Main River. It served as a transportation hub and center for the manufacture of German uniforms. During March–April, 1945, the city was shelled reportedly by three U.S. tanks firing from an overlooking hill. 70 percent of the town was destroyed with a loss of 60 percent of its population. Such was the intensity of the fighting that Secretary of War Henry Stimson stated the following at an April 7, 1945 news conference, his comments relating directly to the newspaper article seen here.

> There is a lesson to be learned to fighting to the end at Aschaffenburg. There Nazi fanatics used the visible threat of two hangings to compel German soldiers and civilians to fight for a week. After a week of fighting, during which the city was reduced to rubble and many Germans lost their lives, the inevitable took place and the fanatics ran up the white flag and surrendered to our veteran 45th Infantry Division.

A reportedly 33,000 Germans were executed by their own military, mostly for desertion which increased dramatically in the last four months of the war as German soldiers sought to escape the ever-escalating and pointless carnage with 300,000–400,000 dying each month.

Top of next page:

April 5, 1945—Würzburg

A U.S. Signal Corp Photo by Sergeant Robert Stubenbaugh dated April 5, 1945, a month before war's end, contained the following caption:

> Infantrymen in background searching building send three men and two women who they found hiding in cellars down the street to their buddies for removal from besieged city. They seem happy to be out of the fighting. (222nd Infantry Regiment, 42nd Division, XXI Corps, 7th Army.

On March 16, 2005 Würzburg commemorated the 60th anniversary of its Second World War bombing by the RAF's elite squadron Group Number 5. Regarded as "precision bombers" having previously struck Heilbronn, Darmstadt, Braunschweig, Munich and Kassel, 236 of the squadron's aircraft reached Würzburg at 9:30 p.m. dropping an estimated 350,000 incendiary bombs resulting in a firestorm with temperatures exceeding 1,000 degrees Celsius. Of the reported 5,000 killed, over 3,700 were women and children. Würzburg, of historical but little military value, had been added to the list for bombing because it had a population over 100,000, the standard set by RAF Air Marshal "Bomber" Harris in order to wear down Nazi Germany's resistance and bring about end of the Third Reich.

Child Gunners

Boys of the *HJ* man a mobile 20 mm AA gun guarding an industrial area. No amount of German anti-aircraft defense could stem the waves of American and British bombers raining high explosives and incendiaries over German military targets and metropolitan centers. Many *HJ* boys and girls remained at their posts, perishing at the expense of the Nazi leadership's order to fight "to the bitter end."

Gebetsandenken

an unseren lieben unvergeßlichen
Sohn und Bruder

Paul Brunner

Zimmermannssohn von Niederwinkling
Soldat in einem Flack-Regiment

welcher am 6. April 1945, infolge schwerer Verwundung sein junges Leben von erst 17 Jahren und 2. Monaten für seine geliebte Heimat lassen mußte.

Er ruht in Seligenstadt bei Hanau

R. I. P.

Barmherziger Jesus gib ihm die ewige Ruhe!

Betet Brüder, daß mein und euer Opfer Gott wohlgefalle.

Flieger

Clemens Mayr

geb. am 16. Nov. 1927 in München

gefallen am 30. April 1945
bei Canov in Mecklenburg

Late Casualty—Flak Soldier—April 6, 1945 (*above left*)

On April 6, 1945, one month before Germany surrendered, flak soldier Paul Brunner, a carpenter's son from Rieberwintling, was killed in action. He was buried in Seligenstadt near Hanover. His age was listed very precisely by his parents as 17 years two months.

Three weeks later, the Red Army began its attack on Berlin. On the 28th, Mussolini was executed by Italian partisans. On the 29th, Hitler married Eva Braun in the *Führerbunker*, followed by their joint suicide.

In the last days of the war, Hitler Youth boys of 14 years or even younger manned some of the last defensive positions including Berlin's bridges. On May 3, an officer of the 57th Panzer Division noted in his diary:

> At dawn, attack on the bridge across the Havel at Spandau. The bridge is captured. It can only be crossed by jumping. But desperation drives a vast mass of refugees of all ages on to it. They drop off in whole rows. The last serviceable tanks and lorries pave a grisly path through confused heaps of human bodies. The bridge is swimming in blood.

April 30, 1945—"Flyer"—A Week before War's End (*above right*)

The family of Clemens Mayr has chosen a childhood photo for his memorial card which shows only Christian imagery and prayers and no image or mention of the Third Reich's cult of death except indirectly via a quotation that reads, "When a soldier takes God with him into battle and falls in the fulfillment of his duty, then he falls in the Army of God."

Mayr is described on the card as a *Flieger* and may have been a young Luftwaffe pilot or cadet. By this date, the vaunted German air force had been destroyed; its last pilots literally boys given minimal training. He died at the age of 17 in the Mecklenburg region of Bavaria, on the very day that Adolf Hitler committed suicide in his Berlin bunker and a week before the end of the war in Europe, Germany officially surrendering to the Allies on May 7, the fighting ceasing on May 8.

"*Ein Volk Steht Auf*"—One Folk Rises Up

The last postage stamp to be issued by the Third Reich depicts the alliance between the regular Wehrmacht, Hitler Youth and the *Volkssturm*, prophesized to win the war at the last moment.

In the final weeks of the war, especially in the last ditch defense of Berlin against Soviet forces, over 200,000 old men and young boys perished. Only when Germany was completely overrun by Allied troops, Hitler dead, Berlin captured and reduced to rubble as were most German cities and towns, did the Third Reich military leaders finally surrender after sending more than a million German men and boys to their deaths in the last few months of a war already long lost.

Death on the Day after the War Ended—May 9, 1945—Zeitlarn

A 45-year old corporal fighting with his local Volkssturm home defense battalion, Josef Högn, previously a landlord from the Bavarian town of Zeitlarn, died in hospital from his wounds on May 9, 1945, two days after the Allies accepted the unconditional surrender of German forces and the official end of the Second World War in Europe, and one day after fighting had formally ended … for the most part … pockets of resistance still holding out.

An incident that occurred in Zeitlarn in the very last days of the Third Reich was symptomatic of murderous Nazi fanaticism. On the night of April 25–26, 1945, some two weeks prior to Högn's fatal wounds, members of the Waffen SS under the command of a Major Pflaum forced 25 Russian POW officers, slave laborers at a local quarry, to lie face down in a truck then drove them to a nearby forest at which point they were made to dig their own graves. Pflaum and his Waffen-SS comrades then shot them. The story was unearthed by Anna Elisabeth Rosmus in her book *Wintergreen-Suppressed Murders*.

Zum Gebetsgedenken an

Josef Högn

Hausbesitzer von Zeitlarn

Obergefr. in einem Landessch.-Btl.

welcher am 9. Mai 1945 im Alter von 45 Jahren, im Lazarett Andernach/Rhein für sein Vaterland gestorben ist.

O Herr, gib ihm die ewige Ruhe!

Buchdruckerei Erdl, Vilshofen.

Den Heldentod auf der Jnsel Texel
starb unser lieber Sohn und Bruder
Franz Achatz
Landwirts-Sohn v. **Auerbach**
Gefr. u. Gefchützführ. einerKüften-Batt.
gefallen19. April 1943 infolge Unglücks-
falles im Blütenalter von 23 Jahren.

Dein Grab im fernen Feindesland
Jst uns wohl eine schwere Pein
Doch nimm das Wort z. Unterpfand
Dein Grab soll nicht verlassen sein
All Abend wenn die Glocken klingen
Zieht betend unser Geist dorthin
Streut Dir liebend Andachtsblumen
Aufs Heldengrab mit frohen Sinn.

Druck: Anton Lackerbauer, Regen, Tel. 78

Died a "Hero's Death" on an Island —The Last Battle of the Second World War in Europe
Franz Achatz appears with a uniform drawn over a civilian photo. He was a landowner's son from the city of Auerbach located in Lower Silesia. Auerbach, meaning "floodmeadow waters," was also the site of the Birkenheim slave labor camp, a satellite of the Organisation Schmelt network set up in Lower Silesia.

Achatz had attained the rank of gun commander of a coastal battery on the German occupied Dutch island of Texel. He apparently died three months after "falling ill to a blood disorder," his passing recorded on April 19, 1943.

The gun commander would not live to see the fate that befell Texel two years later in the last days of the war. The island was fortified as part of the Germans' *Westvall* defensive line. Along with German troops there was a large contingent of Russian ex-POWs from the Georgian Republic (Stalin's birthplace). They had joined the German army in order to escape the POW camps which were basically death camps. Some also were anti-Stalinists as well. But as the war entered its last weeks, Nazi Germany's defeat certain, the Georgians had a change of heart.

Early on the morning of April 6, 1945 (a month before the war in Europe ended), they attacked with knife and bayonet some 400 of their sleeping German ex-comrades, killing them all. However, after alerted to the threat from within, the German coastal gun emplacements were able to hold off the Georgian re-defectors until German reinforcements arrived. The ensuing carnage took its toll on both the combatants and the townsfolk. Canadian troops eventually secured the island, however the fighting extended after the official German mainland surrender, thus earning it the onus as the last battle of the Second World War in Europe. The fate of the Georgian survivors turned over to the Soviets was in keeping with Stalin's dictum about "traitors."

On the day on Achatz's death from some unidentified illness, on the Eastern Front, far from Texel, the battle at the Kuban Peninsula between German and Soviet forces was raging. Also on this day German troops under Himmler's orders began the annihilation of the Warsaw Ghetto as the poorly armed Jews rose up in revolt, at least 56,000 dying. The SS was confident it would crush the resistance in three days, but it took several weeks and some 1,00 German casualties.

May 7, 1945—Protracted Deaths in Yugoslavia (*top of next page*)
Georg Radlsbeck, age 37, a corporal and a medic, died on the day that German forces surrendered unconditionally to the Allies, the document signed by the German General Alfred Jodl in the French city of Reims some 80 miles from Paris.

Soviet forces had entered Yugoslavia several months previously, liberating the capital, Belgrade, on October 10, 1944. In addition to Red Army troops, the Germans faced fierce partisan resistance including the forces of communist leader Tito. The fighting between them and German troops as well as other opposing national forces were particularly brutal. In addition, some 60,000 of Yugoslavia's Jewish inhabitants perished.

While the guns officially fell silent a day after the surrender papers were signed by the Germans at 2:41 a.m. early Monday morning May 7, German forces in Yugoslavia kept fighting until May 15, 1945, perhaps knowing their fate if falling into partisan or Soviet hands. Very likely, the corporal medic was one of the last to die after the war officially ended.

†

Gebetserinnerung
an meinen lieben Gatten,
treubesorgten Vater, Sohn
und Bruder Herrn

Georg Radlsbeck

Obergefreiter in einer San.-Einheit
Landwirtssohn v. Weitfeld b. Walchsin

welcher am 7. 5. 1945 in
Bistrica bei Villa del Nevoso
(Jugoslavien) im Alter von
37 Jahren gestorben ist.

Er ruhe in Frieden!

Herr, gib ihm die ewige Ruhe!
(300 Tage Ablaß.)

Karl Lehr, Passau

Ihr Sternlein, euch leer ich mein Herz nur aus
Ihr bringt meine Wünsche wohl gerne nach Haus
Sagt meiner Gattin, sie ahnt es wohl kaum,
Daß an sie jetzt denkt, ihr sterbender Mann.
Sagt den Eltern, den Geschwistern,
daß das Auge mir bricht
Vor d. Feind muß ich sterben, vergeßt mich nicht
Ihr Sternlein, ihr habt meine Wünsche gehört
Bringt sie der Heimat, euch seis nicht verwehrt.
Bringt den letzten Gruß in mein Heim
das ich nimmer kann sehn
Sagt meiner Gattin und Kinder, Lebewohl
Auf Wiedersehn!

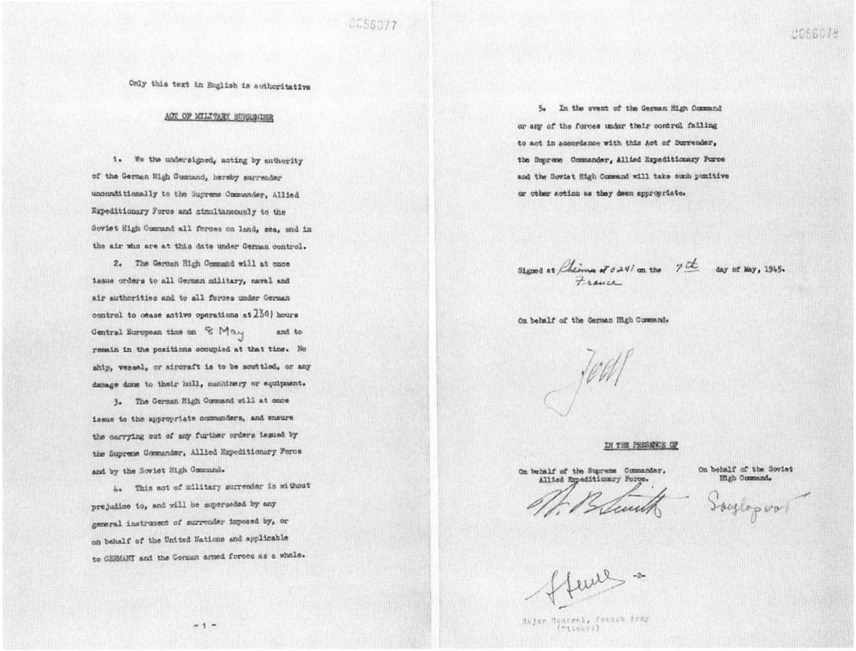

0056077

Only this text in English is authoritative

ACT OF MILITARY SURRENDER

1. We the undersigned, acting by authority of the German High Command, hereby surrender unconditionally to the Supreme Commander, Allied Expeditionary Force and simultaneously to the Soviet High Command all forces on land, sea, and in the air who are at this date under German control.

2. The German High Command will at once issue orders to all German military, naval and air authorities and to all forces under German control to cease active operations at 2301 hours Central European time on 8 May and to remain in the positions occupied at that time. No ship, vessel, or aircraft is to be scuttled, or any damage done to their hull, machinery or equipment.

3. The German High Command will at once issue to the appropriate commanders, and ensure the carrying out of any further orders issued by the Supreme Commander, Allied Expeditionary Force and by the Soviet High Command.

4. This act of military surrender is without prejudice to, and will be superseded by any general instrument of surrender imposed by, or on behalf of the United Nations and applicable to GERMANY and the German armed forces as a whole.

- 1 -

0056078

5. In the event of the German High Command or any of the forces under their control failing to act in accordance with this Act of Surrender, the Supreme Commander, Allied Expeditionary Force and the Soviet High Command will take such punitive or other action as they deem appropriate.

Signed at Rheims at 0241 on the 7th day of May, 1945.
France

On behalf of the German High Command.

Jodl

IN THE PRESENCE OF

On behalf of the Supreme Commander, Allied Expeditionary Force.

W. B. Smith

On behalf of the Soviet High Command.

Sousloparov

F Sevez

-2-

Major General, French Army
(Witness)

Copy of the Original "Instrument of Surrender" Document

On May 7, 1945, brought to a small brick schoolhouse in Reims, France, German Gen. Alfred Jodl entered the meeting room and clicked his heels. But when he extended his hand to the American General Dwight Eisenhower, it was refused. Jodl was the last to sign the surrender document after the British, American, French and Russian representatives had affixed their signatures. At 2:41 a.m. he used an American-made Parker 51 fountain pen to sign the document. Eisenhower, the Supreme Commander of the Allied Expeditionary Force in Europe, then issued a simple message: The Mission of this Allied Force was fulfilled. Various other surrender documents were signed at different locations culminating in Nazi Germany's unconditional surrender. Jodl was arrested, later tried and on October 16, 1946, executed for war crimes.

On the Cover of *TIME* Magazine—February 2, 1942—Submariner Dönitz

Karl Dönitz, a First World War submarine veteran and later an ardent supporter of Hitler, was the originator of Nazi Germany's highly effective U-Boat command. He had called for enlarging the fleet and felt it could have won the war if his recommendations were heeded. As a grand admiral his rank was equal to a field marshal. He would eventually "inherit" the leadership position of Nazi Germany, if briefly.

Wolf in the Water

The low silhouette of a German *U-boot* may have been photographed from another submarine in its wolfpack. A sailor can be see walking across its deck, several more perched on its conning tower, and forward of that the versatile 88 mm deck cannon with which many ships were sunk as well as with torpedoes. In total, German U-boats sank nearly 2,800 ships.

As the war began the Kriegsmarine counted 56 subs of which 24 could operate in the open Atlantic. Each carried a numerical designation such as U-36 or U-578 and usually a crew of 50. By war's end the shipyards at Kiel had built 1,156 with new, larger designs iminent, purportedly some that could carry aircraft or launch rockets but never saw production. As Allied anti-submarine warfare evolved, the *U-Boot* service suffered some 80 percent fatalities, 758 submarines and crews eventually lost, the highest attrition rate of any branch of the Wehrmacht.

Unwanted Position

After Hitler's suicide, having been recommended for the position by *Reichsmarschall* Hermann Göring, Dönitz served as *Führer* for 23 days before being arrested at the end of the war. In prison awaiting the Nuremberg Tribunal he fumed against Göring for putting him in the predicament, not believing he should have been charged at all. Though his submariners caused the deaths of thousands of Allied seamen, he laughed at the concept that he was a war criminal. Considered a brilliant naval strategist even by his wartime enemies, some even defended him against war crimes accusations.

While in Spandau prison serving his sentence, he made the following statements in writing. It again points to the Nazi efforts to lay claim to the loss of the First World War by political betrayal, while the second war was an honorable fight to the finish, something the German people could be proud of and build from. In effect, Dönitz was still functioning from a fascist and racist mindset, one he apparently never renounced.

> In this war there was a just, clean distribution of food up to the end. Nobody starved. Everyone received his share and no one received more. No black market. In the last war 1914–18 there was profiteering everywhere in this regard. Ask the housewives who went through both wars. The state food-purchasing organization of the First World War were Jewish profit enterprises. There was an atmosphere of sabotage, soldiers loitering about who did not salute properly, overflowing with profiteers and Jews, God know that was not clean.

Convicted of lesser charges he served ten years in prison prior to his release in 1956. He lived a free man for the next 24 years before dying in 1980 at age 89.

"Caravan to Nowhere"—Human Catastrophe Compounded

The title to the caption that accompanied this International News photo continues with:

> Germany … These German refugees are typical of many thousands caught in the vortex of war. They fled their own communities and reached the bank of the Elbe. There were no bridges left, so they couldn't cross the river with their horses and wagons, nor could they go back. Use of the roads is denied them, because of pressure of military traffic.

This photo was made near Walternienburg by Fred Ramage, INP Pool Photographer, April 1945.

German civilians, and soldiers, made a life or death rush westward to avoid the approaching Red Army. In addition German *Volksdeustche* living in countries once occupied by the Third Reich, many of whom had displaced the original residents from their homes, now fled not only from the Soviets but from the revenge visited upon them by the people victimized by the German "lebensraum" programs.

In what has been termed the greatest forced human migration in history, some 12,000,000–14,000,000 people were turned into refugees, as many as 2,000,000 dying. Many were even turned away by "true Germans" living in their hereditary homeland.

November 8, 1945—Photo Sent to POW Son

The handwritten notes in German on the reverse of this photo translates to "For our big brother from your family—Siegmund and Mutter," then followed in English with "Berlin, Germany 4 Nov. 1945." As the war in Europe had been over since May 8, 1945, it is possible the family has sent the photo to the older uniformed son seen in the photo who at this time was interred in a British or American POW camp. In the photo he wears a Luftwaffe cadette uniform. The eventual fate of the family is unknown. Treatment of German POWS brought to the U.S. was quite good, some even remaining when released, however assertions have been made that a significant number of German POWs died in crowded post-war French and American prison camps located in Europe due to exposure and lack of food. This is still a controversial subject.

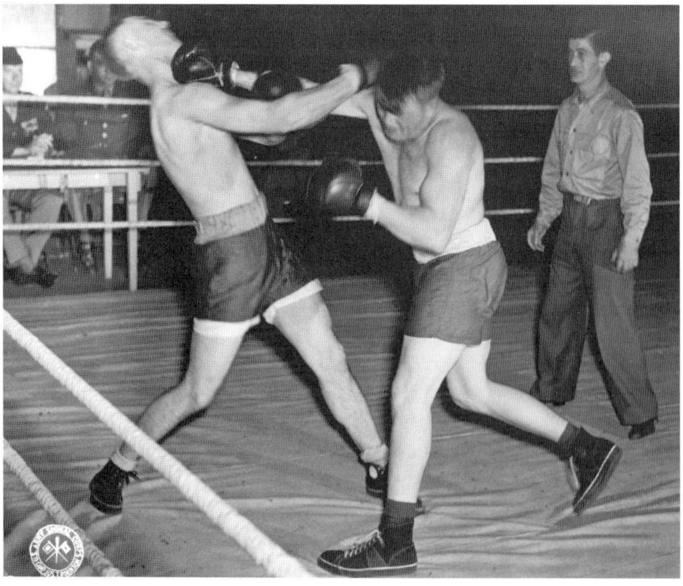

Knock-Out Punch—August 1942—German POWs in the U.S.
German POWs, veterans of the vaunted Afrika Korps battle in the ring at Camp Robinson. *Continued on next page.*

Construction of the facility located on 44,000 acres began on September 9, 1940 and originally slated to accommodate 25,000 U.S. soldiers. By January 7, 1941 it housed 16,000 troop of the U.S. 35th Division and the 153rd Infantry Regiment, later the 92nd Infantry Division and its all black enlisted personnel and some 50 percent of the officers. They were followed by troops of the 66th Infantry Division who while in troop transports crossing the English Channel lost 762 soldiers to German submarines. The German POW section was established in September 1943 and at its peak contained 3,000 Germans captured in North Africa. Four died of natural causes. Coincidentally there was a Fort Robinson in the northwest corner of Nebraska that also housed German POWs, at a maximum of 3,000, the last not repatriated until May 1946. Eventually over 375,000 German POWs were held in camps across the U.S. including the southwest and Florida. There were few escape attempts and at the same time the more fanatical prisoners joined forces and at times passed fatal judgement on their fellow prisoners who they felt violated the "code" of the Third Reich military.

Post-War POWs

Some of the over 5,000,000 German soldiers who surrendered to Allied forces at the end the war were crowded into makeshift open enclosures. Some have dug holes in which to find some relief from the elements as the 1945 summer turned towards winter's rain and cold.

France demanded and received tens of thousands of German POWs as laborers to repair war damages to their country. The conditions in the French camps were harsh resulting in many deaths from disease, hunger and sometimes from fellow prisoners. A number of German POWs released from American POW camps in the U.S. then found themselves transitioned back to Europe and in French camps where their belongings were stolen both by the French guards and their fellow Germans. Some German POWs would spend two years in such labor programs before being allowed to return home.

†

Zur frommen Erinnerung
im Gebete
an meinen lieben Gatten, Sohn
und Bruder, Herrn

Josef Stierstorfer

Schuhmacher von Landshut

welcher am 4. August 1945
in französischer Kriegsgefangenschaft
in Poitiers
im Alter von 40 Jahren
verstarb.

R. I. P.

O Herr, gib ihm die ewige Ruhe und
das ewige Licht leuchte ihm! Laß ihn
ruhen in Frieden! Amen.

Mein Jesus, Barmherzigkeit!
(300 Tage Ablaß)

Trausnitz-Druckerei, Landshut

Liebe Gattin, Eltern und Geschwister mein,
Ich kehre nicht mehr zu euch heim;
Mein letzter Gedanke, letzter Blick,
Eilte noch zu euch zurück.
Als ich starb im Feindesland,
Reichte niemand mir die Hand;
Und eh' mein Auge ward gebrochen,
Sah den Himmel ich schon offen.

Death in a French POW Camp—August 4, 1945

Having survived the war, Josef Stierstorfer, a shoemaker from Landshut, died of unlisted causes in a prison camp in the French city of Poitiers at the age of 40. The family has not identified his rank or military group. Poitiers, a city in west central France, was a German garrison town during the war and a strategic rail network. It was heavily bombed by the Allies on June 13, 1944 during the first week of the D-Day invasion. The soldier's hometown of Landshut, located in lower Bavaria and 60 km north-east of Munich, was founded in 1204 and as such every four years celebrated one of Europe's largest historical pageants. During the war, it was the location of a subcamp of Dachau providing slave labor for local industry. A few weeks after the war's end, many of the Nazi V-2 rocket scientists and their families were gathered and housed in Landshut before transport back to the U.S. as part of Operation Paperclip. When word leaked out that they had been smuggled as illegal immigrants into the U.S. through Mexico, American officials had to re-enact the immigration process.

Top of next page:

Reverse of Stierstorfer Memorial Card

The panel on the right carries the prayer:

> O Sacred Head, Now Bloody and Wounded,
> Full of pain, covered with derision!
> O Divine head wounded
> With a crown of thorns!
> O head, the other teachings and honors
> Worthy of a crown,
> Let me greet with a thousand pious tears

A cynical interpretation for the choice of the prayer might allude to a metaphorical reference to defeated Germany and the never-realized Thousand Year Reich.

Death in an American POW Camp—June 1946 (*right*)

This *sterbebild* was issued in Germany in "loving memory" by the family of Josef Rudolf Ensgraber, a POW in Ft. Custer, an American detention center located in Augusta, Michigan. He died on June 20, 1946 at age 42, one year after the end of the war and just one day before his planned return to Germany.

Ensgraber, who had been taken prisoner while a member of Rommel's Afrika Korps, had seen the war end and repatriation at hand. He was preparing for his departure to New York by airplane to meet up with the ship that would take him back to Germany.

However, one of his comrades at Camp Custer handed him a copy of the camp's newspaper because it featured a photo taken near Ensgraber's hometown of Erbach. As he sat reading the article, he began laughing heartily with joy to see the town's name. In the midst of his laughter, he suffered a heart attack and died.

He is buried with 25 other German POWs in the Camp Custer Cemetery, the last German POW to die at the camp.

From 1943 to 1946, Fort Custer housed several German Prisoner of War camps. Many of the 4,000 prisoners worked on local farms and in vineyards. In Section B of the Fort Custer National Cemetery, once part of the Post Cemetery, there are 26 German graves. Sixteen of the men died as a result of an accident on Halloween, October 31, 1944 when a truck returning from a work detail collided with a train at an unguarded railroad crossing at Blissfield, MI. The other ten died of natural causes while prisoners of war, Ensgraber among them.

Individual marble tombstones marked each of the 26 graves. A bronze plaque commemorated the camp and the 26 dead with the inscription, "Since 1953, German American communities and veteran organizations have sponsored an annual memorial service to honor those who are resting here."

The extensive campgrounds continued to be a well-regarded training site for both the Army Reserve and the Michigan National Guard.

Gedenket meiner im Gebete

Ach, es ist ja kaum zu fassen, daß du nicht mehr kehrst zurück;
So jung mußt du dein Leben lassen, du unsere Hoffnung, unser Glück.
Ein jeder, der dich hat gekannt und auch dein gutes Herz,
Der drückt uns nur noch stumm die Hand, in diesem tiefen Schmerz.
Du Vaterherz ruh still in Frieden, ewig betrauert von deinen Lieben.

†

Zum frommen Andenken
an den in Gott ruhenden
Tischlermeister
August Keßling

Der liebe Verstorbene war geboren zu Mettingen am 15. Oktober 1909 und starb am 14. September 1945 in Sibirien in russischer Kriegsgefangenschaft.

Gott gebe ihm für seinen Opfertod die Krone des ewigen Lebens.

Ablaßgebete.

Jesus! Maria; Josef! Euch schenke ich mein Herz und meine Seele!
Jesus! Maria! Josef! Stehet mir bei in meinen Todesnöten!
Jesus! Maria! Josef! O daß meine Seele mit Euch in Frieden ruhe!

Vater unser . . . Gegrüßet seist du . . .

Zu beziehen durch Alex Konersmann, Mettingen

The Soviet Gulag—War's End Plus Four Months—September 1945
One of tens of thousands of German POWs that perished in Soviet captivity, master carpenter August Keschling, born in Wettingen, Austria, was reported deceased a month before his 36th birthday having died of unidentified causes in an identified Siberian prisoner of war camp.

While German authorities estimate POW deaths in Soviet captivity at 1,000,000, official Soviet figures put forward a third of that figure. An additional 1,300,000 Germans are still officially listed as missing by the German Red Cross and believed to have died as POWs.

On the next page:

July 7, 1947—Letter Home from Fredy Dolgner—Siberian POW camp (*above*)
On thin paper, the size of a small postcard, a German soldier Alfred "Fredy" Dolgner has sent a message, addressed to father Daniel, his parents living in Duisburg located in the western part of the Ruhr Valley and in the British zone of occupied Germany.

Read by Soviet Eyes (*below*)
A POW in Camp 72816/1 for at least two years, in neat handwriting compressed on to the small card, he writes words he knows his Soviet captors will also read:

> My Dear Parents … Finally after six months I have received your message. Until now I have three of the 12 letters mother has sent. Relatively speaking I am doing well as captivity goes. Healthwise I also feel very good. Hopefully I will be home soon.

He also makes some cryptic comment about how the weeds must pass before the Willow reappears. He adds his "heartfelt greetings to Aunt Ria, Uncle Fritz, all other relatives and friends" and requests that his job at the gas station will be there when he returns home to start over. He ends with

> … a thousand kisses for the future. Above all, I wish you good health … Your Fredy.

There is no trace of Dolgner's eventual fate. His parents' city of Duisburg, a major wartime center for chemical, steel and iron production, was one of the mostly heavily bombed German cities, suffering some 299 raids. Apparently Dolgner's parents survived to receive his letters.

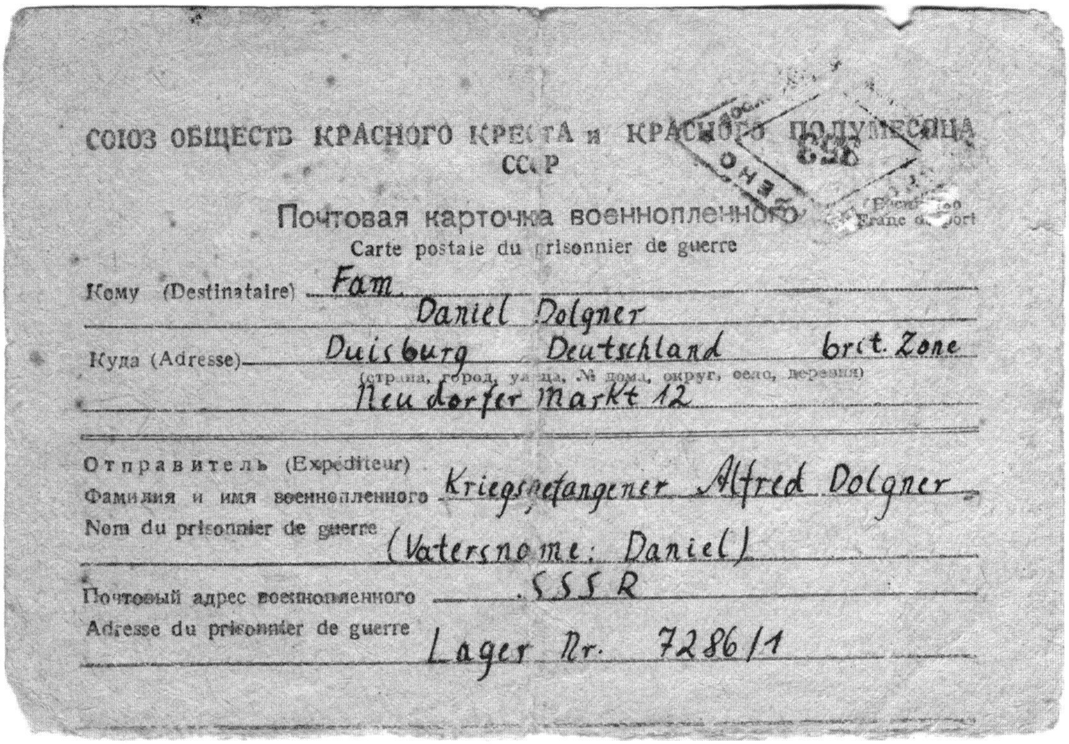

СОЮЗ ОБЩЕСТВ КРАСНОГО КРЕСТА и КРАСНОГО ПОЛУМЕСЯЦА
СССР

Почтовая карточка военнопленного
Carte postale du prisonnier de guerre

Кому (Destinataire) Fam.
Daniel Dolgner

Куда (Adresse) Duisburg Deutschland brit. Zone
(страна, город, улица, № дома, округ, село, деревня)
Neudorfer Markt 12

Отправитель (Expéditeur)
Фамилия и имя военнопленного Kriegsgefangener Alfred Dolgner
Nom du prisonnier de guerre (Vatersname: Daniel)

Почтовый адрес военнопленного SSSR
Adresse du prisonnier de guerre Lager Nr. 7286/1

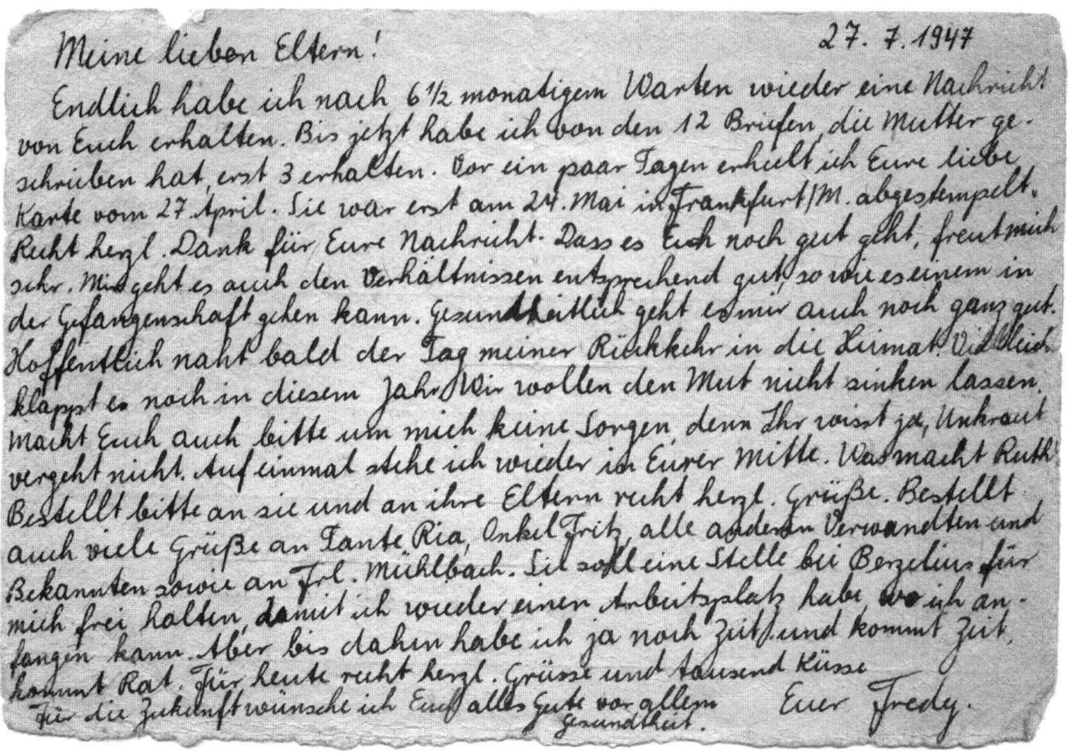

Meine lieben Eltern! 27. 7. 1947

Endlich habe ich nach 6½ monatigem Warten wieder eine Nachricht von Euch erhalten. Bis jetzt habe ich von den 12 Briefen, die Mutter geschrieben hat, erst 3 erhalten. Vor ein paar Tagen erhielt ich Eure liebe Karte vom 27. April. Sie war erst am 24. Mai in Frankfurt/M. abgestempelt. Recht herzl. Dank für Eure Nachricht. Dass es Euch noch gut geht, freut mich sehr. Mir geht es auch den Verhältnissen entsprechend gut, so wie es einem in der Gefangenschaft gehen kann. Gesundheitlich geht es mir auch noch ganz gut. Hoffentlich naht bald der Tag meiner Rückkehr in die Heimat. Vielleicht klappt es noch in diesem Jahr. Wir wollen den Mut nicht sinken lassen, macht Euch auch bitte um mich keine Sorgen, denn Ihr wisst ja, Unkraut vergeht nicht. Auf einmal stehe ich wieder in Eurer Mitte. Was macht Ruth? Bestellt bitte an sie und an ihre Eltern recht herzl. Grüße. Bestellt auch viele Grüße an Tante Ria, Onkel Fritz, alle anderen Verwandten und Bekannten sowie an Frl. Mühlbach. Sie soll eine Stelle bei Berzelius für mich frei halten, damit ich wieder einen Arbeitsplatz habe, wo ich anfangen kann. Aber bis dahin habe ich ja noch Zeit und kommt Zeit, kommt Rat. Für heute recht herzl. Grüsse und tausend Küsse

Für die Zukunft wünsche ich Euch alles Gute vor allem Gesundheit.

Euer Fredy.

Ich weiß Ihr werdet bitter weinen,
Daß ich so ferne sank ins Grab,
Wo nur die lieben Sterne scheinen,
In meine dunkle Gruft hinab,
Doch einmal kommt der Tod zu allen,
Und bricht der Liebe zartes Band,
Drum liebe Eltern weinet nicht,
Ich schau ja Gottes Angesicht,
Mein früher Tod, mein großes Glück,
Drum meine Lieben weinet nicht,
Ich lebe noch und liebe Euch,
In Gottes schönem Himmelreich.

†

Zur frommen Gebetserinnerung
an unseren lieben, einzigen,
unvergeßlichen Sohn

Hans Brenzinger

Student von Obernzell
Uffz. in einer Inf.-Einheit

welcher am 16. Februar 1943, bei Nowo-Spatobka (Rußland) in Gefangenschaft geriet und am 17. Juli 1948, nach 5½ jähr. Gefangenschaft, im Lager 7623 im Raume Tschjabinsk (Sibirien) im Alter von 27 Jahren verstorben ist.

Ehre seinem Andenken.

Mein Jesus Barmherzigkeit!
(300 Tage Ablaß)
Pius X., 20. Mai 1911

Zu bez. durch M. Unfried Obernzell

Death in Siberia—War's End Plus Three Years—July 17, 1948

According to his memorial card, Hans Brenzinger, an *Unteroffizier* (sergeant) in an infantry unit was taken prisoner on February 16, 1943 at Nowo-Spatobka (perhaps Sparovka)) in Russia. After 5½ years in a POW *Lager* (camp 7623) located in the area of Tschjabinski (perhaps Chelyabinsk) in Siberia, his death was reported at the age of 27. Before the war he had been a student in the Bavarian town of Obernzell.

Zum frommen Gebetsandenken
an meinen unvergeßl. Gatten, unseren herzensguten Vater, Sohn u. Schwiegersohn

Karl Schönberger

langj. Kraftfahrer bei Fa. Schwannberger
in Ruhmannsfelden
welcher uns am 27. Juli 1951, als Opfer einer 5-jähr. Kriegsgefangenschaft, im Alter von 40 1/2 Jahren, für immer entrissen wurde.

Zu früh o Gatte und Vater, wurdest du uns entrissen
Ach in so ungeahnter Zeit,
Wie bitter deiner Kinder, Tränen fließen
Und deiner Gattin Herz, schmerzt in tiefstem Leid.

Anton Tackerbauer, Regen Tel. 78
Zu beziehen durch **Frau Wurzer**

†
Christliches Andenken
an Herrn

Dr. Hanns Wichtl

Praktischer Arzt und Strafanstaltsarzt von Garsten, Gemeindearzt v. Aschach a. d. St.

welcher am Dienstag, 8. Juni 1954, um 3 Uhr früh nach längerem, schwerem Leiden, versehen mit den heiligen Sterbesakramenten, im 39. Lebensjahre selig im Herrn entschlafen ist.

„Ich habe den guten Kampf gekämpft, den Lauf vollendet, den Glauben bewahrt, jetzt harret meiner die Krone der Gerechtigkeit."
(2. Tim. 4, 7—8.)

Leichenbestattung M. Hieslmair, Garsten
Vereinsdruckerei Steyr

Death in Captivity—War's End plus Six Years—July 27, 1951 (*above left*)
After surviving some five years in a Soviet prison camp, Karl Schönberger died at the age of 40½. Before the war he had been long-time driver for the family Schwannberger in the small Bavarian town of Ruhmannsfelden which after the war served as a Displaced Persons (DP) processing center.

A Doctor's Nine Year Post-Mortem—June 1954—Residual Effects (*right*)
The relatives of Dr Hanns Wichtl when announcing his passing at 3 a.m. on Tuesday June 8, 1954, some nine years after the war's end, have chosen to use a photograph of the doctor wearing his Third Reich uniform. Dr Wichtl had a professional career as both a municipal physician as well as a prison doctor in the city of Aschach. The cause of death was not specified although he died at age 39 apparently after "long suffering with the trauma of death." The memorial card also contains the Biblical passage from 2nd Timothy, "I have fought the good fight, I have kept the Faith, now don the crown of Righteousness."

Christliches Andenken
an Herrn
Josef Berger
Schuldirektor i. R. und Major d. Res.
in Gallspach 29

welcher am 2. Februar 1957, um 18 Uhr, einen Tag nach Erreichung seines 77. Lebensjahres, mit unendlicher Geduld ertragenem Leiden für immer von uns gegangen ist.

GEBETSANDENKEN
an Herrn
Heinrich Amberger
Rentner von Blossersberg
welcher nach langem Leiden, versehen mit den hl. Sterbesakramenten, am 2. Oktober 1969, im Alter von 63 Jahren im Herrn verschieden ist.

O Herr, gib ihm die ewige Ruhe!
Vater unser — Ave Maria

LACKERBAUER VIECHTACH

Still in Third Reich Uniform 13 Years Later—1957 (*above*)
A memorial card printed in 1957 extols the "infinite patience" of one Josef Berger who passed away at 6 p.m. on February 2, 1957 having attained the age of 77. Notations state he was a school director and a major in the army reserves, having been 55 at war's end. His photo portrays him in his Third Reich uniform; however a Christian Cross has replaced the Iron Cross.

Post-war, the West German government permitted veterans of all branches to wear their Third Reich era medals as long as no swastikas were visible. Even the Waffen-SS wore their awards to meetings and social events. A number of veterans' organizations met frequently, hosting events for decades. It was much promoted that the veterans had been fighting the Communists which somehow glossed over the facts of invasions and mass carnage.

Still in Uniform 24 Years Later—Heinrich Amberger—October 2, 1969 (*left*)
For his memorial card, his relatives have chosen a Third Reich era photo of Amberger in Luftwaffe corporal's uniform. He died at 63, a pensioner living in the Bavarian city of Blossersberg, 59 miles north of Munich.

The Final Indictment

One of the last Germans to die in the war was Hitler himself, committing suicide in his Berlin bunker with his newlywed bride Eva Braun on April 30, 1945. In his "last testament" he blamed the Jews for the war and its loss on his generals as well as the weak will of the people who therefore did not deserve him or the right to survive. While he condemned Germany to utter destruction, ordering the complete destruction of Germany's infrastructure, his decree went largely unheeded.

One of Hitler's last statements was made on April 30 when said his farewells to his personal pilot, Hans Bauer, during which he refused an offered escape plan. Hitler also gave Bauer his portrait of Frederick the Great by Lenbach, a painting Hitler thought to be his "lucky" talisman. Then he offered an observation: "I know tomorrow millions of people will curse me … that's Fate for you."

Two days previously with the Third Reich collapsing upon itself, a conversation was overheard in the bunker involving Hitler's secretary and some say the second most powerful man in the Third Reich, the Head of the Party Chancellery, Martin Bormann. He was engaged in a heated exchange with the Chief of the Army General Staff General Hans Krebs and Hitler's chief adjutant Major General Wilhelm Burgdorf, the three having last drinks as Russian artillery pounded the earth overhead. The conversation was recorded by Wehrmacht officer Berthold Boldt who had been a member of German military intelligence assigned to the *Führerbunker*. The incident was mentioned in his successful post-war book *Die Letzten Tage der Reichskanzlei* (*The Last Days of the Reichs Chancellery*).

> Burgdorf was shouting at Bormann: "Believe me, I have done my very best to smooth things over between Hitler and the Army, so much so that the Army has called me a traitor to the German Officers' Corps. Now I realize that they were right all along, that my work was in vain, my idealism misdirected, no, naive and stupid." Breathing heavily, he paused for a moment. Krebs tried to calm him down and begged him to spare Bormann's feelings.
>
> But Bergdorf went on regardless: "Just leave me to it, Hans, it has to be said for once. In forty-eight hours it may well be too late. Our young officers went into battle full of faith and idealism. They went to their death by the hundred-thousand. But for what? For their Fatherland, for Germany's greatness and future? For a decent life? In their hearts they did, but nowhere else. They died for you, for your pockets, for your boundless ambitions.

> Thinking they were dying for a just cause, our youth allowed themselves to be bled to death on the battlefields of Europe, sacrificing millions of innocent lives, while you, the Party leaders, waxed richer and richer, living it up like lords, accumulating untold riches, stealing vast estates, building castles, reveling in luxury, deceiving and milking the nation. Our ideals, our morals, our faith, our soul—all these you have ground into dirt; mankind was only a stepping stone for your insatiable greed. You have destroyed our ancient culture, you have broken up our nation. That is your only achievement!"
>
> The general's voice had risen to a roar. Now the bunker was quite still. We could hear his breath come in gasps. Then we heard Bormann's cool, superior, and oily voice. All he had to say was this: "My dear fellow, do you really have to be so personal? Even if the others have filled their pockets, I myself am free of blame. That I swear to you by all I hold dear. Cheers my friend, and drink up."

Previously Krebs had taken part in the impromptu court martial of Hermann Fegelein, Himmler's liaison and the husband of Eva Braun's sister who was accused of desertion and condemned to death by Hitler but may have served as a scapegoat for Himmler who had deserted Hitler and sought a separate agreement with the Allies. Conflicting reports says Fegelein was shot by an SS squad outside the *Führerbunker*. Meanwhile Burgdorf was directly involved in the forced suicide of Field Marshal Erwin Rommel who had been accused of complicity in the July 20 assassination attempt on Hitler.

On May 1–2, 1945, a short time after the purported heated exchange in the bunker, both Krebs and Burgdorf committed suicide, their bodies found by Soviet troops. Conflicting accounts state the Bormann was killed by Soviet troops while trying to escape the Berlin bunker while others contest that he escaped to South America. However, his remains were said to have been discovered more recently, indicating he had been killed after fleeing the bunker. Pilot Bauer, though suffering an amputated leg survived eight years in Russian captivity and was released in September 1955, followed by a further five years in French captivity before being released again, but long enough to write about his wartime experiences, living to the age of 95.

Surrender Manifestos—Last Words of the Third Reich

The German high command initially sought to end the fighting on the Western Front, the area controlled by American, British, Canadian and French forces, thereby allowing their remaining forces to continue the battle against the Soviets attacking from the East, and hoping to prevent capture of more of their troops. So in effect, they attempted to end half the war while the other half raged on. Toward that goal on May 5, 1945, the Germans initially surrendered to British forces, a ceasefire affecting north-western Germany, Holland and Denmark. The official announcement by the Wehrmacht stated:

> This ceasefire was agreed at the order of Grand Admiral Dönitz after almost six years of honorable struggle, since the war against the Western powers has lost its meaning and

> is leading only to the loss of precious German blood, above all through the bombing campaign. The resistance to the Soviets, however, will be continued in order to protect as many Germany people as possible from the Bolshevik terror.

Of note is the attempt to cast Germany's war of aggression that destroyed millions of lives as an "honorable struggle" and again calling the Allies to task about the aerial bombing (*terrorangriff* or "Terror Bombing"). The choice of wording also spotlights "Bolshevik terror," an echo of the longstanding Nazi propaganda effort to both demonize the Russians and to sanction their war of annihilation against them. It became a self-fulfilling prophecy when Soviet troops in revenge did kill and rape large numbers of civilians as they entered the land of their invaders.

The German military's efforts to cast themselves as heroic in their struggle, only falling victim to superior forces, and showing concern only for their own losses, was re-affirmed as stated by Dönitz's appointee Lutz Graf Schwerin von Krosigk, the chairman of the post-Hitler government in the last days of the war, when, on May 7, he broadcast the following message to his fellow countrymen:

> On the orders of Grand Admiral Dönitz the Supreme Command of the Wehrmacht today has declared the unconditional capitulation of all fighting troops. After a heroic struggle of unparalleled severity lasting almost six years, Germany's strength has been overcome by the overwhelming power of our opponents. The continuation of this war would have meant only senseless bloodshed and pointless destruction.
>
> A government which possesses a sense of responsibility for the future of our people had to draw the conclusion from the collapse of our physical and material forces and to request a cessation of hostilities from the opponent. It was the most noble aim of the Grand Admiral and of the government supporting him, after the sacrifices that had been demanded, to preserve the lives of as many German people as possible in its last phase. This aim amounts for the fact that the war was not ended immediately and not simultaneously in the west and in the east.

The inclusion of such terms as "most noble aim" juxtaposed with history's most brutal government seems surreal as is the suggestion that the German military "requested an armistice"). While there is mention of saving German lives, there is no mention of the non-Germans still dying in combat or the prisoners still dying by the thousands as the speech is given. Moreover, the Nazi leadership left the civilian population to their own resorts, preferring to protect their military apparatus at all costs, Hitler often refusing to allow civilians to evacuate cities under attack.

The announcement continued with the following:

> We must light the path through the darkness of the future and be guided by the three stars which always were the pledge of true German character: unity and law and freedom.
>
> We want to safeguard and rescue one thing from the collapse of the past: the idea of the people's community that during the years of war found its finest expression in the comradeship at the Front, in the reciprocal readiness to help in all emergencies at home.

> Only if we preserve this unity and do not again break apart into conflicting groups and classes can we survive the difficult time to come.
>
> We must make law the basis of the life of our people. Justice shall be the supreme law and the uppermost guiding principle among our people. We must recognize and respect the law as the basis of relations between peoples out of inner conviction.
>
> We will combine pride in the heroic struggle of our people with determination as part of Christian–Western culture to make a contribution in sincere work for a peace that corresponds to the best traditions of our people.
>
> May God not forsake us in misfortunate, and bless our difficult undertaking.

Despite the protestations that Nazi Germany and its "heroic struggle" represented the best of Western Christian culture, Eisenhower demanded a complete unconditional surrender or the bombing would continue. In fact Eisenhower, in conference with Churchill and Stalin, had advocated shooting all members of the SS while Churchill recommended turning Germany into one large farmland. Oddly enough, rather than mass executions of the war criminals, purportedly it was Stalin who called for an International Tribunal and the public prosecution of the Nazi leadership.

The German high command eventually gave up their conditional demands and surrendered, broadcasting the announcement to its 3,000,000 troops still in the field of combat, some 1,850,000 still being decimated on the Eastern Front.

Prelude to Unconditional Surrender: Final Message

On May 9, the official broadcast from Nazi Germany's "*Reichssender* Flensburg," a radio substation located near the German border with Denmark, and the last "voice" of the German Army High Command (OKW), made the following announcement to its military personnel and the civilian population. It reflects the continual effort to convince the German people that their honor was upheld, unlike the aftermath of the First World War, and that Germany could arise again with its self-respect intact. Its veiled admonition called for history to vindicate Germany's "battle against Communism" and echoed the Nazi mantra for all Germans to uphold "folk and fatherland."

> Since midnight the weapons on all fronts are now silent. On the orders of the Grand Admiral, the Wehrmacht has given up the fight which has become hopeless. Thus the heroic struggle which lasted nearly six years has come to an end. It brought us great victories but also heavy defeats. In the end the German Wehrmacht was honorably defeated by a huge superior force.
>
> The German soldier, true to his oath and with the greatest dedication, has performed deeds which never will be forgotten. The home front supported him to the last with all its powers and suffering the greatest sacrifices.
>
> The unique achievement of the front and the home front will find its ultimate appreciation in a future just verdict of history.

Our opponents too will not refuse their respect for the achievements and sacrifices of German soldiers on land, at sea and in the air. Every soldier therefore can hand over his weapon with honor and pride and begin work courageously and confidently for the eternal life of our people in the darkest hour of our history.

In this dark hour the Wehrmacht is thinking of its comrades who remain with the enemy.

The dead obligate us to unconditional loyalty, to obedience and discipline with regard to a Fatherland bleeding from countless wounds.

For Whom the Death Bell Knells

The last five months of the war brought "carnage incarnate." The level of murderous warfare even eclipsed the ferocity of the preceding five years, the word apocalypse earning its full due. In the single month of January 1945 alone some 450,000 German soldiers died. Allied pilots flying overhead reported the stench of the corpses reaching them high above the battleground now carpeted with the dead.

For the following months of February, March and April 1945, the last months of the war before it ground to a halt in early May with the signing of the unconditional surrender, German military deaths reached 280,000 per month, in total some1,800,000 … and almost all within the borders of Germany, the country imploding upon itself. What remaining hopes of an Allied partnership with the remnants of German forces to turn on the Russians faded as had the delusional reliance on Hitler's "wonder weapons." The Nazi leadership, fanatical to the end, had decided literally to go down in flames and take both its soldiers and civilians with it in the final, literal expression of Ultimate *Heldentod*. In their warped minds, their desperate act would "rescue" the German people from the shame cast upon the national reputation after its defeat in the First World War. Despite lack of fuel for its tanks, aircraft to protect its skies, even bullets for its guns, Nazi Germany fought on in a catharsis of mass suicide. There would be no "stab in the back," and no surrender... defeat, yes, but no dishonor. Death before Dishonor became more than a slogan. It became the gravestone inscription for the entire country.

As Richard Bessel, chronicling the shock of the war's loss to the German mindset in his 2009 book *Germany 1945*, concluded that the response to the loss of the Second World War was a reverse of that experienced following the First World War. That war, its loss and its death toll compounded by the onerous penalties of the Versailles Treaty and the German public's belief it had been betrayed by politicians, fed the delusion that it had been "wronged," and those seeds of festering discontent would fan the flames of the Nazi movement. Those flames would eventually result in the immolation of the Third Reich and Nazi Germany. The utter and total destruction attributed to the false gods of Nazism and its attendant militarism allowed for that post-war paradigm shift, and for fascism to be cauterized from the German psyche, at least to the point they became capable of accepting democracy and all that went with it, in particular a rebuilding of Germany.

With their cities reduced to rubble around them, the much-vaunted German *Kulture* stained by Nazi crimes, and betrayed by their leaders, the German public began viewing themselves as victims. This new "world view" was further compounded by the loss of more than a million civilian lives during the chaotic evacuations in the face of Russian advances and the often brutal dislocations and deportations from previously occupied territories when the victims of the Third Reich now took often bloodthirsty revenge. This post-war German self-generated sense of "victimhood," also served to eclipse their shared responsibility for the fate of the millions crushed under the Nazi boot, boots worn by their fathers, brothers, and husbands. The German survivors of the war found their collective memory fogging over, a haze of self-serving survival rationalization pushing aside the horrors inflicted by a Nazified Germany.

What followed over the ensuing post-war decades was the "white-washing" of the regular German Army and a negating of the duplicity shared by its civilian population and its allies. Beyond the myth of "I knew nothing," and the concerted effort to cast the war as Germany's epic battle to preserve Western values against atheistic Communism, perhaps the greatest expression of moral irresponsibility is the Revisionist movement which seeks to deny the Holocaust.

As these words are written, anti-Semitic campaigns and attacks continue to escalate in Eastern Europe including but not limited to those countries where the Nazi ideology found fervent followers. Previously convicted war criminals are now given medals and paraded as nationalists and anti-Communist heroes. Perhaps that will all fade when the last Nazi does die.

On the next page:

Flotsam of War (*above*)
The corpse of an unidentified soldier has washed ashore, perhaps an airman whose plane fell into the sea.

The words announcing the surrender of German forces, spoken by Grand Admiral Dönitz, acting as Supreme Commander of the Wehrmacht, are telling in their residual arrogance and omission of regret or guilt:

> We have nothing to be ashamed of. What the German Wehrmacht achieved in combat and the German people enduring during these six years is unparalleled in history and in the world. It is heroism such as there has never been. We soldiers stand here without blemishes on our honor.

"Miracle of Evil" is a phrase appearing in the book *In My Own Hands* by Irene Gut Opdyke (Knopf 1999) after she witnessed her first mass execution of Jews in Poland.

Part II

Victims of the Third Reich— "A Miracle of Evil"

***Mordanschlag*—Nazi Murder of Austria's Chancellor** (*right*)
The memorial card includes the announcement, on July 25, 1934, that Engelbert Dollfuss was assassinated (*Mordanschlag*) and died at the age of 42.

As Nazi Germany sought control of Austria, Dollfuss fought against the indigenous Austrian Nazis who struck at administration centers and attacked his supporters. On July 25, 1934, German SS troops wearing Austrian Army uniforms invaded the Federal Chancellery during which the Chancellor was shot in the throat. Preventing medical attention, the Germans allowed Dollfuss to bleed to death. While Austrian authorities rallied and thwarted the initial attempted Anschluss of Austria, German troops rolled into Austria in March 12, 1938 where they were welcomed with flowers by the cheering crowds, the country now absorbed into the so-called Greater Reich.

The Murder of Poland

> If the slightest incident happens now, I shall crush the Poles without warning in such a way that no trace of Poland can be found afterwards. I shall strike with the full force of a mechanized army, of which the Poles have no conception.
>
> Adolf Hitler

Hitler supplied his own "incident" by disguising German troops as Polish soldiers and "attacking" a German radio installation near the Polish border. Corpses were secured from concentration camps and fitted with German uniforms to further implicate Polish "aggression."

Imported Terror
Soldiers transport an armored vehicle and the Swastika across a river. Poland would suffer under the unremittent terror of German occupation until war's end and serve to forge the crucible of brutality that would be unleashed on the Eastern European and Soviet peoples, an all-consuming plague of barbarism that would infect those wearing the Nazi uniform. The wave of violence would in turn sweep back upon the Germans as the Russians exacted a terrible vengeance.

"Assault on Polish Bunker" (*top of next page*)
An illustration appearing in the newspaper *Illustrierter Beobachter* purports to show German troops in the opening days of September 1939 overrunning a fortified position near Łomża, some 90 miles from Warsaw. The city, mostly destroyed in the invasion, was turned over to Soviet forces then in alliance with Germany to divide up Poland between them. German troops re-occupied it after the invasion of the USSR and by August 1941 had already established a ghetto followed by the murder of some 20,000 Jewish civilians rounded up from the surrounding villages and towns, with only a few of Łomża Jews surviving.

First Capture—1939—The New War is New

A handwritten notation on the reverse reads “The first Polish prisoner.” Germany invaded Poland on September 1, 1939 precipitating the Second World War and unleashing their policy of cultural and racial eliminationism upon the entire counry including the calculated destruction of Polish culture as well as the extermination of 90 percent of its Jewish population, the largest concentration in Europe.

Polish Tank

German soldiers investigate a Polish tank, likely disabled when its tracking treads was hit from canon fire from another tank or anti-tank gun. The rubble of a church is visible on the left.

The mechanized onslaught of the German blitzkrieg begun on September 1st succeeded in defeating Polish resistance in four weeks, aided in part by the Soviet invasion of Poland from the East on September 17th, the treachery of Stalin contributing to the Nazi subjugation of the country that began its surrender on September 29, 1941.

Last Stop

The corpses of two civilians, a man and woman, lie alongside a Polish passenger train, the subject of interest for a German soldier's camera. The invasion precipitated the murder of some 5,500,000 Poles including Catholic clergy, intellectuals, academic, medical personnel and military officers and the country's 3,000,000 Polish Jews.

Moment of Confrontation—1939—Polish POW/German Captor

A photo by Heinrich Hoffman, Hitler's primary State photographer, has caught the tense facial expressions of opposing forces. The dramatic scene was presented on one of the commercially available series of stereoview photo cards (*Raumbild*) produced by the German propaganda offices. The caption on the reverse simply states the Polish officer is 55 years old. His fate may be sealed, Polish officers were murdered in large numbers both by the Nazis and the Soviets.

Portrait of a Polish Officer

In addition to the deaths inflicted by the German forces, Poland suffered simultaneously under Stalin. The signing of the German–Russian non-aggression pact had allowed Soviet forces to invade and occupy Polish territory. But after Germany invaded the Soviet Union, the London-based Polish government-in-exile requested the return of thousands of Polish prisoners taken by the Soviets. In response, Stalin announced it was not possible since the Polish POWS "had escaped to Manchuria." In reality, and in an effort to destroy Polish military infrastructure which the Soviets saw as a threat to their planned takeover of Poland, NKVD forces arrested thousands of Polish military officers and shot as many as 22,000 of them. Between 13,400 and 14,000 were discovered in a mass grave in the Katyn forest outside Smolensk, Russia. Initially, the blame was laid at the feet of the Germans, even when suspicions of Soviet involvement became known. The government of Nazi Germany having occupied the area, announced the discovery of the mass graves in April 1943 and invited international observers to the scene. The truth was eventually revealed as the corpses were disinterred and evidence brought to light. American President Truman sought to lay the blame on the Nazis as the Soviets had become allies in the war against Nazi Germany. In the Soviet Union, references and images of Katyn were expunged from all historical and public references.

Polish White Chargers Face German Tanks

The story of Polish lancers on horseback charging German Panzers is now considered one of the "myths" of the Second World War. It may however be based on an actual, and courageous, encounter between elements of the Polish 18th Lancer Regiment, part of the Pomorska Cavalry Brigade (*Podlaska Brygada Kawalerii*) who set themselves against a German infantry position near the town of Krojanty in Pomerania on September 1, 1939, the first day of the German invasion and as a result caused a delay in the offensive led by the German 20th Motorized Infantry Division. The 18th Lancers later suffered disaster when encountering German armored vehicles, the losses including the death of its regimental commander, Colonel Kazimierz Mastelarz.

The lances-against-tanks story also took root thanks to an initial report by an Italian journalist brought to the scene by the Germans, accuracy apparently lost in translation. In addition, a German propaganda film intended to cast the Poles in a negative light, the use of primitive weapons via their lances, had an opposite effect. Produced in 1940 the "documentary" was titled *Schlachtgeschwader Lutzow* (Battle Squadron Lutzow) and included staged cavalry charges versus tank scenes. By 1939 lances had been long abandoned by Polish forces, replaced by Tsarist-era Russian 3-inch guns serving as anti-tank artillery pieces that still proved effective against German armor.

The 60th Anniversary Commemoration Special Single Stamp issued September 1, 1989 was the first in a series chronologically depicting 100 major events during the Second World War. The introduction of the series by the Marshall Islands postal service spanned six years, the length of the war itself. As "ownership" of the Marshall Islands shifted over the years, it first used stamps printed in Germany and then from 1914 to 1944 reverted to Japanese postage. After the end of war, the islands became part of the U.S. Trust Territory of the Pacific and now designs and prints its own collectible postal issues.

Top of next page:

Unexplained

What appear to be Polish cavalry swords, pierce the body of a white horse in a photo taken by a German soldier. The animal may have been injured in battle and thus put out of its misery, but the brutal use of swords rather than a gunshot is a question unanswered. As the swords were left behind, it would indicate their owners had become casualties, their killers in turn wielding the blades.

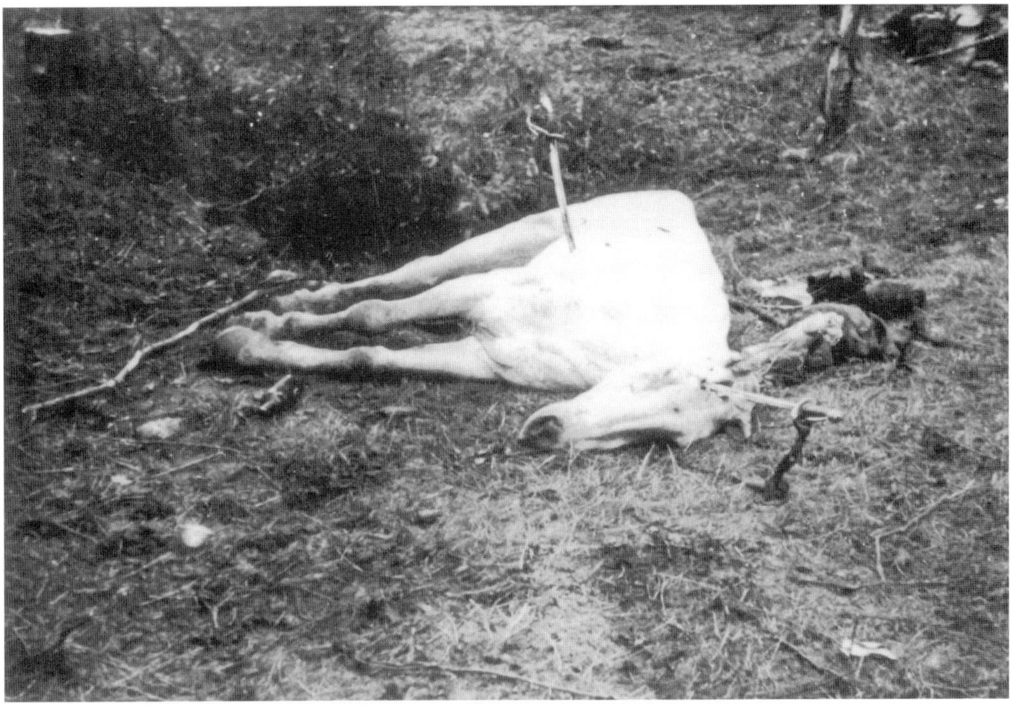

"Neben in Polnische Wagen"
Somewhere in Poland a German soldier stops to photograph the remains of a horse. His neatly inked notation on the reverse translates to the cryptic phrase "Next to the Polish Wagon." An unknown number of horses used by all the European combatants died during the war. The German losses are better recorded. Over 2,750,000 horses and mules serving in the German military died from wounds, the elements or hunger, many of them eaten, especially on the Eastern Front as food supplies disappeared, even those previously buried disinterred.

Out of Range
Three soldiers, two in overalls, appear to find something humorous taking place off-camera while in the background what may be a corpse lies in the field. The style of farm buildings in the background suggest the location is Poland.

Bootless in Death
A notation on the reverse of the photo identifies the corpse as a Polish soldier. His boots have been taken for re-use by a comrade or civilian. Or his boots may have been removed to slow down any escape attempts. Nearby can be seen the boots of a German soldier alongside his Mauser rifle.

9. September

Die Provinz Posen wird ohne feindlichen Widerstand fortschreitend besetzt. Im großen Weichselbogen zwischen Sandomir und Kutno hat der schnelle Durchbruch der motorisierten und Panzertruppen bis an die Weichsel große Erfolge angebahnt. Teile zahlreicher polnischer Divisionen sind um Radom von der Weichsel abgeschnitten und von allen Seiten umstellt. Nordostwärts Warschaus haben die Truppen am Südufer des Bug Fuß gefaßt.

Polnische Gefangene

Polish POWs in Miniature
In one of a series of popular mini-photo books sold to the German public, this example focuses on the Polish campaign, specifically September 9, 1939, a week after the German invasion. Vast numbers of Polish POWs stretch into the distance. The text speaks to the cutting off and surrounding on all sides of several Polish divisions with sudden breakthroughs by motorized and Panzer troops in the area of Radom and the Bug River.

Barbed wire and Polish POWs
A seemingly insubstantial prison fence surrounds some of the 420,000 Polish troops captured during the German invasion launched on September 1, 1939. Some even manage to clown for the camera, unaware of the fate that will befall many.

Photo Detail
Soviet forces soon attacked Poland from the East as a result of the Fascist–Communist alliance briefly formed by the notorious Molotov–Ribbentrop Non-Aggression Pact. As a result of the joint invasion of the country, the Russians also captured some 200,000 Polish soldiers.

Doppelganger
A German soldier has discovered his Polish POW twin, both smiling for the camera.

Uncertain Fate
The Germans constructed an estimated 440 *Polenlager* or Polish prison camps, where some 1,500,000 million Poles were forced into hard labor. The camps were later swelled with Soviet prisoners most of whom died due to the German practice of starvation and abuse after the invasion of the Soviet Union on June 22, 1941.

Photo Detail (*on the next page*)
What appears to be two civilians standing in the front row among the mass of Polish soldiers have noticed their photographer aiming his camera.

Official Polish sources estimated casualties resulting from the German invasion as 63,000 soldiers killed and 133,700 wounded. Among the Polish POWs, some 60,000 were Jewish and taken aside for "special treatment." Some 25,000 Polish soldier prisoners had already died in the German *Stalags* by the spring of 1940 and by war's end only a few hundred still survived.

The occupation of Poland by German forces resulted in the country's division into five districts: Krakow, Lublin, Warsaw, Galicia and Radom, the latter containing some 280,000 Jewish residents who came under the control of SS leader Dr Karl Lasch. Two of the first ghettos designed to concentrate Jews for more efficient destruction were located in the city Radom which lies in central Poland 100 km south of the capital Warsaw and situated between Lublin and Łódź. German troops took control of Radom on September 8, 1939, just a week after the invasion. By April 7, 1941, the Germans had set up two ghettos in the area that had supported a thriving Jewish community, some 30,000 Jews then concentrated into the Radom ghetto. In its streets, beatings and other tortures fell randomly upon the Jews attacked at will by German soldiers. Initially, some 2,000 of the younger, stronger men, and thus a potential resistance threat, were deported to work on anti-tank defenses in the Lublin district, most not surviving the treatment that awaited them.

In the summer of 1942 the Radom ghetto liquidation process was begun by Germany security police and Ukrainian collaborators. On August 5, SS troops shot 600 older people and children. Another 6,000 of the ghetto residents were rounded up and sent to the extermination camp at Treblinka. The Germans in charge of the liquidation of the ghetto included Franz Schipers, Adolf Feucht and Erich Kapke. Specific acts of murder included the use of grenades by SS-Hauptscharführer Erich Schildt to kill a group of children. On November 9, all Jewish children up to 12 years as well as the old and sick were gathered from Radom and the surrounding area and shot in Radom's Biala Street, the execution teams led by SS officers.

A few Jews escaped Radom, joining partisan groups to fight the Germans, though few survived the war. Others were among the 250,000 Polish freedom fighters that later perished in the fated Warsaw Home Army General Uprising.

Field Marshal Walther von Reichneau, commander of the 6th Army from 1939 to early 1942 (prior to its loss at Stalingrad), was attached to Poland where he personally became aware of the massacre of several hundred Jewish civilians at Radom by members of the *SS-Leibstandarte*. Apparently suffering severe anxiety, he wrote a letter to Hitler stating he did not want to accept any more members of the SS into his command. He received no reply. Some contend that his reservations were not with the deaths of the Jews, but that the viewing of the executions by his regular army troops might have a negative impact upon their discipline and composure.

In August 2008, some one hundred multi-colored and well preserved Jewish tombstones *(matzevot)* were unearthed in Radom during new road construction. The discovery represented the largest single find in several years. Many of the artistically designed markers had disappeared when German soldiers desecrated Jewish cemeteries often using the gravestones for paving roads. The newly revealed tombstones were replaced in the Radom cemetery. More such finds, considered archeological artifacts, were reported by the Foundation for the Preservation of Jewish Heritage in Poland.

June 1940—Polish POWs in Germany
A German officer confers with local civilians during the distribution of Polish POWs perhaps for work in the factory seen in the background.

Hundreds of thousands of POWs and civilians were transported to Germany to replace German workers recruited for war service and to provide the large workforce needed to feed the Wehrmacht's war machine. Fed and housed poorly, often mistreated and subject to Allied air raids during which they were denied access to bomb shelters, thousands died.

"Belzian—1940"
The three intertwined bodies appear to be of civilians executed in Belzian, then in Poland (previously part of the Ukraine and annexed by Romania in 1940.) Along with the handwritten notation naming the location and date, a stamp on the reverse indicates the photo was processed at the Van Uchelen studio in the Dutch city of Zeist, the Netherlands having been invaded in May 1940.

Inured to Death

A German soldier, busy with two pails of water, is caught off-guard by the photographer. A body lies where it fell at a barn door.

The German catch-all term "partisans" included "suspected partisan helpers, suspicious individuals, looters, spies, Gypsies, Mongols, Armenians, Muslims, Red Army Commissars and Soviet officials, provocateurs, stragglers" and others considered 'useless eaters.' The edict of the time was that "all Jews are partisans and all partisans are Jews" whether or not they were found with weapons, and thus providing *carte blanche* for summary execution.

Warsaw Tourists

German army soldiers including a medic pose before the destruction visited upon Warsaw as Poles observe the conquerors turned tourists.

The capital of Poland first suffered intensive bombing during the September 1939 invasion, then the destruction of the Warsaw Ghetto during the Jewish resistance of April–May 1943. Some 1,500 young fighters armed with few weapons, mounted a heroic albeit futile uprising. Still it took the SS four weeks instead of the projected three days to "clear the ghetto." Germans losses are an estimated 400 dead, 1,000 wounded while 60,000 Jews were killed during the uprising, a previous 300,000 having been sent to the Death Camps. Some 50 Jewish fighters managed to escape.

The Ghetto revolt was followed by the abortive Polish Home Army uprising in August 1943 which led to the leveling of the city by German forces and the deportation of its remaining population. Nearby Soviet forces stood by without giving aid, deliberately ordered by Stalin to remain in place as he wished the Polish defenders to be destroyed as one less obstacle to his path of takeover.

While Poland did not take part in the Holocaust, it acquired the onus of being the location chosen for the installation of the Extermination Camps. Millions of non-Jewish Poles also died under German domination. While some Polish individuals came to the aid of their Jewish countrymen, Poland, as was much of the rest of Eastern Europe, was infused with anti-Semitism.

Some Poles actively persecuted and even killed Jews without German aid or motivation. A particular case involved the Polish town of Jedwabne where, on July 10, 1941 its non-Jewish inhabitants rose up with club, knife, hatchet, pitchfork, hook and rock, and finally flame, to torture and murder their 1,600 Jewish neighbors. The horrific story was chronicled in the award winning book *Neighbors* written by Jan T. Gross. Published in Polish and English, it created a firestorm of controversy within Poland by bringing to light Polish anti-Semitism and the fate of the country's Jews before, during and after the Second World War.

Kielce, Poland—*Jüdisches Wohnviertel*—Echoes of a Nightmare

A barbed wired encrusted sign posted in German, Polish and Hebrew translates euphemistically to "Jewish Residential Area." The pre-war Jewish population of Kielce was 22,000, the town known for its large lime kilns owned by a Jewish family and which supplied the building material for all of Poland. Another 6,000 Jews fled to the city as the German threat grew, eventually 28,000 were trapped there after the town's occupation on September 4, 1939, but it was not until March 31, 1941 that the Kielce Ghetto was established.

The ghetto's liquidation or *Aktion* took place on August 20–24, 1942 conducted by the Germans with the aid of Ukrainian, Lithuanian, and Polish volunteers. The elderly, invalids and the ill were shot on the spot, an additional 19,000 Kielce Jews sent by train to Treblinka for extermination. It was during this time that an SS officer Kurt Gerstein observed the gas chamber executions. So appalled, he then risked his life in an attempt to bring the crimes to the attention of the West, in particularly by making entreaties to the Vatican, but his efforts were rebuffed.

In post-war Poland, those who rescued Jews kept it a secret in fear of reprisal from their neighbors, many harassed and beaten or even killed when the fact became known. Part of the concern was related to the intense level of residual anti-Semitism but also from the belief, usually untrue, that anyone who hid Jews had been awarded with money and valuables and thereby prime targets for robbery by their neighbors. Expropriating property and assets from Jews as a source of revenue was a main factor in the Nazi extermination plan, their property and valuables amounting to many millions of dollars. Shortly after the death camps in Poland were liberated, Polish civilians turned the areas into moonscapes by frenzied digging in the soil looking for "Jewish plunder" in the form of money and jewels buried moments before the victims entered the gas chambers. The scavengers also dug up corpses, often taking home whole skulls in order to check for gold teeth.

A post-war incident took place in Kielce, Poland that still haunts the country when revealed more recently. The German invaders gone, some 150 surviving Jews returned to their homes only to be met by the residual animosity of their neighbors. On July 4, 1946 rumors spread that Jews had murdered a Polish child for a religious ritual (a common historic ploy for violence against Jews). A mob formed and a pogrom took place. Kielce civilians along with local police attacked, beat and murdered 42 Jews. The boy was later discovered elsewhere unharmed.

Unscheduled Death Train Stop in Poland
Corpses of men and women lie draped over railroad track. Their bodies have been searched for valuables, their belongings littering the ground.

July 6, 1941—*Bauchschusses*—Gutshot—Died in Rohatyn, Poland
Some six weeks after the invasion of Russia, in the Galician Polish town of Rohatyn, at 1:30 in the afternoon, 24-year old Rupert Röhammer died after suffering a stomach wound. He is shown wearing civilian clothes rather than his uniform and unusually there is no mention of what branch of the military he served in, nor his rank, all of which may indirectly reflect the family's feelings about the war.

Rohatyn, Poland, located about 40 miles southeast of Lvov has been described as a small but modern and vibrant town, the avenues wide and tree-lined, the businesses flourishing and supporting museums, libraries and a movie theater. The name is spelled the same in German, Yiddish and Polish. After the Germans established a ghetto, many of its prisoners were sent to their death at the Belzec concentration camp, the remaining ghetto survivors were liquidated in June 1943. Today there is a memorial in Rohatyn to the 3,500 Jews gathered there from Rohatyn and surrounding Jewish settlements including the nearby small town of Burštýn, who were then shot by German execution squads.

Burštýn —A Miracle Among the Murderers

The following, based on an eye witness account, is an excerpt from the *Yizkor Book Project JewishGen, Inc.* 2009.

> Long before the destruction of the Jews of Burštýn we learned about the Germans' evil plans to destroy all the Jews of Galicia. Successive trains filled with Jews passed through the train stations of Burštýn on the way to the crematorium camps. One time 11 Jews jumped off the trains, were caught and brought into town. At that time there was a German stationed there who had a hobby of shooting helpless people. He was particularly cruel to children and it was he who received these 11 Jews as his targets. First he shot nine of them and there remained a mother and her seven-year old child. The murderer ordered the child to turn around and face him as he took out his pistol to shoot him. Then a remarkable thing happened. The boy faced the German with an innocent smile on his face. The murderer was stunned and remained standing as if he had been turned to stone, his gun falling from his hand. This murderer, who had killed hundreds of people, many of them children, this animal in the form of a human, who never before had shown pity to any child who may have crawled before him and begged for his life, was completely overcome by the smile of an innocent child and he fell in a dead faint. When he was revived, he ordered the Ukrainian policeman Schtick, the one who had shot the first ten Jews of Burštýn, to bring the child to the Judenrat making him accountable for the boy's life. This German lay in the Tanka Moskeviten house for many days and would command that the boy be brought to him from time to time because he felt better when the boy was there. When the Jews of Burštýn were killed, the boy and his mother disappeared and no one knows what happened to them.

Cause of Death Unknown

A German soldier has a vantage point to record a funeral possession in a Polish village, the photo dated April 1941. One young girl has caught sight of him and turns in the direction of the camera.

A More Ornate Funeral

A handful of mourners, one pushing a bicycle, follow an elegantly appointed horse-drawn funeral procession through a section of seemingly undamaged Warsaw. The soldier's notation on the photo simply reads: "*Leichenwagen in Warschau*—Hearse in Warsaw."

"*Thus the dead ones are driven to their graves*" (German notation on back of photo) With mourners following in its wake, a coffin pulled by a solitary man, a rope over his shoulder, makes its way through the cobblestoned streets of a desolated Warsaw.

Zum
Andenken
im Gebete
an den
Ogefr.

Johann HURKA

Schreinergehilfe von Furth i. Wald

welcher am 6. 8. 1944 in Sichelsberg (Polen)
im Alter von 21 Jahren verunglückte.

Du gingst von uns mit schwerem Herzen
Und hofftest auf ein Wiedersehn;
Doch größer sind jetzt unsere Schmerzen,
Da dieses kann nicht mehr geschehn.
Du warst so gut, Du starbst so früh,
Wer Dich gekannt, vergißt Dich nie;
Du gutes Herz, ruh still in Frieden
Ewig beweint von Deinen Lieben.

Warsaw Polish Army Uprising Casualty—August 8, 1944
Johann Hurka, a carpenter's helper from the Bavarian/Czech border town of Furth im Wald, died at age 21 on August 8, 1944 in Sichelsberg, Poland, as the result of an "unlucky wound," so states the deathcard's inscription.

Commentary on Warsaw Uprising—A Late War Letter from Fredi
Mailed on Aug. 12, 1944, *Gefreiter* (Corporal) Fred Hilse sent the following and oddly uncensored letter to his wife Hilde. (English translation):

> My dear wife—Just to let you know that we left here on time without any casualties and that was important, but my mood went down to zero as you might imagine. We got back to battalion and everyone was happy to see us. A lot has changed now in the 5th year of the war and the losses have been big. They've made 2 battalions out of 5 companies now and one company is still in Holland, the other in Riga–Latvia. Our Assault Battalion participated in the Warsaw Uprising and has helped the city stay in our hands. But we had horrible losses too and all officers except 3 were killed and many new comrades were killed. Well, I don't want to write more about it now. The replacement company is up to full strength again, so more cannon fodder for the front. We have 200 men put aside to go to the front but we don't know what happens to us next. The company sergeant said he has nothing to do for us and might send us on home leave if we don't get an order to move up front. All the older sick men are back on duty now. I'm going to see the medic tomorrow to see what he says, if the report is ok, I might be going to the front too. That's the situation here my dear. I saw Hans here, he told me their division retreated from France and arrived here in Königsgratz. Bremen was bombed out so we hear, total loss of the house but the family is ok, they were in a bunker during the raid. Just now I'm reading the latest news and it says the Volkssturm is our new weapon, but don't worry, all things will end one day. Sleep well and kisses, Fredi.

Den Heldentod für das Vaterland
starb der Grenadier
in einer Geb.-Jäg.-Division

Alois Seidl

Wagnermeisterssohn von Lochfeld
gefallen am 14. August 1944
bei Treblinka in Polen
im 19. Lebensjahre.

Geliebter Sohn und Bruder,
du liegſt begraben
In fremder Erde Schoß,
Als Held biſt du gefallen,
Das Leid um dich iſt groß.
Leb' wohl, du tapf'rer Kämpfer,
Der Abſchied war ſo ſchwer,
Deine Lieben mußteſt du ſo früh verlaſſen,
Seh'n dich auf dieſer Welt nicht mehr.

Xaver Wittmann, Roding

Death Card—Treblinka—August 14, 1944

The announcement records the battlefield death of Alois Seidl, the son of a master coach builder from Lochfeld. The 19-year old member of a German mountain troop division fell on August 14, 1944 near Treblinka, Poland while fighting Soviet troops liberating the area. The Treblinka death camp had already ceased to exist as of July 1943, leveled by the Germans, a year prior to Seidl's death. Whether he had knowledge of the infamous extermination center is unknown.

Constructed in a remote area of northeastern Poland near the village of Treblinka and the railway depot of Malkinia, the death camp was approximately an hour by train from the Warsaw Ghetto from which 300,000 Jews were sent to their fate. The camp had become operational in 1942 eventually utilizing 13 carbon monoxide gas chambers capable of killing 3,800 people at a time. Time scheduled for "processing" between arrivals of trains carrying victims to the final disposition of the corpses was two hours.

Approximately 35–40 German SS and Police staffed the camp with another 90–120 Ukrainians serving as guards. During July 1942–August 1943 an estimated 900,000 Jewish men, women and children were fed into its gas and flame. As an unfathomable mathematical computation, some 150 men murdered almost a million people.

> The entrance to the Gas Chamber was covered by a Jewish ceremonial curtain, taken from a synagogue, where it had been used as a covering for the Ark. Either on the curtain or on the building was the Hebrew inscription "This is the Gateway to God. Righteous Men will pass through." The gable over the entrance bore a large Star of David. To reach the opening of the building, the victims had to climb five wide steps, decorated on either side with potted plants.
> (www.HolocaustResearchProject.org)

A revolt on August 2, 1943 resulted in the escape of 200–750 prisoners of which almost all were tracked down and killed. It is believed only 60–70 people survived Treblinka. Later, as the Russian Army approached, the Germans attempted to eradicate all traces of the camp by plowing it under and planting groves of trees. Today very little remains of the camp itself but a memorial exists, that of a field with 17,000 stones inscribed with the individual names of some of the towns from which the camp's victims had been rounded up and deported.

Nachrichtentruppe **Demonstration—Arm Forces Day**
As signal corps soldiers adjust an antenna on a communications vehicle, school children gather with interest during a public demonstration. The mobile units, equipped with the latest electronic communications gear, were pivotal to the success of Germany's blitzkrieg tactics.

Elevated Target
A soldier attaches telephone or telegraph lines while comrades stand guard. Constant repair to lines of communication often severed by enemy troops or partisans often left communications repair teams in jeopardy.

Page from a German Soldier's Photo Album—Travelogue to the Invasion
No doubt due to the fact that he was a member of a communication (*Nachrichten*) group, the captions are neatly printed and the photos well organized on an album page titled *Vorkommando von Velden nach Russland* or "Advance Party from Velden to Russia." Velden is the name of a Bavarian town. Reading clockwise from top left, the captions translate: "Afternoon tea at the Strand Hotel; During the journey; Polish Jews; Parking lot in Brünn (Czech city of Brno); My Control Panel troop—Kolb, Lerciz, Giesche—June 24, 1941; and Armored car in Przeworsk (Poland)—June 29, 1941."

"On the Way"
Apparently the soldier, his communication team and their equipment including specially built vehicles are on their way to join the invasion of the Soviet Union just launched a few days earlier on June 22, 1941. A closer examination of the second photo reveals an officer aiming his camera at the soldiers resting in the ditch.

Company Communications Unit Commander Communicating

The vehicle is identified as a Kfz 17, a closed-bodied communications vehicle built on the standard medium uniform chassis. The plethora of widely different vehicle designs as well as weapons platforms, promoted by competing companies eventually caused a major problem in parts replacements and qualified mechanics on the battlefield, the major portion of trucks becoming disabled later in the war, horses often filling the gap in transport vehicles.

"Parking Lot in Brünn" (Czechoslovakia)

In the "Brünn" photo, three of the four names of the communications soldiers are listed on the album page notations, leaving one unnamed and mostly likely the owner of the photo album. The vehicle itself is of an unusual design and appears to blend an automobile cab was a truck body for carrying equipment.

On Location Reporting in Yugoslavia

A war correspondent holds a large microphone for recording the comments of the communications unit commander at this point in their travels stopped in the Yugoslavian town of Bosanska Krupa (now part of Bosnia and Herzegovina), located 130 miles north-west of Sarajevo. German forces took control of the region in April 1941. (Some 50 years later it would be the location of death camps created during the Bosnian War).

Yugoslavia Anti-Nazi Protest—27 March 1941—Belgrade

Under extreme duress, the Yugoslavian government succumbed to Nazi Germany's ultimatum to join the Axis Tripartite Pact; the documents signed on March 25, 1941. Two days later, in a popular anti-fascist uprising, the Serbian people and elements of the army took to the streets of Belgrade, chanting, "Rather war than the pact, rather death than slavery." The government was overthrown, the Serbs taking an anti-Nazi stance. German retaliation quickly followed.

Belgrade Bombed

Yugoslav civilians under German supervision clear bomb damage.

In response to the Serbian defiance, Hitler ordered the destruction of Yugoslavia as a military power and sovereign state. Belgrade was subsequently bombed on April 6 resulting in more than 17,000 deaths. Four days later German forces and their Italian, Hungarian and Bulgarian allies, later joined by Croatian fascists attacked the country, overpowering the Yugoslav national forces within two weeks. An armistice was signed on April 18, a pro-Nazi fascist government returned to power. The Germans then carved up the country, creating an independent Croatian state.

The Croatian fascist *Ustaše*, allied with the Nazis, engaged in their own ethnic violence against Serbs, Gypsies and Jews. In the Jasenovac Croatian concentration camp some 600,000 perished under conditions of barbarity surpassing the Nazi Extermination Centers. 250,000 more civilians were expelled and 200,000 forcibly converted to Catholicism. The acts of the *Ustaše* concentration guards even revolted their SS counterparts. One of the guards boasted that in a competition he had cut the throats of 1,360 new arrivals.

Nachrichten **Album Page—Passing Through Poland**

The communications unit has reached Poland. Many of the building windows are open indicating the heat of the summer. While the older man, wearing the required armband marking him as a Jew, looks away from the German's camera, the young boy can't resist smiling. Next to him curbside can be glimpsed one of the communication crew's vehicles.

Top of next page:

Nachrichtentruppen **Arrival in South-Eastern Poland**

The photographer has captured a *Leichte Panzerspähwagen* Sd. Kfz.221 (armored reconnaissance vehicle) in motion in front of the military post office. Capable of 50 mph on roadways, 40 off-road, it was equipped with a special wrap-around communications antennae. In the background other motorized vehicles along with horse-drawn wagons are visible as well as the faint figure of a soldier gazing upon the scene from the balcony (upper right). *Continued on next page.*

The location is identified as Przeworsk, a town then located in south-eastern Poland, dating back to 1394 and very close to the Soviet border. At the time of the German occupation it was also the home of a Jewish settlement or *Shtetel* established in 1583 and on the day of German occupation of September 12, 1939 listed a population of 1,781. The German troops immediately burned down the 17th Century Renaissance synagogue and either expelled or killed all but 27 of the Jewish residents.

Die aufrecht durchs Leben gingen,
werden den Frieden finden.

Frommes Gebets-Andenken
an

Toni Höfle

Obergefr. in einer Nachrichten-Abteilung
Inhaber des E.K. II,
des Verwundeten-Abz. u. der Ostmedaille
geb. 20. 12. 1920, gefallen 23. 10. 1943

Geliebte, wenn mein Geist geschieden,
So weint mir keine Träne nach,
Denn, wo ich weile, dort ist Frieden,
Dort leuchtet mir ein ewger Tag.
Wo aller Erdengram verschwunden,
Soll Euer Bild mir nicht vergeh'n,
Und Linderung für Eure Wunden,
Für Euren Schmerz will ich erfleh'n.
Weht nächtlich seine Seraphsflügel
Der Friede übers Weltenreich,
So denkt nicht mehr an meinen Hügel,
Denn von den Sternen grüß ich Euch.

O Herr, gib ihm die ewige Ruhe!

October 23, 1943—Toni Höfle—Communications Battalion

Having been awarded the Iron Cross 2nd Class, the Wound Badge for a previous battle injury, and the East Medal for service on the Russian front, Corporal Höfle, bearing an unusual first name, was killed while serving as a member of a communications battalion. The location of his death is unspecified, but most likely the Russian Front.

France and Adjoining Countries Conquered

"On the Luxembourg Border—May 10, 1940"
After Poland, Hitler and the German military set their sights on France and the Low Countries. Here twenty-eight German soldiers, five of them smiling, pose for a celebratory photo on the day of the Luxembourg invasion, the date inscribed on the back of the image. Several wear their white denim fatigues.

German forces invaded the Duchy of Luxembourg (population 266,000) on May 10, 1940 when attacking Belgium and the Netherlands. The people of Luxembourg strongly resisted Nazi occupation and suffered for it. As an example, when the Germans initiated a military draft of its citizens in August 1942, the response was a general strike. During its suppression twenty-one strikers were executed, thousands arrested and tortured and hundreds more deported to concentration camps, a little known story of courage and resistance against Nazi oppression.

Luxembourg Passage—*Wochenend Ausflug?? Aber wohin?*
A page in a German soldier's personal album featured a captioned photograph of refugees including priests and civilians pushing bicycles and carrying their belongings. A sign post indicates the Luxembourg Pass. The cynical caption for the photo translates to "*Leaving for the weekend? But where to?*"

At the outbreak of war, some 3,500 Jews were citizens of the small country. Some 2,500 were allowed to leave, many ending up in France where they ultimately were sent to their deaths. On June 17, 1943, Nazi authorities announced Luxembourg to be *Judenfrei*. Various sources cite 683 Jews deported, of whom only 36–43 survived, others cite 1,950 deaths and an additional 1,000 or more Jewish refugees from other countries who had sought sanctuary in Luxembourg also perishing in the death camps.

Rapid Victory

German troops have mounted a disabled French tank, the success of the six-week of summer May–June 1940 campaign seemingly throwing Europe open to Nazi domination.

The French were the first to produce what was considered a modern tank with the Renault FT during the First World War, and had by the Second World War produced 20 different tank models of some qaulity for their military inventory. This example may be a predecessor of their FCM F1 Super Heavy Tank. However the Germans better deployed their panzers strategically as leading assault tools while the French held back their tanks as more defensive troop support.

French Tank Recovered

A Luftwaffe corporal has entered a French Souma S35 medium tank and holds one of its cannon's shells. The Germans would "repurpose" many of the captured French tanks into their arsenal as well as the Czech made designs after occupying that country and its famous Skoda Works factories.

The Camera Brings Peace

German soldiers and French POWs seem to lay aside their animosities in favor of a photographer's attention. Note two of the co-belligerents including the German NCO have crossed their arms in defensive body language.

During the occupation of France thousands of civilians died as hostages or were executed as members of the Resistance while others suffered in the torture chambers of the Gestapo and their French Vichy allies-in-terror, the *Melice* or French Secret Police. In addition to French soldiers killed and injured during the German invasion, an estimated 60,000 French POWs died in German captivity and 107,000 members of the Resistance were killed. Furthermore, 79,000 civilians died as a result of the war including 18,000 gypsies (Sinti and Romani) and 79,000 French Jews—the latter collected in cooperation with French authorities.

"Here rests a brave French soldier"

A German *kradschützen* motorcycle trooper poses before the grave of an enemy for which he has offered his acknowledgment of bravery.

Victims of Another Color

Under escort, three French soldiers walk toward captivity. While the black soldier is required to keep his hands raised, the white French soldiers are more casually regarded.

During the First World War, the French has relied on their colonies to provide foot soldiers. Prior to the outbreak of the Second World War, more than 100,000 of the French forces were men recruited from French West Africa (Mauritania, Senegal, Niger, Somalia) and generally referred to as *Tirailleurs Senegelais.* Soldiers, often of lighter skin, were also recruited from North Africa, Morocco, Madagascar and Indochina. German forces when encountering these "soldiers of color" reacted with a variety of responses … from curiosity to murderous intent. Of the colonial infantry, some 63,000 troops manned the front lines. Of that number 40,000 were involved in the short-lived but deadly combat during May and June 1940.

Souvenir Photo

Two colonial POWs wearing traditional French berets have attracted the attention of a group of blond German soldiers. The photo was originally attached to a soldier photographer's service album.

The precise number of French African colonial conscripts who died as combatants in the Second World War is unknown, although the estimates run to many thousands. It is known that German troops, spurred on by Nazi propaganda and the ferocity of close combat, often took no black prisoners during battle, executed the wounded and took part in mass shootings of those captured as POWs. While there was no systematic program for their elimination, many Afro-Germans also perished in Nazi concentration camps.

German Medics Secure a Souvenir Photo with an "exotic" French African Colonial POW.

A Summer Day in France

German Luftwaffe ground troops rather tentatively examine dead French artillery troops, their cannons still in position, an ammunition cart upended, the shells visible. A closer examination reveals the corpse is that of French African colonial soldier.

The Coupe-Coupe

German racist propaganda characterized the French African soldiers as barbarous savages who used their *coupe-coupe*, large machete-like knives, to mutilate German soldiers. In this photo, at least one Colonial soldier lies dead, cartridges spilling from his ammo pouch, the special battle knife prominently in view.

The German High Command forbade anyone, including French civilians, from decorating the graves of black soldiers, in many cases requiring the bodies of black soldiers to be left unburied and to rot where they lay. However the French, well aware of the sacrifice of thousands of colonial soldiers, most without the benefits or rights of French citizenship, sought during and after the war to memorialize their actions and gravesites, considering it a national duty.

The East—*Vernichtung*—A Policy of Annihilation

Police Forces—Advance Guard of the Holocaust
A staring match seems to be in progress between two regular police and an SS policeman somewhere in France, 1940. German police served in many forms—as traffic controllers, border guards, customs agents, railroad security, investigators of civilian crime, military policemen, but some also as "racial soldiers" ultimately responsible for the murder of over 1,000,000 Jewish men, women and children, the so-named "Holocaust by Bullets" conducted by roving execution squads operating in Eastern Europe.

PB 322 at Play
During July–October, 1941, members of Police Battalion 322 added more than 35,000 Jews and purported partisans to their ledger of death.

Sleeves Rolled
Two policemen of different generations, their distinctive dark uniform cuffs rolled up against the summer heat, pose for their photo somewhere in Russia.

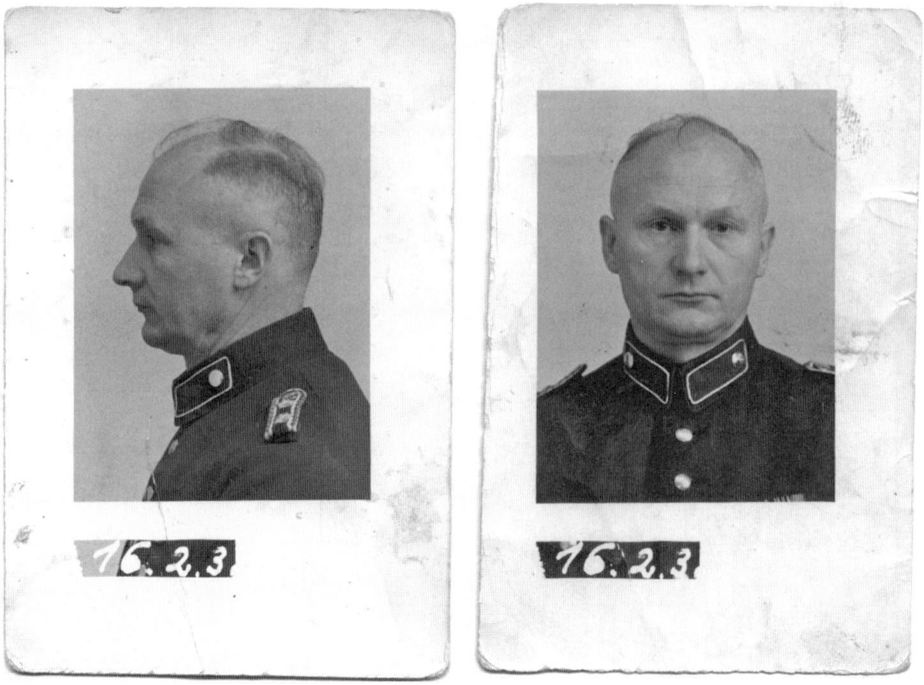

I.D. card photos for a policeman
Not all policemen were mass executioners. Some functioned as true policemen protecting German citizens from criminals and criminal acts. In fact, upon occasion the police brought charges against even the SS, for example, their investigations into the corruption and brutality of Hilmar Wackerle, an early commandant of the Dachau concentration camp.

Located some 12 miles northwest of the Bavarian city of Munich, the camp was initially used to incarcerate and "educate" political opponents. The police initiated charges against Wackerle and others of his staff for the murder of camp inmates. This occurred early in the history of the Nazi takeover of the country and in this case the victims were "Aryan" Germans as opposed to "racial enemies" of the Third Reich. The families of the dead prisoners caused a public uproar which brought bad publicity, much to the annoyance of Himmler and other Party leaders. It should be remembered that a public outcry, including protests from both Catholic and Protestant German clergy, brought an end to the euthanasia program liquidating the mentally and physically handicapped. No such outcry resulted from the treatment of Germany's Jewish population.

Er war uns
lieb im Leben.
Gedenken wir
auch seiner
im Tode.

Gedenket im
Gebete des ge-
fallenen Helden

Hans Holler

Mauerers- und Landwirtssohn von Haag b. M.
Gefr. in einem SS-Polizei-Schützen-Regt.,
welcher am 21. August 1941 im Osten
im Alter von 21 Jahren fürs Vaterland starb.

O Eltern und Geschwister mein
Ich kehre nicht mehr zu Euch heim,
Der letzte Gedanke, der letzte Blick
Der eilte noch zu Euch zurück
Als ich starb im Feindesland,.
Reichte niemand mir die Hand,
Doch als mein Auge war gebrochen
Sah den Himmel ich schon offen.

Heil. Herz Jesu erbarme dich seiner!
Süßes Herz Mariä sei meine Rettung!
Vater unser . . . . Ave Maria.

Druck von Jg. Forstner, Oberviechtach

August 21, 1941—SS-Policeman—KIA in The East

In civilian life back home in the Bavarian village of Haag, Hans Holler had been a mason, a bricklayer. A 21-year old corporal in a SS *Schutzpolizei* regiment, he was killed during the first summer of the German advance into Russia. His cap bears the distinctive emblem of the Police.

The *Schutzpolizei* or "Protection Police" were charged with regular police duties in pre-Third Reich Germany, then incorporated into the SS where they took part in anti-partisan warfare and upon entry into Eastern Europe the mass executions of "racial enemies of the State."

Many of the policemen sent to the East were over 40, others too young for regular combat service, others culled from the ranks of the wounded and disabled.

It was often literally overnight that police regiments were transported from urban environments like Hamburg and Vienna to conquered territory in Eastern Europe where they became the vanguard in the extermination of the Jewish populations and tasked with combating partisans or "bandits." The latter Nazi terminology was a catch-all term that allowed for treating partisans outside the pale of the Geneva Conference rules, in effect "legalizing" the wholesale murder of men, women and children.

The killers conducted their *Aktions* with ruthless, seemingly impossible efficiency. For example, in the case of the Babi Yar massacre at Kiev, Ukraine during the two days of September 28–29, 1941, some 34,000 Russian Jewish men, women and children were shot to death by a few handfuls of Germans including members of Police Battalions 45, 303 and 314, the corpses stacked in a trench 60 yards long and eight feet deep. Later the Germans had Jewish prisoners dig up the bones and grind them to dust in an attempt to hide their crime; the prisoners were then killed. However, at least one escaped to tell the story.

Often the victims were made to walk long distances to the execution sites in order to weaken them, then forced to lie in the hot summer sun for hours without water to further debilitate them as the mass graves were dug, then filled with their fellow victims before their eyes. Subterfuge was a main weapon of controlling the victims prior to their murder, including promises of work, promises of remaining with their families, promises of more food. Moreover the victims could not fathom they were being led to their mass deaths. Even the Germans were amazed at how easily their victims seemingly acquiesced to the procedure ... deriding them as "like sheep to the slaughter."

The executioners counted on mothers and fathers unable to abandon their children and elderly grandparents and the fact that the Jews had nowhere to escape to for in most cases their fellow non-Jewish countrymen either shunned them for fear of reprisals by the Germans or in many cases collaborated for rewards with the killers.

Banditen hinter der Front

Wie der Wehrmachtbericht schon des öfteren mitteilte, haben sich im besetzten Gebiet der Sowjetunion kleinere Gruppen der in den verschiedenen Schlachten Geflüchteten und Versprengten zu Banden zusammengeschlossen. Durch Überfälle auf schwache deutsche Abteilungen und durch die Ausraubung von Güterzügen bildeten diese Banden eine dauernde Beunruhigung des geregelten Nachschubverkehrs. Es war deshalb notwendig, dieses Bandenunwesen in militärischen Einzelaktionen zu vernichten.

PK-Aufnahmen: Kriegsberichter Heine (Atl.) 6

Als letzten Ausweg haben sich die eingekreisten Mitglieder der Bande in den Häusern verbarrikadiert, die von den deutschen Soldaten in Brand geschossen werden (links)

Es ist gelungen, den Anführer der Bande zu fassen. Sein Schicksal ist besiegelt. Denn gegen Banditen kennt die deutsche Wehrmacht kein Erbarmen. Sie stehen außerhalb des Kriegsrechts (rechts)

be- chen ihre teil

Neben dem Schienenweg hat ein deutscher Soldat, im Kampf gegen die bolschewistischen Banden gefallen, seine letzte Ruhestätte gefunden. An dieser Stelle hatten bolschewistische Banditen im Schutz der nahen Wälder einem deutschen Güterzug aufgelauert und ihn in die Luft gesprengt. Der deutsche Soldat hatte dabei den Tod gefunden

***Sein Schicksal ist besiegelt*—"His Fate is Sealed"—"Bandit Behind the Front"**
So states the text accompanying a feature article appearing in the July 1942 issue of the illustrated newsmagazine *Die Wehrmacht*, an official German military publication. The story concerns the activities of "bandits" i.e., civilian partisans harassing German forces behind the lines of combat, and the special efforts to annihilate them … *zu vernichten*. The Russian partisan seen in the photo is further identified as the group's leader … his Fate sealed.

Comradeship
Enjoying beer and a songfest, several dozen *Polizei,* including at least one wearing SS runes along with the distinctive dark cuffs of their uniform, relax while on assignment in Krakow, Poland in 1941.

On June 6, 1942, 6,000 Jews were deported from Krakow's ghetto to the Belzec death camp and another 600 were killed inside the city.

It was in Krakow that Oscar Schindler, a Sudeten German, successful businessman and Nazi party member of "Schindler's List" fame operated his enamelware factory, a refuge for Jews. Schindler saved many hundreds from death.

Music Break—SS Police Band

In the early days of the mass shootings, the male prisoners were shot first, followed by the women and children. But then it was thought better to mix in the women and children rather than leave them for the last, since a concentration of solely women and children put more strain on the killers who often returned splattered with blood and brain matter. To further counter the stress and strain of the various execution teams' activities, the Reich Security Office called for donations of light reading materials, chess and checkers, games, cards, dice, record players and even table tennis equipment.

Members of police and other execution squads were given the option to decline participation in the shootings without fear of punishment. A few did abstain, but in general there was an overabundance of volunteers especially after individuals became inured to the slaughter. The meticulous documentation by the Germans themselves accounted for every last murder, the statistics broken down into men, women and children thus providing ample and undeniable evidence of their crimes.

SS Police *Aktion* in Lublin Ghetto—photo published in *Illustrierter Beobachter* newspaper

German troops entered Lublin, an important Jewish cultural center, on September 18, 1939, some two weeks after the initial invasion of Poland. By war's end, of the 40,000 Lublin Jews, 1,300 survived. The Lublin Ghetto was the first "liquidated" by the Germans and served as a model for future round-ups, deportations, transports to death camps, and eliminations of other ghettoes across Europe.

Naming Themselves—1943 *Harvest Festival*
On the reverse side of his photo of three policemen, one of their number has neatly typed: *Erntedankfest Sept. 43 in Radziecho. Rechts Kamerad Schubert, links Wm. Rheinhardt.* The individual in the center does not name himself for the photo was included in his personal service album.

Neatly Typed

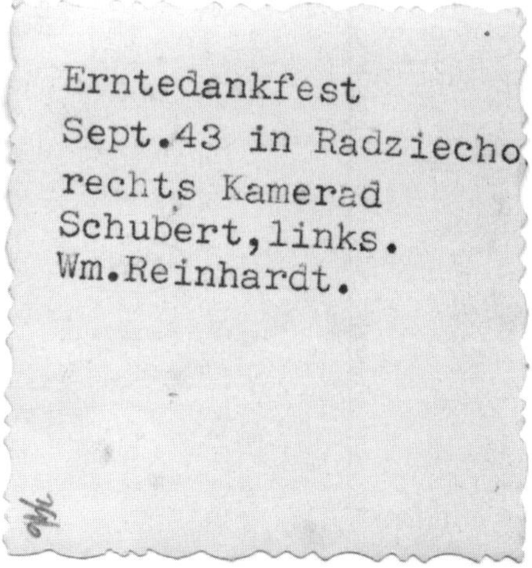

Erntedankfest translates to Harvest Appreciation Festival, a traditional annual German celebration. In the fall of 1943 the shortened form *Erntefest* or Harvest Festival became the code name for the German effort to exterminate the last surviving Jews remaining in the Lublin District of the *Generalgouvernement* (occupied Poland). The Germans claimed it was in response to incidents of Jewish resistance and revolts in various camps and ghettoes including Warsaw.

"Erntefest" began at dawn on November 3, 1943 when SS and Police units surrounded the Trawniki and Poniatowa labor camps. After rounding up the prisoners, they forced them into nearby pits and shot 6,000. At the Majdanek/Lublin camp, another 17,000 people were shot. To conceal the sound of gunfire and screams of the dying, the Germans played music through loudspeakers at both Majdanek and Trawniki. The killing operations at Majdanek and Trawniki were accomplished in a single day. Two days were required at Poniatowa, where some 42,000 Jews were killed. Often the mounds of earth over such mass graves would days later heave and "groan" as the bodies, expelling gases of decay, swelled and ruptured, local villagers observing the event.

SS Policemen Attend Social Gathering—Friednau Berlin Neighborhood 1939
Polizei often had wives and children of their own back in Germany and Austria, yet they often shot, individually and at close range, several hundred people during a day's work. Occasionally their wives and girlfriends would visit them and invited to witness mass executions. Sometimes the women would provide refreshments during breaks in the shooting.

Unflinching Gaze
A family portrait of a Customs Policeman and his family bears the effects of time as it was taken on March 18, 1944, Germany being pounded into rubble if not submission from all sides. The Allies were advancing up the Italian boot after the Anzio landings in January and on the Eastern Front the Red Army continued to decimate German troops pushing them back toward Germany's borders. The Customs officer may soon be exchanging uniforms and sent to the front as the Third Reich began thrusting all able-bodied into the escalating carnage during the last months of the war.

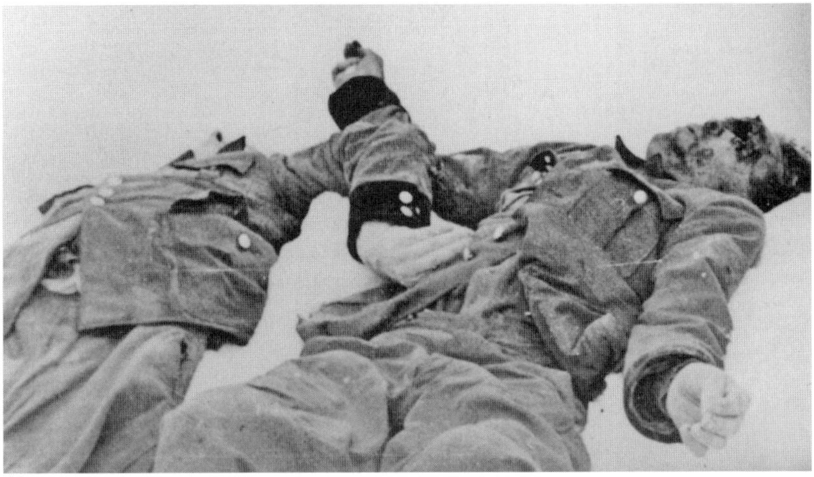

Rarely Photographed

The bodies of two dead policemen found in the Russian snow have been discovered by another German soldier. They may have been killed fighting Soviet Army forces, during partisan skirmishes or executed when captured. One appears to have been shot at close range in the face as Russian troops were aware of their murderous activities.

Policeman in Postscript

In this post-war press photo, a rifle-toting Tommy walks directly between two German policemen, his body language indicating his attitude towards the individuals who until perhaps hours earlier had been enforcers of the Third Reich. They in turn ignore him and focus on the cameraman taking their photo. An American jeep can be seen in the background further indicating the Allies' control of the city. Due to manpower shortages and language needs, and thinking of them as police officers similar to their own at home, the Allies frequently detailed German policemen to maintain order among their fellow POWs and to patrol recently occupied German towns and cities, unaware that some were guilty of crimes themselves. Many of those mass murderers returned to Germany after the war, resumed their civilian police positions and were thus able to protect themselves and their comrades from disclosure and prosecution.

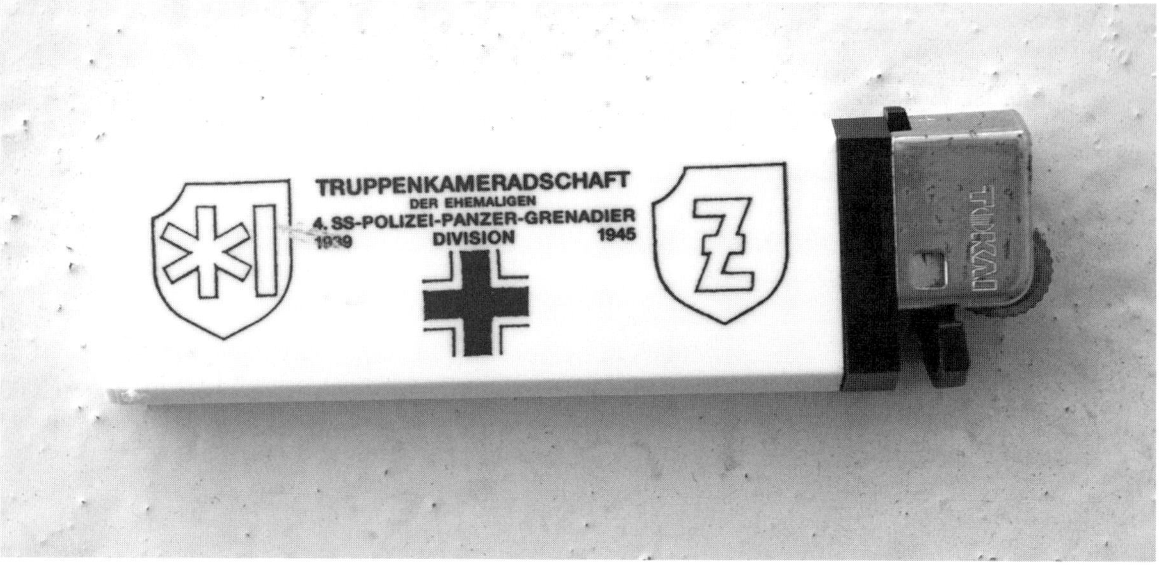

Found on the Internet: SS Polizei Reunion Commemorative Lighter

The inscription marks a 1980s "Troop Fellowship" reunion of the surviving members of the former Police 4th SS-Panzer-Grenadier-Division 1939–1945.

One could say the lighter helps to shed light, if unintentionally, on the war crimes record of the unit. Initially composed in 1939 from German civilian police units (*Ordnungspolizei*) that had come under the sway of SS leader Heinrich Himmler, it was one of the 38 Polizei Divisions he sought to incorporate into the Waffen-SS. Officially incorporated in 1942 it was reformatted as the *4th SS-Polizei-Panzergrenadier Division*. In various forms, this police division saw combat in France, Russia and Pomerania against Russian and Allied forces and also took part in anti-partisan warfare including actions in Greece. It was here that the police unit committed one of the most publicized war atrocities.

Prior to the incident, in August, 1941, the 4th was engaged in heavy action against Red Army forces at the Luga bridgehead where it suffered 2,000 killed in action including the divisional commander, Arthur Mülverstadt, but still eventually overcame Soviet resistance in the area. In January 1942 its members switched out of their regular police insignia for Waffen-SS insignia. It then took part in more direct combat including the Leningrad front.

The 4th Division was transferred to northern Greece where its combat honor was stained by its crimes against the civilian population including the action known as the Distomo Massacre. Reportedly it was a reprisal raid stemming from a previous partisan attack that caused German casualties (6 dead, 15 wounded). Troops of 4th SS Polizei Panzergrenadier Division then attacked Distomo's civilian population on June 10, 1944, just four days after the D-Day landings in Normandy. Under the command of *SS-Hauptsturmführer* Fritz Lautenbach, they set fire to the town and murdered 218 civilians. Witnesses reported the German SS police bayoneted babies in their cribs, stabbed pregnant women, and beheaded the village priest; 45 adolescents and 20 babies were among the dead.

Lautenbach was in fact brought to a military Secret Police tribunal by fellow officers when it was learned that the partisan connection had nothing to do with Distomo. Nevertheless the German reviewers found him not at fault but that he had been "motivated by a sense of responsibility to his men."

The remaining members of the 4th left Greece in August 1944 to meet the Red Army penetration of Yugoslavia, suffering more losses, first withdrawing into Slovakia, then Pomerania where they engaged in more holding actions against Soviet Forces advancing toward Germany. Initially trapped in Danzig, the division survivors escaped and fought their way to surrender to U.S. forces near Wittenberge-Lenzen.

After the war a German soldier identified as Hans Zampel was accused of responsibility in the murders and sent back from his hiding place in Paris to Greece, but after a return by authorities to West Germany he was never returned to Greece to face prosecution. Post-war reparations were paid to Greece in the 1960s by West Germany, but the personal claims by relatives of the Distomo survivors were denied when suit was brought in 2003.

Distomo was not an isolated instance of atrocity perpetrated by German troops in Greece. In December 1943 the 117th Hunter Division destroyed the small town of Kalavryta and 24 surroundings villages during which they shot some 1,300 male inhabitants. During the 1941–1945 German occupation, 460 Greek villages were destroyed and approximately 60,000 men, women and children killed. 65,000 Greek Jews were deported and killed in Auschwitz. None of the murderers of Distomo or any other massacre in Greece was ever tried by a German court.

Yugoslavia/Serbia
Masses of Serbian POWs have been concentrated in a gully between hillsides. As fighting spread to the Balkans, Wehrmacht troops occupied Yugoslavia, Bulgaria and Northern Greece as Hitler sought to protect his southern flank. Yugoslavia's Marshal Tito mounted successful partisan warfare which in turn brought terrible retribution.

Serbia—Carnage Incarnate
In this rare photo taken by a German soldier, the indistinct shapes of bodies lie scattered about, some half buried within the chaos of corpses. A comparison with photographs exhibited by the Hamburg Institute for Social Research suggest this may be a scene from the massacre of 1,755 hostages in Kraljevo in Central Serbia in October 1941. The official German report labeled the mass murder as an act of "atonement".

Lithuania—Swastika On the Border
German Soldiers and a Lithuanian volunteer pose at the "new" border of Nazi Germany and Lithuania. With the invasion of the Baltic countries on June 22, 1941 during the invasion of the USSR, Lithuanian nationalists rose up against the Red Army in retreat and initially welcomed the German forces as liberators.

Lithuania—*Greif-Division, Einsatz in Kowno, Flüchtlinge, 1942*
Well-dressed civilian refugees are seen walking along Kovno's cobblestone street, their destination unknown. The photograph was taken by a members of the Greif Division or Cross Division, the nickname for the German 122nd Infantry Division. Composed of three regiments (infantry, artillery and support units) and part of the 16th Army, it fought on the Eastern Front. By 1942, the infantry had been reformed as grenadier regiments in support of mechanized units and as shock troops. *Continued on next page*

Kovno is the Russian name for the historic Lithuanian city of Kaunas and once home to some 40,000 Jewish citizens, one-quarter of the city's population, composing much of the city's commercial, cultural and educational leadership. The Soviets when occupying Lithuania had persecuted the Jews, but the Nazis and their collaborators increased the terror. In an early action 4,000 Jews were rounded up in Kaunas, taken to a hastily established concentration camp at one of the city's historic forts, and murdered often in barbaric ways involving public spectacles attended by Lithuanian civilians. During the Nazi occupation, some 20,000 Lithuanians were killed along with 30,000 Jews.

Greif ("Snatch") was also the code name for a proposed, though unimplemented German operation employing troops dressed in American uniforms and set to capture the Meuse River bridges during the Battle of the Bulge.

Latvia—Cigarette Break (*above left*)
In a pre-war photo, two young Latvian soldiers assume a jaunty pose. Latvia, created on November 18, 1918 as the result of the collapse of Germany in the First World War was occupied by the Soviet Union in June 1940, then by Nazi Germany in June 1941.

On the Road to Riga (*above right*)
A German sign encapsulates the massive assault on the Soviet Union that also engulfed the Baltic countries includinlg the Latvian capital of Riga.

Riga, Latvia—A. Vitolis Photo Studio Portrait

With the German–Soviet Non-Aggression Pact in place, the USSR took control of Latvia in late 1939, establishing a puppet government and brutally suppressing anti-Soviet opponents. Then in June 1941, upon invading the Baltic countries on their way into the Soviet Union, the Germans entered Latvia where they were joined by public uprisings against their Soviet occupiers. Eventually some 140,000 men joined the Latvian Waffen-SS divisions.

By early July, German troops controlled the country. Almost immediately they concentrated on the destruction of the Latvian Jewish population including 3,000 killed in the capital city of Riga. During December 7–9, another 25,000 were transported from the ghetto to the nearby Rumbula Forest and systematically shot by the police forces of *Einsatzgruppe A*. As a prelude to the mass execution, the SS entered the ghetto hospital and threw some thirty Jewish babies from the upper windows to their death as their mothers watched.

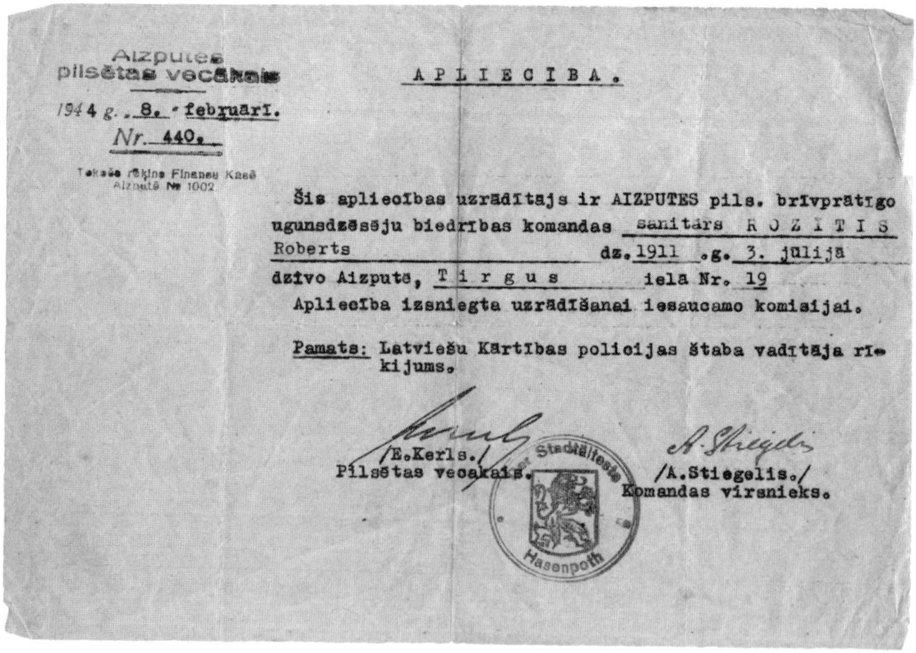

Aizputes
pilsētas vecākais
1944 g. 8. februārī.
Nr. 440.
Tekošā rēķins Finanšu Kasē Aizputē № 1002

APLIECIBA.

Šis apliecības uzrādītājs ir AIZPUTES pils. brīvprātīgo ugunsdzēsēju biedrības komandas sanitārs ROZITIS Roberts dz. 1911 g. 3. jūlijā dzīvo Aizputē, Tirgus iela Nr. 19

Apliecība izsniegta uzrādīšanai iesaucamo komisijai.

Pamats: Latviešu Kārtības policijas štaba vadītāja rīkijums.

/E.Kerls./
Pilsētas vecākais.

/A.Stiegelis./
Komandas virsnieks.

Stadtälteste Hasenpoth

Application for Membership in Latvian SS

A 33-year old Latvian named Roberts Rozitis has on February 4, 1944 applied as a medic in the Latvian *Freiwillige* SS legion, the form filled out in Riga. *Continued on next page*

On January 23, 1943, Hitler had ordered SS leader Heinrich Himmler to form a Voluntary Latvian SS Legion. When this February application was signed, the Germans still occupied Latvia but were fighting to halt the Soviet Advance. In March, the second Latvian SS Legion (19th Division) was formed then joined with the former unit to face Soviet forces on March 16 in the battle of the Velikaya River which later became memorialized as the Legion's Memorial Day in post-war Latvia. Russian forces re-entered the country in July, 1944 resulting in some 150,000 Latvians evacuated to German controlled territory. By October 13, 1944 the Soviets occupied Riga. During the three occupations by the Soviets, the Germans and then the Soviets again, some 300,000 Latvians died. Post-war, some 120,000 Latvians chose to remain in the West.

Latvians as Anti-Soviet German Allies (*above*)
As Soviet forces advanced, the remaining Germans and Latvians held the rapidly deteriorating front weathering several major Russian offensives until the war ended. According to German estimates, during the protracted fighting, Soviet army casualties included 390,000 soldiers, dead, wounded or captured. Material losses included 2,388 tanks, 659 planes, 900 cannons, and 1,440 machine-guns. By May 23rd, several days after the war had officially ended, some 180,000 German troops surrendered to Soviet captivity. When captured among them, those Latvian Legion soldiers who had fought as allies of the Germans were shot as Soviet traitors. Recent memorials held in Latvia honored the Latvian SS as national anti-Communist heroes.

The Battle of Kurland—November 3, 1944 — "Honor His Memory!" (*right*)
German Flak Soldier Anton Brtl met his death in Kurland, the Latvian Baltic peninsula where by mid-October some half a million German and 20,000 Latvian Waffen-SS troops were trapped by Soviet forces. A few weeks previously Soviet troops had liberated Riga from German occupation. Latvian Waffen SS Legion troops fought alongside German troops evacuating the capital city and prevented Red forces from encircling and capturing the German garrison. Anti-fascist Latvians, including the 130th Latvian Riflemen, also fought on the Soviet side, aiding in the liberation of the city from Nazi control.

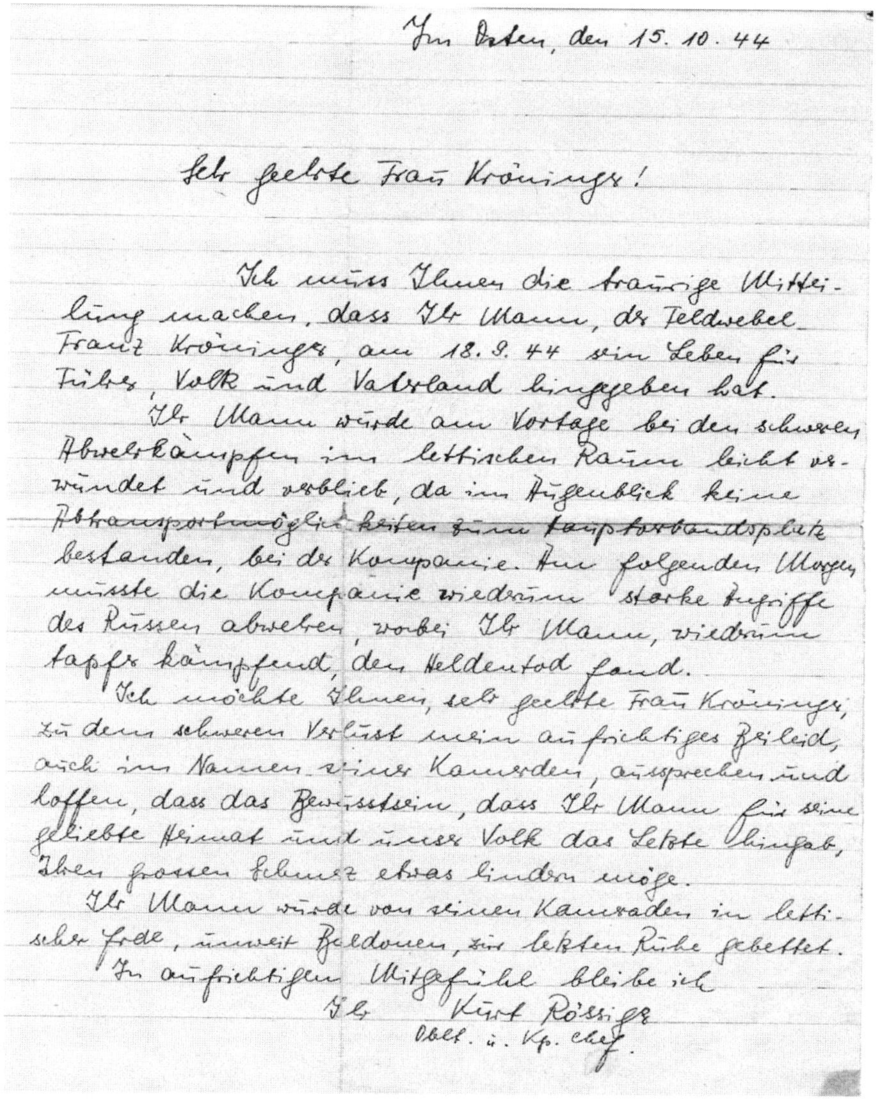
Im Osten, den 15. 10. 44

Sehr geehrte Frau Kröninger!

Ich muss Ihnen die traurige Mitteilung machen, dass Ihr Mann, der Feldwebel Franz Kröninger, am 18. 9. 44 sein Leben für Führer, Volk und Vaterland hingegeben hat.

Ihr Mann wurde am Vortage bei den schweren Abwehrkämpfen im lettischen Raum leicht verwundet und verblieb, da im Augenblick keine ~~Abtransportmöglichkeiten zum Hauptverbandsplatz~~ bestanden, bei der Kompanie. Am folgenden Morgen musste die Kompanie wiederum starke Angriffe des Russen abwehren, wobei Ihr Mann, wiederum tapfer kämpfend, den Heldentod fand.

Ich möchte Ihnen, sehr geehrte Frau Kröninger, zu dem schweren Verlust mein aufrichtiges Beileid, auch im Namen seiner Kameraden, aussprechen und hoffen, dass das Bewusstsein, dass Ihr Mann für seine geliebte Heimat und unser Volk das Letzte hingab, Ihren grossen Schmerz etwas lindern möge.

Ihr Mann wurde von seinen Kameraden in lettischer Erde, unweit Baldonen, zur letzten Ruhe gebettet.

In aufrichtigem Mitgefühl bleibe ich

Ihr Kurt Rössigs

Oblt. u. Kp. chef.

German KIA Latvia–October 15, 1944- Condolence Letter

Dear Mrs. Kröninger!

I have to give you the sad news that your husband, 1st Sgt. Franz Kröninger, on Sept. 18th 1944 gave his life for Führer, Folk and Fatherland. Your husband had participated in the battle in Latvia the day before and was slightly wounded. During the battle we had no transport available to bring our wounded to the rear so the wounded stayed overnight with us. The following morning the Russians attacked again and during the battle, your husband was killed.

Dear Mrs. Kröninger, on behalf of my Comrades and myself, I would like to give you our deep condolences and be assured that your husband gave his very best for his beloved Fatherland. May this lessen your grief. Your husband lies in Latvian soil not far from Baldonen.

With my deepest sorrow,

Kurt Rössigs, 1st Lt. and Company Commander

(On the preceding August 19th, Russian forces completed their encirclement of fifty-five German Divisions on the Baltic Coast. As the German front collapsed, Sgt. Kröninger was caught within that maelstrom. Both doctors and wounded when found in field hospitals were shown no mercy by either side.)

Romania—Batons of Power

German *Feldmarschall* Wilhelm Keitel (right) and Romanian Prime Minister Ion Antonescu raise their symbols of authority as they take part in a parade during Keitel's state visit to the Romanian capital of Bucharest.

Although Hitler's chief military adviser he had threatened to resign because of the plan to invade the USSR. He however considered Hitler a genius and himself as the *Führer's* "loyal shield bearer" and later also highly approved of Hitler's treatment of Russia. He was also responsible for implementing the *Nacht und Nebel* (Night and Fog Decree) mandated by Hitler where a "threat to the State" instead of being arrested and executed, the person would literally be disappeared into the fog without any trace. Tried at Nuremberg for war crimes and found guilty on all counts, he was hanged on October 16, 1946. Antonescu was also convicted of war crimes post-war and shot by firing squad in Romania on June 1, 1946.

Romanian Object of Derision

As recorded by a German soldier's camera somewhere in Romania, everyone is laughing except the old man. There is a word unique to the German language … *schadenfreude* … that translates to "taking delight in the suffering or misery of others" or "malicous joy."

German and Romanian soldiers join together for a photo—1940

Romania was a strategic target for both Axis and Allied assaults due to its large oil refineries that Hitler needed to fuel his blitzkrieg. The fascist Iron Guard was led by the dictator Ion Antonescu who came to power in Romania in September 1940 when King Carol went into self-exile with his mistress Elena Lupescu. In June 1941 Antonescu allied Romania with Nazi Germany and joined in the invasion of the Soviet Union.

The Germans held their Romanian allies in low repute as soldiers. Soviet forces would often target the weaker Romanian defensive lines in order to breach German positions. On August 23, 1944, with the war turning against the Third Reich, Antonescu was overthrown and the new government of Romania changed its allegiances and joined the Soviet forces in fighting their ex-allies.

538,000 Romanians fought against the Axis in 1944–45 with some 167,000 casualties. A total of 370,000 Romanian soldiers were killed including those who died fighting both with and against Germany.

Eager Accomplices (*previous page, below*)
Nominally more anti-Soviet, then pro-German, the Romanians nevertheless were enthusiastic in their efforts to eradicate their Jewish population. During the summer of 1941 over 100,000 Jews were shot to death by Germans and Ukrainians but in largest part by Romanian soldiers. By February 1942 the area which was once home to 180,000 Jews was declared *Judenrein*, "cleansed of Jews." In total, Romanian soldiers took part in the killing of as many as 380,000 men, women and children. In addition over 25,000 Romanian Sinti and Romani peoples perished during Romania's collaboration with Germany.

An official 2004 Romanian government report concluded:

> Of all the allies of Nazi Germany, Romania bears responsibility for the deaths of more Jews than any country other than Germany itself. The murders committed in Iasi, Odessa, Bogdanovka, Domanovka, and Peciora, for example, were among the most hideous murders committed against Jews anywhere during the Holocaust.

Memorial Pin— "Behind this Gate the Earth Groans"
While several of the larger Nazi Concentration and Death Camps are well-known, thousands more of varying scale remain lost in the history of the Holocaust. Such is the case of Salaspils. A monument at the Latvian concentration camp reads "Behind this gate the Earth groans." Designated by the Germans as Stalag-350-s, it was used to imprison Soviet POWs, 43,000 of whom died behind its barbed wire. A second camp built in the nearby forest was designated for "work and education." Between 50,000 and 100,000 civilians perished there. In the period December 1941 to August 1942, of the 15,000 prisoners entering the camp, only 192 survived. The camp was also a center for Nazi medical experiments focusing on Soviet children of whom 150 reportedly died daily. An estimated 12,000 children were funneled through the camp for the purpose of extracting a portion of their blood for use by wounded German soldiers. Soviet authorities commemorated the site on October 31, 1967.

Bulgaria—"The Devouring"—*Zigeuner*
Three family members wearing their finest traditional garments pose for their photograph at a professional studio in Sofia, Bulgaria.

The Sinti and Romani peoples were targeted for extermination by Nazi racial directives as "asocials," some 200,000 (and as many as 500,000) Roma and Sinti peoples were gathered from all over Europe. They were often tattooed with numbers beginning with "Z" for *Zigeuner*, German for gypsy. Their own term for the mass murder of their people, similar to the term "Shoah" regarding the Holocaust, was *Porraimos* or "The Devouring."

In Auschwitz–Birkenau, a special camp for gyspy families allowed them to remain together as the Germans found them amusing, often calling upon for them for music and dancing as entertainment. SS doctor Mengele was obsessed with them and was said to be distressed when the order went out to send 21,000 of them to the gas chambers. The gypsy children called him "Uncle Pepi" as he often gave them sweets. Upon the order for their extermination, he again used candy to draw the last of the gypsy children into his car at which point he drove them to their deaths. Only one German was ever convicted of crimes against the Roma and Sinti, the West German courts freeing all others on the grounds that the gypsies were "executed" as criminals rather than victims of genocide.

The Great Patriotic War

Death March of Millions
Endless lines of Soviet POWs stream along a dirt road in the Ukraine. During the month of July 1941 German troops occupied Latvia then invaded the Ukraine where some 750,000 Red Army soldiers fell victim to captivity, and for most, subsequent death.

Replacement
In this photograph Soviet leader Joseph Stalin has been decapitated, a German soldier taking the opportunity to repurpose the statue for his souvenir photo. The defacing of sculptures of Stalin, Lenin and Marx was a common practice among German forces who embraced the "total war" Nazi mindset seeking the complete eradication of Russian Bolshevism and its followers.

Body Language
A German NCO, wearing an Iron Cross and Silver Wound Badge, assumes an aggressive posture when posing with two Russian women whose body language and expressions display opposing reactions to their German liberators or at least to the camera.

Sport in Soviet Lands
Battle hardened German soldiers surround two Russians, possibly father and son, and have them pose for a souvenir photo. Two carry MG34 machine guns slung on their shoulder, another carries a stick grenade tucked in his belt. The fate of the two men unknown but sealed if considered partisans or determined to be "undesirables."

Blue-eyed Russian Twins

A German soldier's camera mesmerizes a Russian family, the children's mouths agape. Perhaps it is the blue "Aryan" eyes that has attracted the soldier's attention. Thousands of Eastern European children bearing the "correct" physical traits such as blue eyes and blond hair were forcibly taken from their parents and sent back to Germany, most never returned to their families. However the Russians as a whole were considered Slavic *untermenschen* or subhumans and, as Göring described them, "useless eaters" and thus the Nazi planners, once the war had been won, scheduled 30,000,000 for mass extinction via starvation to make room for German colonists. In the end, bullet, bomb and flame killed some 30,000,000 Russians including millions of children.

Die Spitze einer Aufklärungsabteilung ist auf die noch vom Feind besetzte Stadt gestoßen.

„Stadt M. feindfrei!"

Unsere Waffen-SS säubert einen Bolschewisten-Ort vom Gegner.

Bild rechts: Aus dem Rauch der brennenden Ortschaft rast ein Kradmelder zurück.

"City Made Enemy Free!"

A Berlin newspaper features images from the Soviet invasion focusing on the activities of the Waffen-SS, the soldiers seen in ther special camouflage uniforms.

Russian Hay
A less glamorized image of German soldiers taken with a comrade's camera.

Traversing a "Corduroy Road"
A German motorcycle trooper navigates logs set up to ford muddy roads caused by the twice-yearly spring and autumn thaw and rainy seasons *(Rasputitsa)*. The knee deep morass bogged down both man and machine to a crawl.

"Motorized Scouts in the Soviet Union"—Commercial postcard—Feldpost postmarked August 10, 1943
With a MG42 machine gun in the forward position, apparently removed from its pedestal mount seen in the foreground, soldiers enter a dense Russian forest. On the preceding August 4th Soviet troops recaptured the Ukrainian city of Orel with German forces in general retreat along the Eastern Front. The postcard was addressed to the family of Emiel Heizmann in Baden, Germany. The sender however was a member of the 243rd Static Infantry Division and thus stationed far from the Eastern Front. The 243rd was stationed in France and thus faced the Allied Invasion on D-Day June 6, 1944. It was subsequently destroyed in the Battle of Normandy, its last elements perishing in the German defense of Cherbourg.

A Single Guard
While one Russian prisoner holds the rein of the horse cart, the German corporal checks on the endless line of prisoners following in its wake, perhaps noticing the man standing by the roadside.

Divided Attentions
As the guard grips his rifle as if alerted, the Russian POW, one hand holding the cart reins, the other a small whip, stares into a German's camera.

Trophies
A German soldier assumes the hand-in-the-tunic "Napoleonic" pose while his young Russian POWs stand in a bewildered huddle as they face the camera.

So poorly equipped were Russian soldiers in the early months of the war that they were sent as human waves often without so much as a rifle against superior German arms. They were instructed to pick up the weapons of the dead who fell before them. Often they were chained to their bunkers or sealed into their tanks. NKVD troops stood behind assault waves, shooting anyone who turned back, such was the nature of the war in the East.

Three Red Army Comrades

Russian soldiers in contrast to the Germans had few personal cameras and less opportunities for their photos to be taken in the field, this appearing to be a studio photograph. An officer is flanked by privates wearing the traditional Russian *Budenovka* cap and one adding a jaunty cigarette holder. Often such photos were taken from the bodies of the dead as part of German intelligence gathering or simply as war souvenirs.

In this case, one of individuals, the soldier on the left of the botton row, has been identified by his grandson currently living in Moscow as Michail Varlamov who was initially called up to fight in the Soviet–Finnish War, then went on to the battlefields of The Great Patriotic War facing the Germans. When his regiment went into retreat, he was left to take up a defensive position. Wounded and taken prisoner, he died in a German prison camp in 1942.

Momento—Russian Women Joined in the Battle of National Survival

"A Soviet prisoner is searched for weapons"
The photo and caption appeared on the cover of the July 15, 1941 issue of the *Deutsche Illustrierte* periodical published in Berlin. At the beginning of July, SS/SD leader Heydrich was ordered by Göring to begin the extermination of the Soviet Union's Jewish population. The SS *Einsatzgruppen* killing units followed in the wake of the German army and began mass executions.

Uncertain Fate
A tableau of Russian POWs of all ages has attracted the attention of a German soldier and his camera. While the men wear boots, the boy wears wrapped cloth leggings and a pair of relatively new looking shoes, the latter a rare commodity.

The Face of the Russian's War (*above left*)
A German's camera has focused on one of the enemy, the Red Army soldier perhaps joined by his younger brother, both pressed into service, often as cannon fodder.

Smiling for the Camera (*above right*)
A tall Russian POW has been singled out while an amused German soldier appears to juggle a "potato masher" handgrenade.

Entertainment
German soldiers enjoy poking fun at a Russian soldier who apparently wears a moustache similar to the Führer's. He is no doubt thankful he has received something to eat and drink, perhaps his last, as some 3,000,000 Red Army soldiers were deliberately starved to death. Regarding these crimes, in 1949 charges were brought against Gottlob Christian Berger, SS Inspector General of Prisoners of War. He was found guilty and sentenced to 25 years in prison, but two years later was released by the West German authorities. He lived another 24 years and died on 5 January 1975 in Gerstetten at the age of 77.

A Gift of Food
A Russian POW's expression reflects the fear brought about by his German captors' response after an old woman has given him bread, often a forbidden act that could cost both of them their lives.

Opposite Directions
Thousands of Red Army POWs jammed into open railway cars await transportation to an unknown destination while German soldiers crowd the windows of their passenger compartments. While their view of the mass of prisoners might impress them with the power of their military, the sight also indicated the endless supply of manpower that Russia could and would eventually place on the battlefield when the momentum of the war and the trains switched directions.

***Das Gesicht de Geners*—"The Face of the Enemy"—Russian POWs**

One of a series of commercially printed postcards featuring original illustrations by German soldier/artists, this example captioned on the reverse with "Soviet Russians from Nizhny-Novgorod," the artwork was signed by the artist and dated 1942. Nizhny-Novgorod, founded in 1221, is strategically located on the intersection of the Oka and Volga Rivers. Initial German attacks forced Soviet troops to retreat with many of them being captured. The city was also the birthplace of the Russian General Andrey Vlasov who defected to the German side, leading the German-armed, anti-Stalinist Russian Liberation Army of some 120,000 fighting against the Red Army until his capture and later trial and execution by hanging in Moscow on August 1, 1946.

Mother Russia Defiant

Singled out from the mass of male POWs, a woman prisoner glowers into the camera. Over 800,000 women wore the Red Army uniform during the war, many as medical personnel, but also as active combatants, some 2,000 further trained as snipers. Others served as tank crew members and flew as pilots, others fought in partisan bands. Some 200,000 were awarded decorations including eighty-nine earning the highest accolade, Hero of the Soviet Union.

Interrogation (*above*)
A crowd of soldiers rings a female Soviet POW as she is questioned by a Russian speaking German. In the foreground, one soldier has brought out his advanced 16 mm Siemens movie camera to film the event. Another trio of soldiers stand with their arms folded across their chest, a classic body language expression of self-defensiveness in the face of a perceived threat.

Back in Germany when newsreels showed Russian women soldiers, the women in the audience often shouted out angrily and called for their deaths.

Final Resting Place (*left*)
A German camera records the death of a young Russian woman who has either been killed in her defensive dugout or her body tossed into a fresh grave. The scattered papers indicate her body has been searched.

Walking Wounded
Russian POWs, their faces showing the toll taken by the effort to carry themselves and their wounded, will find themselves trapped in a barren location with no food, water or shelter. The young German soldiers watching them pass wear a variety of expressions, perhaps realizing their faces and those of the enemy are almost identical.

Forest March to Oblivion
Apparently shooting from waist level, a German camera captures the haggard faces of Russian POWs plodding through a forest. Most carry their standard issue sleeping blanket slung over their shoulder, while one carries an all-important pot that can be used for a variety of purposes, another has fashioned a walking stick.

Pause for a Photo

A German corporal has his photograph taken with Russian POWs. He seems to be staring at the Soviet soldiers dressed in rags, the Nazi image of an *untermensch*. Standing next to the German, a Russian soldier wears the leather helmet of a tankman, most of the men transfixed by the camera, perhaps the one and only time their image will be recorded.

POWs as Art—
"Gefangene Bolschewisten"

A lone German guard marches a colum of Russian POWs through a forest setting, the image drawn by a soldier/artist identified as Martin Guhl. Often a lone German would guard scores of prisoners due to manpower shortages. In some cases the prisoners were just pointed in the direction and left to march on to captivity as they had nowhere else to go or any further interest or means to continue fighting.

Rifle Butts and Bread

A German soldier's camera records the scene at a a temporary holding area as Ukrainian civilians attempt to bring food to a throng of Red Army POWs. The few handfuls will not sustain the millions of Russian prisoners, very few, including those seen in this photo, surviving captivity.

Not Seven Loaves

A young Ukrainian woman turns and smiles having noticed the photographer. She has not noticed the German guard aiming his rifle butt at a hand reaching through the wooden fence for food.

Thin Bars do a Prison Make (*above left*)
A young Russian soldier captures the attention of a German's camera at one of the hundreds of makeshift prison camps scattered across the vast empty spaces of Soviet Union. Far from any civilization, exposed to the elements in both summer and winter without food or shelter, as many as 50,000 at a time were left to starve to death behind a few strands of barbed wire.

Temporary Compassion (*above right*)
Russian or perhaps German medics have tended to the severe wounds of a Red Army soldier. Another German has stopped to take his photo. The officer still wears his cap and rests his bandaged head on his backpack.

Portrait of the Enemy
A German camera has singled out another wounded Red Army prisoner, one of hundreds of thousands captured in the early weeks of the invasion. The injured had little chance of survival, left to suffer a slow death by infection and starvation. Soviet POWs were also the first to die as test subjects in the Auschwitz gas chambers.

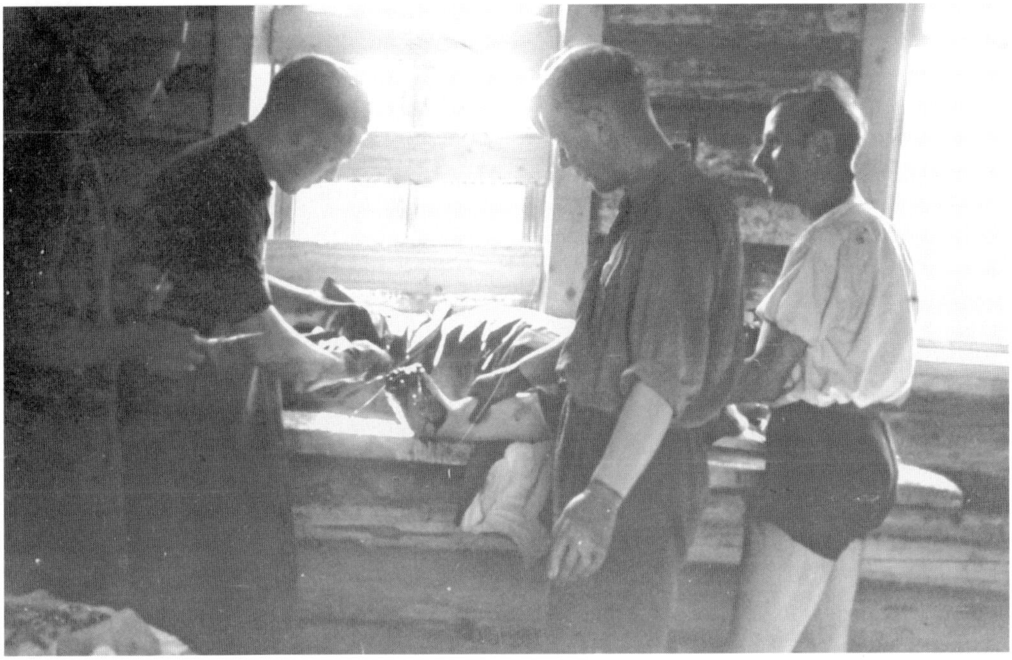

"Traumatic Amputation"
German medical personnel treat a wounded Russian POW who has just lost his forearm and hand.

Fear of mutilation was greater than fear of death for most Russian soldiers, the dread related to rejection by women. It turned out to be well-founded in the sense that post-war treatment of maimed and crippled veterans by Soviet authorities was beyond abysmal. Many of the scarred and maimed were shipped off to distant locations near the Arctic Circle in order to eliminate the "eyesores" of amputees. A common term of the times was "samovar," the name of the traditional cylindrical metal container for heating water often for tea, in this case used to describe soldiers who had lost all their limbs.

At Gunpoint
Although his life hangs in the balance, a Russian prisoner is drawn to the camera capturing his image.

Bilingual Warning
German executioners have attached placards wrttien in both Russian Cyrillic and German stating that such a fate awaits all partisans, a catchall term applied as needed to place the stamp of legitamacy upon murder.

On the previous page:

"Shot While Escaping" (*above*)
Two alleged "partisans" bound together by a rope are led down a dusty Russian village road to their fate. A third individual pushes a bicycle and unbound, his part in the scene unknown. The smaller legs and a cap of a fourth person, perhaps a young boy, can be glimpsed between them as a German corporal glances back at the camera.

Dead Men Standing (*below*)
Four Russian men, young and old, stand huddled in a field, awaiting their fate as they have been judged "partisans" as stated by the German notations on the reverse of the card.

Executive Action

On the 24th anniversary of the Communist October Revolution held in November 1941, the German killing team *Sonderkommando* 1b, a division of *Einsatzgruppe* A, and led by SS *Oberführer* Erich Ehrlinger, presented the city of Minsk with a cynical celebratory exhibit. From gallows hastily erected across the city, on its street, at its parks, markets as well as on the outskirts of town, Ehrlinger and his men hanged some 100 Russians and Byelorussians. They were left hanging with placards that called out their crimes as "partisans." At the same time, SS, Police units and Lithuanian militia dragged out local Jewish men, women and children, forcing them to put on their best clothes then parading them in front of German propaganda movie cameras. They were ordered to smile for the film makers as they carried banners hailing the Soviet Revolution. Later they were trucked to a nearby killing site where 6,624 were shot by Sonderkommando 1b, according to the unit's own official tally.

Ehrlinger, a lawyer by profession, "disappeared" at the end of the war in May 1945. He was later found working as a Volkswagen salesman under his own name. He was arrested in 1958 and finally brought to trial in 1963, a Frankfurt court sentenced him to 12 years in prison. In December 1964, a Karlsruhe court revoked his sentence, freeing him in August 1965. After 1969, he was declared medically unable to be tried. He then lived another 35 years until 2004 and the age of 94.

Epitaph on Justice

Of the thousands of Germans and their East European collaborators who took part in mass murder, the post-war West German judicial system investigated some 1,700 killing squad members of whom 136 were brought to trial. Fifty-three sentences were handed out during the span of four decades between1950–91. Eight of the convicted received life sentences, the others prison terms ranging mostly from 2–4 years with many of the sentences later shortened or commuted.

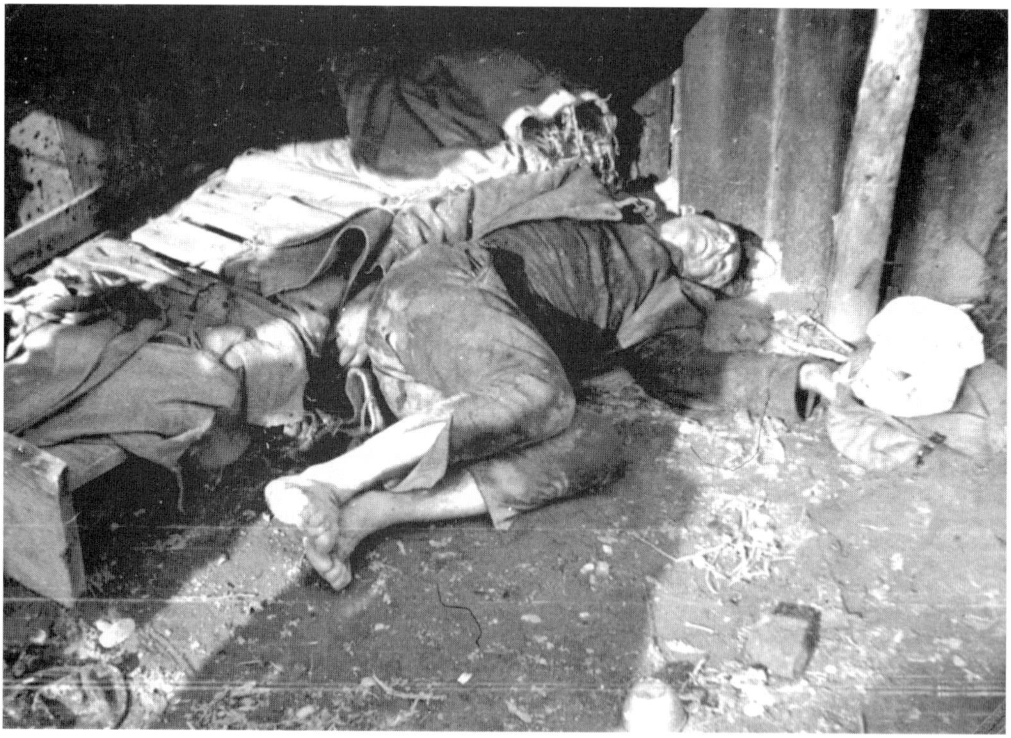

The Hunted

A German soldier has recorded the killing of a Russian as he slept in his makeshift bed, his "crime" … partisan, Jew, political commissar … unknown.

Forest Capture of a Commissar

The photo suggests that the Russian soldier (center) with longer hair relative to the short-cropped heads of the Russian Asiatic troops gathered around him is either their officer or political commissar or both, either of which carries a death penalty.

Focus of Attention—Death Hangs in the Balance

His German captors stare at him with a malevolent curiosity. The largest of them (center) unfolds a camera while another's camera is also recording the scene, perhaps the longest moment in the Russian officer's life, one very likely about to end violently as the result of Hitler's "Commissar Order."

Sowjet-Funktionäre, die mit Waffen in den Händen aufgegriffen wurden, werden abgeführt.

Taken Away (*above*)

"Soviet functionaries, found with weapons in hand, will be taken away." The photo and caption appeared in the July 15, 1941 issue of the *Deutsche Illustrierte* periodical published in Berlin. "Taken away" is a euphemism for summary execution, the fate of all captured Communist party officials, male or female.

A Park in Kiev, Ukraine (*left*)

This photo, with notations, pasted into a German soldier's photo album, apparently shows the bodies of a man and two women killed where they sat on a park bench.

Last Step
A German soldier with his camera at the ready, snaps an image of a Red Army POW under escort by another soldier apparently unaware that the Russian has stopped, turned and about to step off the enbankment. What lies below or how far is unknown as is the man's motivation, since any attempt to escape would be fatal.

Holding Their Ground
Two Soviet soldiers have died in their shallow foxhole. In the early phases of the war Russian soldiers were sent in suicidal charges often without weapons literally to soak up German ammunition. The German practice of killing Russian prisoners also inspired Soviet troops to fight to the death.

Flamethrower
Untouched by the flames that incinerated his camerades, a Soviet soldier lies at the end of trench overrun by his German enemies who have paused to snap his photo.

Reflections on Death
A German soldier has stopped to bring out his camera to record the composition of rock, water, reflective sky and the half submerged corpose of a Russian soldier. Clinging to the edge of his watery grave, the image is punctuated in the foreground by one heel protruding above the surface. The photo was found preserved for more than six decades in a *Dienstag*, a personal war service album.

Outgunned (*top of next page*)
The bodies of Russian infantrymen lie scattered around the hulk of a T-26 series light Soviet tank, no match for the heavier armored German panzers. Tankmen were often sealed into their machines by Soviet security personnel.

By war's end, Russian firing squads had executed some 135,000 of their own countrymen under Stalin's not-one-step-back decree. Born in the Soviet Georgian Republic, as Iosif (Joseph) Besarionis (aka Vissarionovich) dze Dzhugashvili (aka Jughashvili), Stalin's adopted and much shortened name, was well-earned, meaning "Man of Steel." It was gained during his younger Bolshevik revolutionary days when he purportedly placed a blade of grass between his teeth before walking through a double phalanx of anti-communist Russian Imperial soldiers who proceeded to beat him with truncheons and clubs. Stalin reached the end of the beatings, then opened his mouth to show the leaf of grass he had placed between his teeth remained unbitten, testimony of his strength of will.

The Litter of Battle

The bodies of dead Russian soldiers and horses stretch to the far horizon. The corpses have been searched for documents and valuables, their personal papers littering the ground, their weapons missing.

Russian Common Grave
A German has photographed the burial place of ten Russian soldiers. Whether buried by friend or foe is unknown. One helmet appears to show evidence of a sniper's work.

Seeking a Foothold
Like many others, this photo was found in a German soldier's personal album that would be shared with family and friends. The dead Russian appears to be clutching a handgrenade while the damage to back of his helmet indicates the cause of death by shrapnel or bullet.

Holding Ground
A Russian soldier has fought to the death in his snow dug foxhole, his rifle lying by his skis.

Still Life
A German soldier has captured a tableaux of death discovered in a Russian field, perhaps the result of his own hand. Their bodies have been searched, a Russian newspaper partially covering the body in the background.

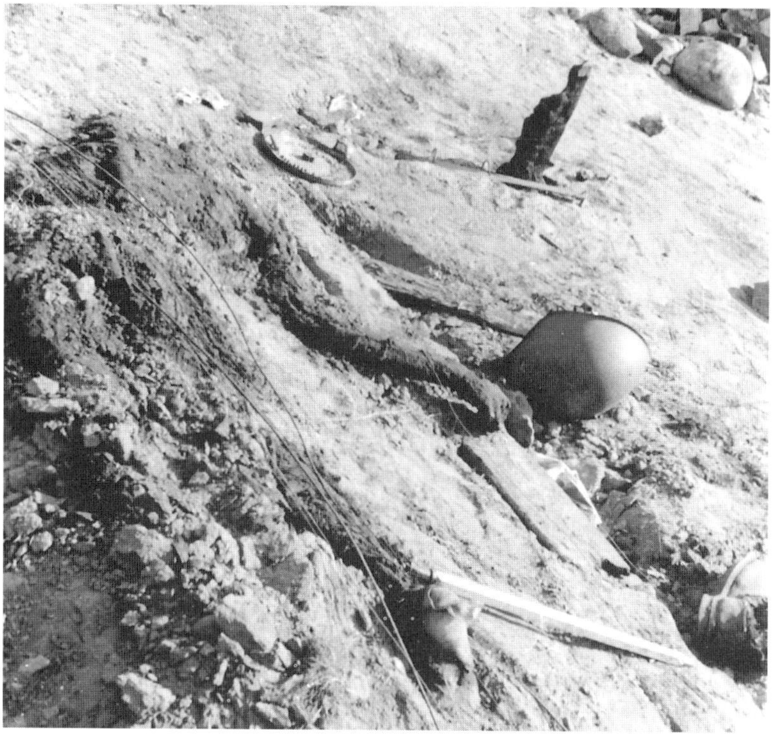

Remnants
Beyond the bayonet and the Russian helmet, it is difficult to distinguish the remains of the Russian soldier crushed into the ground perhaps by the tank treads of a German Panzer.

Death of a Sniper
A horse, its last hoof prints still visible, has fallen alongside two Soviet soldiers. The standard issue Russian rifle, the Mosin-Nagant, one fitted with a sniper's telescopic sights, lies across the head of one body, perhaps posed there by the German photographer.

Reclamation
Russian civilians including children are seen removing clothing from corpses littering the frozen ground. It is difficult to distinguish from among the bodies stretching into the distance as to whether they are civilians or soldiers, Russians or Germans. There is some indication that this photo was taken near Kerch, a seaport in the Ukrainian Crimea that was the scene of a see-saw occupation by German and Soviet forces. First taken by the Germans in November 1941, a Russian naval operation then liberated the area on December 30,1941, but it was recaptured the following year by the Germans then finally liberated again in April 1944. Soviet military losses were estimated at over 160,000 men, killed or taken prisoner. During the German occupation of Kerch some 15,000 civililians were murdered, another 14,000 deported.

Unknown Buried by the Unknown
As a German officer watches from the background, bodies are tossed into a freshly dug mass grave. A cart with more bodies is visible in the background. There is some evidence that this location may be Vinnitza/Vinnystsia in the Ukraine, the site of the 1937–38 murder of 9,000–11,000 Ukrainian civilians by the Soviet NKVD during one of Stalin's mass purges, the corpses discovered by the Germans when they occupied the area in 1943. In addition, the NKVD killers would often murder large numbers of political prisoners held in their prisons to prevent them from being liberated by the Germans advancing into the area.

Unaccountable

Stalinist policy implemented a "Do Not Divide the Dead" doctrine and as result Jewish victims of atrocities and mass executions were not identified as such, rather they were lumped into one sum, the mass of suffering inflicted upon the Soviet peoples. This was in part to present a unified front but also due to Stalin's anti-Semitism as well as an effort to obscure the complicity of Soviet citizens who took part in the German extermination program.

Mass Murder Pardoned *En Masse*

American and British authorities were eager to get Germany back on its feet on the side of the West as the Cold War with the Soviet Union intensified. Denazification was basically a matter of filling out forms and rubber stamping. In the process thousands of fanatical SS men were discharged back into the general population. In fact several worked on repairing bomb damage to the buildings involved with the Nuremberg Trials while other ranking Nazis gained access to political office and government posts.

February 6, 1959, Bonn, Germany—Re-opened Wounds

Some 14 years after the war's end, a German court, upon the insistence of the Soviet Union, tried two former SS guards from the Sachsenhausen concentration camp, Gustav Sorge and Wilhelm Schubert. Though sentenced and imprisoned previously (1947) by Russian authorities, they were among several German war criminals repatriated to West Germany on the condition they continued paying for their crimes. The trial was held by the West German judical system in an effort to dissuade the German public that the charges were trumped up by the Communists. In fact, both defendents readily admitted that "they had taken part in the slow and systematic murder, night after night, for six weeks, of 10,800 mainly invalid Russian prisoners of war and murders for which they had questioned neither the motive nor the necessity." The two SS men were sentenced to life imprisonment.

Although some members of the Waffen-SS were guilty of substantial war crimes, post-war pronouncements by various Waffen-SS groups and their advocates sought to paint themselves as honorable soldiers fighting for their country. Their rebuttal to documented crimes often resorted to Holocaust-denial. Many Waffen-SS veterans left Germany either toward the end or after the war and made their way to various countries particularly those with a strong anti-Communist stance. A 2009 tabulation of then current Waffen-SS personel revealed some unexpected statistics. For example while 128 were known to be still living in Argentina, there were 1,882 accounted for in Canada and 3,337 in the U.S.

Know Thy Enemy
Derived from a U.S. Army training filmstrip *The German Soldier*, this 98 page booklet was produced by the Director of Military Training, Army Service Forces. It was published in 1944 during wartime and was aimed at informing the American soldiers about his German foe. The foreword begins with:

> What Kind of fellow is the German soldier? The answer to this question depends on whom you ask.
> If you ask a Czech who saw the German Army goosestep into Prague, he might say, "He is a precise and heartless robot."
> If you asked a pole who faced him Warsaw, the answer might be, "He is the last word in destruction. His skill and speed are paralyzing."
> If it were a Frenchman: "He is the master of the unexpected. He is superbly trained. He is a smooth functioning cog in a strong and ruthless machine."
> A Russian might say, "He is a wild animal, sly and murderous. Men, women and children—he kills or maims every helpless thing in sight. But he can be hunted down and shot like any other mad dog."
> His former ally, the Italian, should know him well: He is selfish and treacherous. He will sacrifice his friends to save his own skin. In victory, he is arrogant. In defeat he is vicious and mean, destroying people, property and civilization itself in his anger and disappointment."

The message makes the point that not all German soldiers are savages but efficient fighting men. It does include one mention of atrocities near the very end of the booklet when it states:

> … in this German soldier's mind there was ignorance and hate based on this ignorance—hate of so-called inferior peoples—peoples in other countries whom he as a superman had been taught to look down on. Or if he didn't actually hate them, he played along with the others who did, and shot hostages and murdered Jews and "depopulated" whole areas without mercy….

In the booklet, the American soldier is then told to make up his own mind based on the evidence, but points out that the German soldier is a formidable enemy but one who can be bested. The remainder of the booklet delves into the historic background of the German military mindset and Nazi indoctrination as well as weapons, training and the German military campaigns.

Polish Ghetto Street Scene (*above*)
Two men notice a German soldier snapping their photograph. The crowded conditions, lack of food and sanitation debilitated the trapped occupants as part of the orchestrated plan to weaken the victims prior to deportation to the Death Camps.

SD Police target Polish Jews (*left*)
Security Police confront Jews rounded up in Lublin appear in a photograph published on November 9, 1939 in a popular German illustrated newspaper. German media often presented images of Jews in ragged condition to bolster their racist rhetoric. Poland would also serve as the deadly terminus for Jews, gypsies, Soviet POWs and other "undesirables" shipped by rail from all over the continent to the death camps at Auschwitz, Belzec, Chelmno, Sobibor, Treblinka and Maidenek. In actuality the thousands of other camps, large and small, set up by Nazi Germany all over Europe, whether described as concentration camps or labor camps, were in fact all death camps designed in one way or the other to torture and destroy minds and bodies.

Zu den Aufräumungsarbeiten werden diejenigen herangezogen, die das Arbeiten noch nicht gelernt haben. Das Ghetto ſpeit ſie aus, die Peſt Polens.

Sie kennen keine körperliche Arbeit, ſie wiſſen nicht einmal, wie eine Schaufel anzufaſſen iſt.

Polish Ghetto—Photos Published in *Illustrierter Beobachter*
German soldiers take turns taunting an orthodox Jewish man made to repair the street. Nazi propaganda always characterized the Jews as "shirkers" who never did honest work. Victims were often forced to perform meaningless tasks, the small tortures often leading to larger cruelties, "worked to death" taking on its full meaning.

Top caption: *Ones who have not yet learned to work, clean. The ghetto spit them out, the Polish pestilence.*
Bottom caption: *They have done no physical work, so don't even know how to use a shovel.*

Round-up of Jews—Ukraine
A German soldier, his shadow just visible (left), has photographed a closely packed group of prisoners, boys and men, standing near the center of what appears to be a fenced-in garden. In the background a local Ukrainian white-coated volunteer deals with a smaller group of prisoners. Others can be glimpsed to the far right, their heads and caps just visible as they lay prostrate on the ground awaiting "processing" by their captors.

Closer Inspection—Two Rows of Seven
Further cropping and magnification reveals the spectrum of emotions evident on the prisoners' faces.

As they carried out the state-sponsored extermination program, Death Squads of German and their Lithuanian and Ukrainian collaborators followed the advancing German army throughout Eastern Europe eventually shooting to death over 1,100,000 Jewish men, women and children before the industrialized Extermination Camps came on line. Only one bullet was allotted per victim, a means by which researchers have been able to calculate the number of victims when a new mass grave is uncovered, still an ongoing process. The calculations did not take into account that infants and toddlers were usually clubbed or bayonetted to death or tossed alive into the mass graves in order to conserve ammuntion. On occasion Jews were made to clean streets to pay for the cost of the bullets needed to kill them.

Wall of Death

A body lies where it fell. A German soldier has had time to take out his camera and compose this photograph. Corpses often lay unburied for long periods, sometimes deliberately as a warning. Bodies grew black and bloated with the passage of time, the scent of death carrying long distances.

While it was thought that most German murder squads conducted their business far from prying eyes, deep in forests and under the cover of darkness, many mass executions, particularly of Jews, took place in broad daylight often in the middle of towns and villages … schoolyards, town squares, farmers' fields, home gardens. Very often local townsfolk including children were forced by the Germans to dig the graves, trample down the bodies to make room for more, then fill the graves and collect the victims' clothing. They would have to cook for the killers while they carried on their shooting and even wrench the gold teeth from the condemned, often while the victims were still living.

"Execution Tourism"

The secretly recorded conversations of ordinary German soldiers, airmen and naval personnel held in a British POW facility were published in English in 2012, the bestselling book first published in German in 2011 by German military historian Sonke Neitzel after discovering the documents in the British National Archives. Titled *Soldiers: Diaries of Fighting, Killing and Dying*, it exposes the widespread knowledge of genocide and in fact its enthusiastic support by the German Army rather than solely SS "fanatics". The following excerpts concern the matter of what was termed "execution tourism".

> The splendidly named General Edwin Graf von Rothkirch und Trach explained to a fellow inmate; "I knew an S.S. leader in Kutno, Poland, and we chatted about this and that and he said; 'God, when you want to film something, why didn't you say so? I mean, timewise, it doesn't matter. We shoot them in the mornings, but if that is inconvenient, we have others that we can always shoot in the afternoon'. Lieutenant Mueller-Riezenburg, in a transcript made on Christmas Day 1943, said; 'The S.S. invited us over for a Jew-shoot. The whole troop went off with their weapons and joined in. Everyone was allowed to pick which one they wanted to shoot."

The term *Holocaust* is inadequate as pointed out by Claude Lanzmann, the French filmmaker of the benchmark 9½ hour documentary titled "Shoah" which is the Hebrew word for catastrophe or disaster whereas holocaust actually means a burnt offering to a god. As Lanzmann opined, a burnt offering of 1.5 million Jewish children to reach God renders the word unusable. The film, 12 years in the making since the effort began in 1973, has been shown extensively and continually in European theaters and on TV since it was released. Seeing less public showings, Shoah was first premiered in the U.S. in October 1985, then in 1987 first broadcast on PBS television, available on VHS in 2000, and in 2010 on DVD.

Special Treatment

Fastidious documentation kept by the so-called *Schriebtischtater* ("armchair killers") emphasized the "orderly processing" attached to the mass murder of the Jews. The following communication, a transcribed telephone message, was recorded on March 8, 1943 concerning the transport of deportees from Berlin and Breslau to Auschwitz.

> Main Office for the Economy and Administration Department D II Oranienburg
>
> Subject: Transport of Jewish Workers
>
> The following prisoner transports arrived on March 5 and 7:
> Transport from Berlin, arrival March 5, 1943, total strength 1,128 Jews. 389 men were assigned for work (Buna), and 96 women. 151 men and 492 women and children received special treatment. Transport from Breslau, arrival March 5, 1943, total strength 1,405 Jews. 406 were assigned for work (Buna), and 190 women. 125 men and 684 women and children received special treatment. Transport from Berlin, arrival March 7, 1943, total strength 690 including 25 prisoners in protective custody. 153 men and 25 prisoners in protective custody were assigned for work (Buna), and 65 women. 30 men and 417 women with children received special treatment.
>
> Signed: Schwarz
> SS Lieutenant

On the next page:

Mauthausen—"The Stairway to Heaven"

Heinrich Himmler (facing camera), head of the SS terror network responsible for millions of deaths visited Mauthausen concentration camp on March 6, 1941.

Located on a hill above the Upper Austrian market town of Mauthausen, the main camp of a complex of camps, it was one of the first built and the last to be liberated by the Allies.

The two main installations, categorized by the Nazi administration as "Grade III" camps, were designed to exterminate "Incorrigible Political Enemies of the Reich" and were geared to working prisoners to death. Their victims were comprised of the intelligentsia of many countries brought by train from all across Europe as the Third Reich conquered new territory. They included artists, scientists, Boy Scouts, university professors, socialists, anarchists, communists, Hungarian and Dutch Jews, Spanish Republicans, Bible students and Jehovah Witnesses, Soviet POWs ... all sharing the same fate.

Although the main form of extermination was through brutal labor (*Vernichtung durch Arbeit*), it was also one of the few KZ in the West that had its own gas chamber. Through deliberate starvation, prisoners were often reduced to an average weight of 88 lbs, but still forced to carry granite blocks weighing as much as 110 lb up the 186 steps of the granite quarry nicknamed the "Stairway to Heaven." A number of Allied airmen were condemned to death by this means.

The camp also "rented" out its inmates to some 45 German companies and local municipalities. During the latter part of the camp operations, much of the slave labor was provided by Polish, Czech, Russian, and Balkan teenaged prisoners. The Mauthausen KZ system became the most profitable of such Third Reich slave labor and manufacturing facilities.

In addition to some sixty-two means of murder devised by the German guards as well as various medical experiments, the SS often threw prisoners off the quarry cliffs for sport, calling it the "Parachutists' Wall." The victims were given the option: push a fellow prisoner to their death or be shot. Those too weakened to work were also sent to the nearby Hartheim Castle, an early center for euthanasia. Individuals from some twenty-seven countries died in the camp. Because of poor or destroyed documentation, the estimated total number of dead ranges from 55,000 to 200,000 while the data indicates that of the 320,000 prisoners interred in the sub-camps of KZ Mauthausen-Gusen throughout the war, approximately 80,000 survived. Simon Wiesenthal, hunter of Nazi war criminals, was one of the camp's survivors. In the years following the war, the camp area at Gusen was developed into a residential neighborhood.

Mauthausen was also the point of manufacture for the special vials made from Mauser bullet casings that were employed to hide ampules of cyanide. Some 950 of the ampules were ordered near the end of the war for dissemination among the Nazi hierarchy to avoid capture, especially by the Soviets.

Hermann Göring, once one of Hitler's favorites and *Reichsmarschall* of the Luftwaffe among many other titles and offices, used such a capsule to commit suicide shortly before his scheduled hanging after his conviction by the Nuremberg War Crimes Tribunal. During his year of incarceration he had shed over 100 lbs from his previously obese 300 lb weight carried on a 5 foot 7 inch frame. He also "kicked" his long standing drug habit.

Göring, imagining he would be sentenced to exile rather than prosecuted, had brought 17 vehicles laden with personal treasure when surrendering to the Americans. Learning otherwise, he relied on the poison hidden in a jar of his special skin cream and through his charm and wit secured access to it from his guards. He left a note to the warden who had sworn none of the war criminal prisoners under his watch would be able to commit suicide. As a parting jab, Göring wrote that they could find a second capsule in another of his cream jars. Himmler when captured by British troops, bit down onto a cyanide capsule hidden in his mouth.

Final Words from the Third Reich

Anti-Jewish Instructions—Implausible Deniability

The commonly heard protestations voiced by post-war Germans civilians, and often its soldiers, were that they had no knowledge that Jews were being murdered *en masse*. In point of fact, anti-Semitism, the fuel for the Holocaust, was endemic throughout German society, even among Germans who had never even met a Jew.

Repressive Nazi legislation that turned Jews into non-citizens (and non-beings) was rigorously, and very visibly, promulgated by edicts enforcing divestiture from education, banning from social activities and the professions, and open verbal and physical public violence against them in the streets. In addition their mass deportations from Germany, confiscation and redistribution of Jewish property, first-hand reports and even photos of executions sent home from the Front … all was common knowledge. While there was a public uproar against the euthanasia of physical and mentally afflicted Christian Germans, resulting in the termination of its overt practice, no such outcry was voiced concerning the treatment of the Jews except in the case of a group of Aryan German women who in February 1943 staged a week long public demonstration on the Rosenstraße, a Berlin street where they resolutely faced Gestapo machine guns, bravely demanding the return of their Jewish husbands, some 1,700 held in custody in one of the last of the German capital's round-ups and destined for deportation and death. As a result the authorities finally relented, freeing the Jewish men to their courageous wives.

The 1996 book *Resistance of the Heart: Intermarriage and the Rosenstrasse Protest in Nazi Germany* written by Florida State University historian Nathan Stoltzfus first brought public awareness to the event. It served to argue against the longstanding post-war German argument that that the public could do nothing to prevent the treatment of its Jewish neighbors. It could be argued that it took, at very least, public acquiescence to permit the Final Solution; a plan that once placed into motion was maintained even to the very last days of the war.

Public Education—Openly Expressed Justification for the Final Solution

The following is an excerpt from materials issued on May 5, 1943 by the *Redner-Schnellinformation* (Speakers' Express Information), an official Nazi government organization that provided speakers with guidelines for conducting public meetings across Greater Germany. It was presented under the heading "The Jewish Question as a Weapon at Home and Abroad."

> It has become apparent that the reduction of public discussion about the Jewish Question has misled a great part of the public, who now are starting to see the Jewish Question as a weapon we can do without, since the Jewish Question has, after all, been solved in Germany. This view is dangerous and false. Were it correct—and this line of thinking has been often used—the church could have ended its meetings hundreds of years ago, since everyone was Christian, and the Christian Question was therefore resolved. It is true that we have solved the Jewish Question in Germany, but it has become even more important outside Germany during this war, for this war is a war of the Jews against Germany and its allies. Just as the domestic struggle in Germany ended in an anti-Semitic revolution, so, too, this war must end in an anti-Semitic world revolution.
>
> The best foundations for that have already been laid. There are already important anti-Semitic movements in nearly all the nations of Europe, along with more or less advanced Jewish laws aimed at diminishing the influence of the Jews. Even in enemy nations, anti-Semitic voices are so strong that leading newspapers and leading politicians and churchmen have to face the matter in public.
>
> In Germany, we have made the whole nation anti-Semitic by always pointing the finger at the Jews, as hard as they tried to hide themselves. We always ripped the mask from their faces. The Jews attempted often enough to divert the public from the subject by busying them with other matters, since our propaganda was most unpleasant for them. That was still more reason to stubbornly continue that propaganda.
>
> The Jewish Question must be the central issue in the meeting waves of the immediate future. Each German must know that everything he suffers in this war, all the unpleasantness, shortages, overtime, bloody terror against women and children and bloody losses on the battlefield, are the fault of the Jews.
>
> Each meeting must include the following line of thinking:
>
> The International Jew wanted this war. He possessed the key economic positions within every enemy people and in every enemy nation, and used his power to ruthlessly drive the peoples into war.
>
> He today controls public opinion in enemy nations, owning the press, radio, and film, and uses them as the voice of these peoples. Still, knowledge of the nature of Jewry has taken hold in enemy nations, and is increasing.
>
> There is no crime in which the Jew is not involved. Just as was once the case in Germany, well over half of all those engaged in financial crimes, cases of fraud, bankruptcy, corruption, and stock speculation are Jews.

Where Jews do not want to appear as important men themselves, they have bought leading personalities in public life to do the Jews' work for them.

Jews earn money from war, and therefore have an interest in a long war, though hardly a Jew bears a weapon himself, or earns his living by his own hands. Just as was once the case in Germany, Jews let others fight and work for them.

The Jews incited this war as a final attempt to maintain their power in the world and to defeat all those who saw through them. This war will end with an anti-Semitic world revolution, and with the destruction of Jewry in the world, which is the prerequisite to a lasting peace.

The key thought is this: Everything is the fault of the Jews!

Visitors make a pilgrimage to the empty Nuremberg Stadium
The massive Zeppelin field was the scene of the annual Nazi Party rallies, as many as 1,000,000 attending in 1938, all gathered to hear Hitler speak, the last such monumental event prior to the onset of war. It was at the various Nuremberg Rallies that Leni Riefenstahl filmed her epic *Triumph of the Will* film, where Hitler announced the anti-Jewish Nuremberg Laws and where he also proclaimed that the Third Reich would last a thousand years. Nuremberg would also serve as the location for the 1946 Nuremberg Tribunals, the post-war trials of some of the Nazi Germany leaders and which would expose the crimes of the Third Reich to the world.

Gauleiter Frank of Poland Photographed
A still image captured from a German propaganda film spots a photographer aiming his state of art Zeiss-Ikon Contax 35 mm camera at Hans Frank during a parade in his honor. He is quoted as saying, "I have the power of life and death over the people of Poland."

Of the twenty-two defendants tried at the first Nuremberg Tribunal in 1946 several offered their "realizations" as to the nature of the Third Reich, particularly after their sentences were announced. Their "last words" were recorded by an attending American physician at Nuremberg, Dr. John K. Lattimer and found in his illuminating book first published in 1999 and titled *Hitler's Fatal Sickness and Other Secrets of the Nazi Leaders.*

Most complained about their imprisonment, denied responsibility and made various excuses, several fervently advocating that the Allies and Germans "team up" to throw back the Russian Bolsheviks. A few seemed to experience some form of epiphany about the true nature of the Third Reich when time was running out, the gallows beckoning. For example, Hans Frank, the governor-general of Poland from 1939 to the war's end, home to the main Extermination Camps, after first seeing the Tribunal's evidence, then hearing the death sentences for himself and some of his cohorts, exclaimed:

> Do they get on their knees and pray to God for forgiveness? No, they worry about their own little necks and cast about for all sorts of excuses. Can't they see that this is a horrible tragedy for mankind and that we are all symbols of an evil that God is brushing aside?

During his Nazi reign in office, Frank kept meticulous diaries that included details of the murderous brutality and was apparently eager to hand them over to the Tribunal prosecution. When asked why, he said:

> God knows what I did so mankind might just as well know the whole truth. All of it, the good and the bad. I know they are going to hang me. Now only the truth will remain.

Rambling Regrets

Robert Ley, head of the *Deutsche Arbeit-Front*, the German Labor Front, held sway over some 25,000,000 workers controlling salaries, insurance, education, elder care, and the disabled. As a loyal Hitler supporter, Ley was initially rewarded with the position of *Gauleiter* of the Rhineland, then control of the DAF despite the fact that his actions were often affected by a severe head injury sustained while a flier during the First World War. Prone to outlandish statements, including an interest in death rays and rabbits, and subject to incoherent ranting, his aberrant behavior was augmented by heavy drinking. Despite his mental condition or perhaps because of it, he often spoke in place of Hitler, giving long, rambling speeches prone to undeliverable promises, in effect a scapegoat Hitler employed if there was a problem he wanted to distance himself from.

Ley considered himself to be a patriot, professed no knowledge of the Nazi crimes and vehemently refused to accept his description as a criminal. After his capture, he composed a document describing the means by which Germany could rehabilitate itself. In part it read:

> We have forsaken God and therefore we were forsaken by God. Anti-Semitism distorted our outlook and we made grave errors. It is hard to admit mistakes but the whole existence of our people is in question. We have to declare to the youth that it was a mistake. The youth will not believe our opponents. We have to go all the way. German people, reconcile yourselves with the Jew. Invite him into your home (with you.) We cannot stop the excited sea at once but must let her calm down gradually, otherwise terrible repercussions would result. A complete reconciliation with the Jews has priority over economic or cultural reconstruction. We outspoken anti-Semites have to become the first fighters for the new ideas. We have to show our people the way.

However, a review of Ley's sojourn in the Nazi Party reveals a virulent anti-Semite, in fact owning a newspaper in order to attack Jews. In a 1942 public speech he declared, "The Jews have got to be exterminated!"

Leaving a note saying he could not live with the shame of charges of criminality, Ley managed to hang himself in his cell, tying a towel over a toilet pipe. Göring, hearing of the suicide, responded: "It's just as well that he is dead, because I had my doubts about how he would behave at the trial."

Nuremberg Tribunal Summation

For some, the twenty-two Nuremberg defendants represented only the tip of a vast iceberg of evil incarnate. The oft heard lament from the Third Reich officials as well as the general population that they "knew nothing" of the mass murder of innocents holds no ground except perhaps that they didn't know the "gory details" having never visited a mass shooting or a extermination camp in process, however they all knew that the Jews were "disappearing to the East," and many had seen "souvenir" photos sent back by their soldiers. The fact of mass murder was obvious, only the cries of the victims unheard and the corpses unseen, thus allowing for "plausible deniability," even from the leading Nazi defendants. Many members of the German public blamed the crimes on Himmler and the SS, Hitler in their eyes still unblemished.

After hearing the Tribunal defendants consistently deny knowledge of and responsibility for the atrocities and for the war of aggression that scorched Europe, the Tribunal's British prosecutor Sir Hartley Shawcross addressed the Court with these telling words: "What special dispensation of Providence kept these men ignorant of all these things? Years ago Goethe said of the German people that some day Fate would strike them ..."

> ... would strike them because they betrayed themselves and did not want to be what they are. It is sad that they do not know the charm of truth, that mist, smoke, and berserk immoderation are so dear to them, pathetic that they ingenuously submit to any mad scoundrel who appeals to their lowest instincts, who confirms them in their vices and teaches them to conceive nationalism as isolation and brutality.

Adding that Goethe was indeed prophetic, Shawcross, indicating the defendants sitting in the dock, offered to the Tribunal and the world that these were "the mad scoundrels who did these very things."

A Police Unit arrives by train in Nuremberg
As part of the Nuremberg proceedings, an "Einsatzgruppen Trial" took place in 1947, lasting eight months with twenty-three indictments. Three of the convicted were executed. In other war-related trials the French convicted 2,107, sentencing 104 to death. Belgium convicted seventy-five with ten executed. In later postwar trials conducted by West Germany in 1958, seventy-nine received life sentences but were reduced or commuted. There were no executions. Later German judicial inquiries into *Einsatzgruppen* crimes resulted in the investigation of 1,770 members of the killing teams. 136 were brought to trial. Eight defendants received life sentences, commuted to fifteen years or less. Eight received 11–15 years. Sixteen received 7–10 years. Seventy-two received sentences of six years or less Twenty-five were acquitted. Many others complicit in mass murder were excused for health reasons or because the prosecution was unable to locate "witnesses."

The number of German *Einsatzgruppen* members are estimated at a minimum of 3,000. This does not include the thousands of Ukrainian, Lithuania or Latvian volunteers or regular Wehrmacht accomplices. The murders committed by shootings in the field by these units are estimated at a million or more. Most of the greatest mass murderers in history were never brought to justice.

On the next page:

U.S. Army Signal Corps—"For Official Use Only, Not for Publication"—February 14, 1946—Munich (*above*)
Several months after the war's end, soldiers of the 42nd Cavalry arrested a well-dressed former Nazi Party member Adam C. Eckardt during a series of coordinated raids looking for hidden weapons, black market goods, and former Nazi Party officials.

Nazi Party Member Eckart Undergoing Interrogation (*below*)
A U.S. Army lieutenant examines the prisoner's Nazi Party membership documents. Meticulous record keeping by the Third Reich proved the source of much of the evidence for its supporters' crimes.

As the Cold War commenced, many committed Nazis and their sympathizers found themselves useful to the Allies, frequently re-instated into important West German government and military positions as well as recruited for American scientific research projects. Many nodded knowingly when the Allies now agreed that the "real" enemy was Bolshevism, their past Nazi sins now seemingly forgiven.

Truth Be Told—They Knew Everything

In January 2012, a two-volume diary titled: *Vernebelt, verdunkelt sind alle Hirne Tagebücher 1939-1945* (All Minds are Clouded and Darkened) written by Friedrich Kellner was published in Germany. It was published in English in 2018 as: *My Opposition: The Diary of Friedrich Kellner—A German against the Third Reich.* Its contents, chronicling life inside Nazi Germany as it happened from 1939 to just after the end of the war in 1945, was described as "devastating" especially when contrasted with the oft-heard "I knew nothing" espoused by German civilians. As the diary noted, the fate of Jews and other enemies of Nazi Germany was in fact well-known. In one of Kellner's diary entries that he penned during the war, he stated:

Those who wish to be acquainted with contemporary society, with the souls of the "good Germans," should read what I have written. But I fear that very few decent people will remain after events have taken their course, and that the guilty will have no interest in seeing their disgrace documented in writing.

Post-War Poll

Taken a few months after the war ended by Allied authorities, 37 percent of those Germans polled believed the extermination of Jews and Poles was justified in order to defend Germany. None who responded to the poll believed that they, the German people, as a whole were responsible for the fate of the Jews.

Russian Dead—German Camera

Final Tabulations

According to German Red Cross estimates, the military deaths of German, Austrian and East European ethnic Germans numbered 3.1 million killed in action and 1.2 million missing in action and presumed dead for a total of 4.3 million with an additional 600,000 civilians killed in Allied bombings. Russian soldiers fighting the invaders killed 80 percent of the German soldiers who died in the war of mutual annihilation and as a result bore the brunt of the war's carnage. Soviet military wartime casualties are estimated at 8.8–10.7 million plus 12.25 to 14.15 million civilians not including over 1,500,000 of its Jewish population. More recent estimates raise the total number of Soviet deaths to over 30,000,000 with the total European death toll surpassing 50,000,000, perhaps as many as 70,000,000.

One Example of Justice Delayed

Albert Helmut Rauca—Shirt and Tie Mass Murderer—1983

Arrested in 1983, some 40 years after his crimes were committed, Rauca, 73 at the time, became the first Nazi living in Canada to be extradited for war crimes. A Gestapo specialist in Jewish Affairs, he evaded capture, making his way to Canada in 1951 where he lived a reclusive but pleasant life as one of an estimated 1,000 war criminals having made Canada their home after the war.

Over the years, efforts to prosecute both German and Nazi collaborators in that country have met resistance from the government and some ethnic communities. Although Rauca was traced to Canada in 1961 where authorities were notified, it took them ten years (1972) to find him even though since 1956 he was a full Canadian citizen living and working under his real name with a passport and driver's license. Authorities blamed it on "computer glitches." Then it took nearly another ten years to bring extradition charges in 1982.

While an SS Master Sergeant within the *Einsatzgruppe A, Kommando 3*, he was charged with murdering 11,584 Jewish men, women and children. In the Lithuanian city of Kaunas, Rauca directly made the selection of 9,200 who were then shot all in a single day at the infamous Fortress 9. Rauca was the subject of a 1983 book titled *War Criminal on Trial* as written by Sol Littman, a community affairs specialist for CBC News who conducted research for a documentary concerning Rauca and who also attended the 1982 trial that saw the Canadian court authorize Rauca's extradition to West Germany. Rauca, while in a German prison awaiting trial, died of natural causes in 1983.

The Day the Last Nazi Died?—2008

It should be remembered that not all Germans were Nazis, and that not all Nazis were German. On Sunday July 21, 2008 Dinko Ljubomir Šakić died at the age of 86. He had gained the status, or onus, as the last living Second World War-era concentration camp commander. *Continued on next page*

Šakić, a Croatian *Ustaše* fascist while serving the Nazis puppet state run by Ante Pavelić, had commanded Jasenovac, an infamous concentration camp known as the "Auschwitz of the Balkans." Handsome in appearance, he was known for wearing a tailored black uniform, riding a white horse and carrying a whip and a submachine gun as he brought terror and death to the camp prisoners.

In 1999 Šakić was found guilty of killing more than 2,000 Serbs, Jews and Gypsies at the camp, his crimes also included torturing prisoners with a blowtorch, and personally shooting others, including two for smiling. Witnesses also stated that Šakić oversaw the execution of several hundred Jewish women and children. A protégé of Vjekoslav "Maks" Luburić, an *Ustaše* Major and director of all Croatian concentration camps, Šakić had begun serving at Jasenovac at the age of 21 and only 23 when successful in working his way up to camp commander in 1944, retaining that position for seven months until the fascist regime fell to Soviet forces. While post-war death tolls vary, the Belgrade Military Museum lists 77,200 victims of murder at the Jasenovac camp, 41,936 of whom were Serbs. Other estimates run from 200,000 to as many as 700,000 although the current Croatian government offers lower figures. A damning bit of evidence was found in records kept by the German SD (*Sicherheitsdienst*) that in 1943 recorded a death count of 120,000, with still more than a year in operation to increase its murderous operation.

Located 60 miles south-east of Zagreb, Jasenovac was one of 20-some concentration camps established after the German invasion of Yugoslavia in April 1941 that resulted in the creation of the fascist Independent State of Croatia. The Nazis themselves found the conditions of the camp, a 150 square mile complex of facilities, appalling, one German describing it as "Dante's Inferno" or hell on earth. The Croatian guards had even created a special knife specially designed to cut throats which they kept at easy reach on their belt. Here murder was not by gas chambers and crematoria, but literally hands-on in most cases. Photos show Croatian fascist guards gloating over the corpses of their victims.

Post-war Šakić made no effort to hide himself or his achievements at the concentration camp. Having fled Croatia at the war's end, he took up residence with other expatriate Nazis in Argentina. He eventually owned a successful textile company and reportedly also ran a "rest camp" during the 1950s for former Croatian fascists living in Paraguay with the aid of his friend, the Paraguayan dictator and fellow Nazi-ophile Alfredo Stroessner.

An outspoken member of the 10,000 Croatian community in Argentina, in 1990, Šakić's photograph and an interview were published in a Croatian newspaper (*The Feral Tribune*) in which he spewed hatred upon Serbs and lauded the fascist *Ustaše* government. Then in 1994, during a state visit to Argentina by then Croatian President Franjo Tudjman, Šakić was interviewed by *Magazin*, another Croatian magazine in which he stated, "I'd do it all again," stating that he was proud of what he had done, would gladly do it again, and wished more Serbs had died at Jasenovac. He also added, "I sleep like a baby."

In 1997, in yet another interview, Šakić proclaimed that the only deaths in the camp had been from natural causes. Survivors, offered an alternate view, stating that since bullets were in short supply the majority of killings were done by hand, with mallets or axes, sticks, hammers and various other tools, often nails driven through the mouth into the brain. While hanging was also a well-used method, many prisoners died from overwork and starvation.

The court's verdict came several years after Croatia gained independence from Yugoslavia in 1991 at which point President Tuđjman and his government began publicly questioning the number of Jews killed by its fascist predecessors during the war and attempted to re-cast the killers as heroic, anti-communists. As a result, members of the notorious *Ustaše* fascist organization responsible for numerous atrocities, were "rehabilitated" by the government, given rewards and invited to government celebrations. Eventually, after considerable time and international pressure, both Argentina and Croatia cooperated in Šakić's extradition and trial. Šakić had married fascist leader Vjekoslav Luburić's sister, Nada, who, at age 16, started working with him at the camp. The 1998 indictment stated that Šakić and his wife had three children. She was also extradited from Argentina, and although survivors have offered testimony to her personally murdering a number of women prisoners by strangulation, the Zagreb court dropped charges against her.

When Šakić's Argentinean neighbors were interviewed after his extradition to Croatia for trial, they commented that they sometimes noticed him mowing his lawn or hugging his wife goodbye. In response to the court's verdict, Šakić, who had often worn a smug smile during the proceedings, clapped his hands and laughed in derision.

Šakić died in a hospital in Zagreb while serving a 20-year sentence for crimes against humanity as Croatia has no death penalty. However, Šakić's legacy lingered on even at his funeral when the presiding Croatian priest Vjekoslav Lasić, stated, "The court that convicted Dinko Šakić, convicted Croatia and the Croatian nation," and then added, "Every honorable Croat should be proud of Šakić's name."

In apparent counterpoint, the Croatian judge, Dražen Tripalo, who sentenced Šakić said at the trial's end, "I hope the sentence will be a warning that all those who committed crimes in the near or distant past will not escape justice." The fact that Šakić had lived comfortably and untouched by justice for 55 years, as did the majority of the Second World War war criminals, left that statement with a hollow ring.

April 6, 1945—"Living and Dead in Frankfurt"
The press photo caption reads: German civilians walk along a littered street in Frankfurt, passing their own soldier-dead, after this area of the city was cleared by the U.S. Third Army. (Photo by Bryon R. Hollins, AP photographer)

A post-war observation by an educated German woman as reported by historian Modris Eksteins in the book *The Boys Crusade* by Paul Fussel:

> One can only regard our present situation as the quintessence of irony in the whole history of the world. We will never get over this bloody Calvary. We have grown old and weary to death. One sits and searches one's brain for an explanation. What was the point of it all, what rhyme or reason was there for this desperate, ruinous destruction? Was it just a satanic game?

Bibliography

AILSBY, Christopher, *The Third Reich Day by Day*, Zenith Press 2005.

BARENBAUM, Michael, *Witness to the Holocaust*, HarperCollins, New York, 1997.

BARNOW, Dagmar, *The War in the Empty Air—Victims, Perpetrators, and Postwar Germans*, Indiana University Press, Bloomington, IN, 2005.

BAXTER, Ian, *SS: The Secret Archives—Eastern Front*, Amber Books, London, England, 2003.

BEER, Edith Hahn with DWORKIN, Susan, *The Nazi Officer's Wife*, Perennial, New York, 1999.

BERGSCHICKER, Heinz, *Der Zweite Weltkrieg*, Deutsche Militarverlag, Berlin, DDR.

BERNADAC, Christian, *The Death Train*, Ferni Publishing House, Geneva, 1978.

BESSEL, Richard, *Nazism and War*, Modern Library, New York, 2006.

BESSEL, Richard, *Germany 1945*, HarperCollins, New York, 2009.

BETHELL, Nicolas, *Russia Besieged*, Time Life Books, New York, NY 1977.

BEEVOR, Anthony, *Vasily Grossman—A Writer at War*, Vantage, New York, NY, 2007.

BLANDFORD, Edmund, *Under Hilter's Banner—Serving the Third Reich*, Castle Books, Edison, NJ, 2001.

BLEUL, Hans Peter, *Sex and Society in Nazi Germany*, J. B. Lippincott Co., Philadelphia and New York, 1973.

BLOOD, Philip W., *Hitler's Bandit Hunters—The SS and the Nazi Occupation of Europe*, Potomac Books, Dulles, VA, 2006.

BROWNING, Christopher R., *Ordinary Men—Reserve Police Battalion 101 and the Final Solution in Poland*, HarperCollins Publishers, New York, NY 1992.

CARREL, Paul, *Hitler Moves East 1941–1942*, Little, Brown and Co., New York, NY, 1965.

BROWNING, Christopher R., *Collected Memories—Holocaust History and Postwar Testimony*, The University of Wisconsin Press, 2004.

CONOT, Robert E., *Justice at Nuremberg*, Carroll & Graf, New York, NY, 1983.

COWDERY, Ray and Josephine, *Papers Please! Identity Documents, Permits and Authorizations of the Third Reich*, Victory Publishing, Rogers, MN, 1996.

DAVIS, Brian L., *Badges and Insignia of the Third Reich 1933–1945,* The Cassell Group, Wellington, England, 1983.

DAVIS, Brian L. *German Army Uniforms and Insignia 1933–1945*, London: Arms and Armour Press, 1992.

DE BRUHL, Marshall, *Firestorm—Allied Airpower and the Destruction of Dresden, Random House*, New York, 2006.

DESBOIS, Father Patrick, *The Holocaust by Bullets*, Palgrave MacMillian, New York, NY, 2008.

DINARDO, R. L., *Mechanized Juggernaut or Military Anachronism? Horses and the German Army of the Second World War*, Stackpole Books, Mechanicsburg, PA, 1998.

DOLLINGER, Hans, *The Decline and Fall of Nazi Germany and Imperial Japan*, Bonanza Books, New York, 1965.

DOYLE, David, *Standard Catalog of German Military Vehicles*, KP Books, Iola, WI, 2005.

DUPUY, Col. R. Ernest and BREGSTEIN, Lt-Col. Herbert L., *Soldier's Album*, Houghton Miflin, Boston, MA 1946.

EISNER, Jack, *The Survivor*, William Morrow & Co., New York, 1980.

ENSOR, R. C. K., *A Miniature History of the War—Down to the Liberation of Paris*, Oxford University, New York, 1945.

ETLIN, Reichard A., *Art, Culture and Media under the Third Reich*, The University of Chicago Press, Chicago and London, 2002.

EVANS, Richard J., *In Hitler's Shadow—West German Historians and the Attempt to Escape from the Nazi Past*, Pantheon Books, New York, 1989.

FEIG, Konnilyn G., *Hitler's Death Camp—The Sanity of Madness*, Holmes & Meier Publishers, New York—London, 1981.

FOEDROWITZ, Michael, *The Flak Towers in Berlin, Hamburg and Vienna 1940–50*, Schiffer Military History.

FRANKS, Lucinda, *My Father's Secret War*, Hyperion, New York, 2007.

FOWLER, Dr Jeffrey T., *Axis Cavalry in World War II*, Wellingborough, UK: Osprey Publishing, 1998.

FOWLER, Will and ROSE, Mike, *Their War—German Combat Photographs From the Archives of Signal*, Conshohocken, PA: Combined Publishing, 2000.

FUSSEL, Paul, *The Boys' Crusade*, The Modern Library, New York, 2003.

GEHLEN, Wilhelm and GREGORY, Don, *Jungvolk*, Casemate, Philadelphia, 2008.

GILBERT, Martin, *The Holocaust—Maps and* Photographs, Hill and Wang, New York, 1978.

GILBERT, Martin, *The Routledge Atlas of the Holocaust*, Third Edition, London, 2002.

GLANTZ, David *et al.*, *Slaughterhouse—Encyclopedia of the Eastern Front*, The Military Book Club, Garden City, NY 2002.

GOETZ, Samuel, *I Never Saw My Face*, Hudson House, Poughkeepsie, NY, 2001.

GOLDHAGEN, Daniel Jonah, *Hitler's Willing Executioners—Ordinary German and the Holocaust*, First Vintage Books, New York, 1997.

GOODFRIEND, Capt. Arthur and GARRETT, Lt J. G., *The German Soldier*, Infantry Journal, Inc., Washington, D.C., 1944.

GROSS, JAN T., *NEIGHBORS*, PENGUIN BOOKS, NEW YORK, 2002.

GROSS, Jan T., *Fear*, Random House, New York, 2006.

GROSSJOHANN, *Georg, Five Years, Four Fronts—The War Years of Georg Grossjohann*, Aegis Consulting Group, Bedford, PA 1999.

GRUGE, Frank and RICHTER, Gerhard, *Alltag im Dritten Reich—So Lebten die Deutschen 1933-1945*, Hoffman und Campe, Bonn, Germany 1981.

GRUNBERGER, Richard, *The 12-Year Reich—A Social History of Nazi German 1933–45*, Da Capo Press, New York, 1995.

Ed: Hamburg Institute for Social Research, *The German Army and Genocide—Crimes Against War Prisoners, Jews, and Other Civilians, 1939–44*, The New Press, New York, NY 1999.

HATHEWAY, Jay, *In Perfect Formation, SS Ideology and the SS-Junkerschule-Todz*, Schiffer Military History, Atglen, PA, 1999.

HAUPT, Werner, *Army Group South—The Wehrmacht in Russia 1941-1945*, Schiffer Military History, Atglen, PA, 1998.

HAYDEN, Mark, *German Military Chaplains in World War II*, Schiffer Military History, Atglen, PA, 2005.

HELLMAN, Peter and MEIER, Lili, *The Auschwitz Album*, Random House, New York 1981.

HILLBERG, Raul, *Perpetrators, Victims, Bystanders—The Jewish Catastrophe 1933-45*, HarperCollins, New York, NY, 1992.

HINRICHSEN, Horst, *German Military Motorcycles of the Reichswehr and the Wehrmacht 1934-45*, Schiffer Military History, Atglen, PA, 1997.

HIRSCHMANN, Maria Anne, *Hansi—The Girl Who Loved the Swastika*, Tyndale House Publishers, Wheaton, Illinois, 1975.

HOGG, Ivan V., *The Guns 1939-45*, Ballantine Books, New York, NY, 1970.

HOLT, Toni and Valmai, *I'll Be Seeing You—Picture Postcards of World War II*, Mooreland Publishing Co., Ashbourne, England, 1987.

HUNT, Robert and HARTMAN, Tom, *Swastika at War*, Doubleday & Co., Garden City, NY, 1975.

JACKSON, Julian, *The Fall of France—The Nazi Invasion of 1940*, Oxford University Press, Oxford, NY, 2003.

JOHNSON, Eric A. and REUBAND, Karl-Heinz, *What We Knew—Terror, Mass Murder, and Everyday Life in Nazi Germany*—An Oral History, Basic Books, 2005.

JOHNSON, Marc J. and JOHNSON, Kristi A., *"I Died For You, Too!"—A Collector's Guide to German World War II Death Notices*, Syracuse, NY. 2001.

KARPOV, Vladimir, *Russia at War 1941-45*, The Vendome Press, New York, NY 1987.

KATER, Michael H., *Hitler Youth*, Harvard University Press, Cambridge, MA, 2004.

KESSLER, Leo, *Kommando*, Leo Cooper Publishing, London, England, 1995.

KIBLER, Thomas, *Combat Helmets of the Third Reich*, Reddick Enterprises, 2003.

KIRCHNER, Ann, *Sala's Gift—My Mother's Holocaust Story*, Free Press, New York, NY, 2006.

KIRCHUBEL, Robert and ZGONNIK, Dmitriy, *Luftwaffe Field and Flak Divisions*, Concord Publications Company.

KLEE, DRESSEN, RIESS—Editors, *"The Good Old Days"*, Konecky & Konecky, Old Saybrook, CT, 1991.

KNAPPE, Siegfried and BRUSAW, Ted, *Soldat—Reflections of a German Soldier 1936-49*, Orion Books, New York, NY, 1992.

KRAWCZYK, Wade, *German Army Uniforms of World War II in Color Photographs*, Motorbooks International, Osceola, WI 1996.

LANGERBEIN, Hans, *Hitler's Death Squads—The Logic of Mass Murder*, Texas A&M, 2004.

LATTIMER, John K., (Physician at Nuremberg) *Hitler and the Nazi Leaders—A Unique Insight into Evil*, Hippocrene Books, New York, 2001.

LITTLEJOHN, David, *Foreign Legions of the Third Reich, Vols. 2, 3, 4*, R. James Bender Publishing, San Jose, CA, 1985.

LOCHNER, Louis P., Editor, *The Goebbels Diaries—1942-43*, Doubleday & Co., New York, 1948.

LUKAS, Richard C, *Did the Children Cry—Hitler's War Against Jewish and Polish Children 1939-45*, Hippocrene Books, New York, 1994.

LUMSDEN, Robin, *A Collectors Guide to: The Allgemeine SS*, Ian Allen Publishing, Hersham, England, 1992.

MACDONOGH, Giles, *After the Reich—The Brutal History of the Allied Occupation*, Basic Books, New York, 2007.

MACLEAN, French L., *Quiet Flows the Rhine—German General Officer Casualties in World War II*, J. J. Fedorowicz Publishing, Winnipeg, Canada, 1996.

MACLEAN, French L., *2000 Quotes from Hitler's 1000-Year Reich*, Schiffer Military History, Atglen, PA, 2007.

MARKHAM, George, *Guns of the Third Reich—Firearms of the German Forces, 1939–1945*, Arms and Armour Press, London, England, 1989.

MAYER, Milton, *They Thought They Were Free—The Germans 1933–45*, The University of Chicago Press, Chicago, 1966.

MASSAQUOI, Hans J., *Destined to Witness—Growing Up Black in Nazi Germany*, William Morrow and Co., New York, 1999.

MEGARGEE, Geoffrey P., *War of Annihilation—Combat and Genocide on the Eastern Front, 1941*, Roman & Littlefield, New York, 2007.

MENDOLSOHN, Daniel, *The Lost—A Search for Six of Six Million*, Harper, New York, 2006.

MERRIDALE, Catherine, *Ivan's War—Life and Death in the Red Army 1939–45*, Picador, New York, 2006.

MITCHAM, Samuel W., *Hitler's Field Marshals*, Scarborough House, Chelsea, MI, 1990.

MOORE, Albert L., *Postal Propaganda of the Third Reich*, Schiffer Military History, Atglen, PA, 2003.

MULLER, Werner, *German Flak in World War II*, Schiffer Military History, Atglen, PA, 1998.

MICHAELIS, Rolf, *German War Decorations 1939–1945—Army–Waffen-SS–Police*, Michaelis-Verlgan, Berlin, Germany, 2003.

MULLER, Werner, Sound Locators, *Fire Control Systems and Searchlights of the German Heavy Flak Units 1939–45*, Schiffer Military History, Atglen, PA.

MUNOZ, Antonio J., *Hitler's Green Army—The German Order Police and their European Auxiliaries 1933–45, Western Europe and Scandinavia*, Europa Books, Inc., Bayside, NY, 2005.

MUNOZ, Antonio J., *Hitler's Green Army—The German Order Police and their European Auxiliaries 1933–45, Eastern Europe and the Balkans*, Europa Books, Inc., Bayside, NY, 2006.

MUNOZ, Antonio J., *Generalgouvernement—Internal Security of the Eastern Occupied Polish Territories 1939-45*, Europa Books, Inc., Bayside, NY.

NICHOLAS, Lynn H., *Cruel World—The Children of Europe in the Nazi Web*, Vintage Books, New York, NY 2005.

NOVOTNY, Alfred, *The Good Soldier*, The Aberjona Press, Bedford PA, 2003.

OVERY, Richard, *Interrogations: The Nazi Elite in Allied Hands, 1945*, Penguin Books, New York, NY, 2001.

POLIAKOV, Leon, *Harvest of Hate—The Nazi Program for the Destruction of the Jews of Europe*, Holocaust Library, New York, NY, 1979.

PONTING, Clive, *Armageddon—The Reality Behind the Distortions, Myths, Lies, and Illusions of World War II*, Random House, New York, NY, 1995.

PONTOLILLO, James, *Murderous Elite—The Waffen-SS and Its Complete Record of War Crimes*, Leander & Ekholm Publishing, Stockholm, 2009.

Preuss Publishers, *Fallen for the Fatherland—Translation of Original Third Reich Book to Comfort the Families of the War Dead*, 2001.

PUEKERT, Detllve J. K., *Inside Nazi Germany—Conformity, Opposition, and Racism in Everyday Life*, Yale University Press, London and New Haven, 1987.

REES, Laurence, *War of the Century—When Hitler Fought Stalin*, The New Press, New York, NY, 1999.

REESE, Willy Peter, *A Stranger to Myself—The Inhumanity of War: Russia, 1941-45*, Farrar, Straus, Giroux, New York, 2003.

RICHTER, Klaus Christian, *Cavalry of the Wehrmacht 1941–1945*, Schiffer Military History, Atglen, PA, 1995.

RIKMENSPOEL, Marc J., *Waffen-SS The Encyclopedia*, The Military Book Club, Garden City, New York, 2002.

RHODES, Richard, Masters of Death- *The SS-Einsatzgruppen and the Invention of the Holocaust*, Vintage Books, New York, 2003.

ROGOW, Sally, *Faces of Courage, Young Heroes of World War II*, Granville Island Publishing, Vancouver, 2003.

ROSMUS, Anna Elizabeth, *Wintergreen—Suppressed Murders*, University of South Carolina, Columbia, SC, 2004.

RURUP, Reinhard, *Topography of Terror—SS and Reichssicherheitshauptamt on the Prinz-Albrecht-Terrain*—A Documentation, International Documentation and Study Center, Verlag Willmuth Arenhovel, Berlin, 1989.

SACHAAR, Abram L., *The Redemption of the Unwanted*, St. Marten's, New York 1983.

SCOTT, Mark and STINGER, Ann, *"Bravo, Amerikanski" and Other Stories from World War II*, 1st Books Libraries.

SEGEV, Tom, *Soldiers of Evil—The Commandants of the Nazi Concentration Camps,* Domino Press, McGraw-Hill Book Co., New York, 1987.

SHECK, Raffael, *Hitler's African's Victims*, Cambridge University Press, Cambridge, 2006.

SHIRER, William L., *The Rise and Fall of the Third Reich*, Simon & Schuster, New York, 1960.

SMITH, F. D., *Photography and the Holocaust*, The Journal of Progressive Judaism, 1993.

SNYDER, Louis L., *Encyclopedia of the Third Reich*, Wordsworth Military Library, Cumberland House, UK, 1998.

SPEER, Albert, *Inside the Third Reich*, Avon, New York, NY, 1970.

STARGARDT, Nicholas, *Witnesses of War- Children's Lives Under the Nazis*, Knopf, New York, 2006.

STEPHENS, John Richard, *Weird History 101*, Fall River Press, New York, 2006.

STEPHENSON, PhD, June, *Poisonous Power: Childhood Roots of Tyranny*, Diemer, Smith Publishing Co., 1998.

STEINWEIS, Alan E., Art, *Ideology, & Economics in Nazi Germany*, University of North Carolina Press, Chapel Hill, NC, 1993.

SYNDOR, Jr. Charles W., *Soldiers of Destruction-The SS Death's Head Division 1939-45*, Princeton University Press, Princeton, NJ, 1977.

TERRENCE, Marc, *Concentration Camps-A Traveler's Guide to World War II Sites*, Universal Publishers, 2003.

THOMAS, Nigel, *The German Army 1939-45* (1)—*Blitzkrieg*, Osprey Publishing, Elms Court, UK, 1997.

THOMAS, Nigel, *The German Army 1939-45* (4)—*Eastern Front 1943-45*, Osprey Publishing, Elms Court, UK, 1999.

TROPPER, Harold and WEINFELD, Morton, *Old Wounds—Jews, Ukrainians and the Hunt for Nazi War Ciminals in Canada*, The University of North Carolina Press, Chapel Hill, NC, 1989.

Tsouras, Peter G., *The Great Patriotic War*, Greenhill Books, London. 1992.

Tubbs, Floyd R., *Stahlhelm—Evolution of the German Steel Helmet*, The Kent State University Press, 2000.

Ungerer, Tomi, *Tomi: A Childhood under the Nazis*, The Roberts Rinehart Publishing Group, Niwot, Colorado, 1998.

Van Meers, Rachel, *Lost in the Fog—Memoir of a Bastard*, Academy Chicago, Chicago, 2008.

Volakova, Hana (Editor), *Children's Drawings and Poems—Terezin 1942-1944*, McGraw-Hill Co., New York, 1962.

Weber, Louis, *The Holocaust Chronicle*, Publications International, Lincolnwood, IL, 2001.

Westermann, Edward B., *Hitler's Police Battalions- Enforcing Racial War in the East*, University of Kansas Press, Lawrence Kansas, 2005.

Williamson, Gordon, *German Army Elite Units 1939-45*, Osprey Publishing, Elms Court, UK, 1999.

Williamson, Gordon, *Germany Security and Police Soldier 1939-45*, Osprey Publishing, Elms Court, UK, 2002.

Williamson, Gordon, *The SS: Hitler's Instrument of Terror*, Barnes & Noble, New York, 2006.

Wilson, Paul J, *Himmler's Cavalry-The Equestrian SS, 1930-45*, Schiffer Military History, Atglen, PA, 2000.

Winnick, Myron, *Final Stamp-The Jewish Doctors in the Warsaw Ghetto*, Author House, Bloomington, IN, 2007.

Wistrich, Robert, *Who's Who in Nazi Germany*, Bonanza Books, New York, 1982.

Additional Resource Materials

German-English Dictionary of German Administrative Terms—U.S. War Department Pamphlet No. 31-69—July 3, 1944

German Military Abbreviations—reprint of Military Intelligence Service—War Department, April 12, 1943—Service Publications

Germany—Handbook for British soldiers entering post-war Germany—published November 1944.

Original documents and photographs—Police Battalion 322 (Author's Collection)

www.yad-vashem.org

"Shoah"—Complete Video Series—Claude Lanzmann

Mein Krieg—directed by Harriet Eder and Thomas Kufus—Kangurum Film—Video Kino—1991

The Simon Wiesenthal Collection—8 documentaries—Moriah Films

Index